W9-BWP-822

GLOBALIZATION OF THE AUTOMOBILE INDUSTRY

GLOBALIZATION OF THE AUTOMOBILE INDUSTRY

The United States, Japan, and the People's Republic of China

Xiaohua Yang

Westport, Connecticut
London

Library of Congress Cataloging-in-Publication Data

Yang, Xiaohua.
    Globalization of the automobile industry : the United States,
Japan, and the People's Republic of China / by Xiaohua Yang.
        p.   cm.
    Includes bibliographical references and index.
    ISBN 0–275–94837–4
    1. Automobile industry and trade.   2. Automobile supplies
industry.   3. International business enterprises.   4. Competition,
International.   5. Automobile industry and trade—United States.
6. Automobile industry and trade—Japan.   7. Automobile industry and
trade—China.   I. Title.
HD9710.A2Y36   1995
338.4'76292—dc20   94–37887

British Library Cataloguing in Publication Data is available.

Copyright © 1995 by Xiaohua Yang

All rights reserved. No portion of this book may be
reproduced, by any process or technique, without the
express written consent of the publisher.

Library of Congress Catalog Card Number: 94–37887
ISBN: 0–275–94837–4

First published in 1995

Praeger Publishers, 88 Post Road West, Westport, CT 06881
An imprint of Greenwood Publishing Group, Inc.

Printed in the United States of America

The paper used in this book complies with the
Permanent Paper Standard issued by the National
Information Standards Organization (Z39.48–1984).

10 9 8 7 6 5 4 3 2

Contents

Tables and Figure

TABLES

FIGURE

Abbreviations

AMC	American Motor Corporation (Now Chrysler)
BICE	Beijing Internal Combustion Engine plant
CAD	Computer-aided-design
CAIGC	China Auto Industry General Corp.
CNAIC	China National Auto Industry Corp.
CNTIC	China National Technical Import-Export Corp.
DFI	Direct foreign investment
EOS	Economy of scale
FAW	First Auto Works, China
FTC	Foreign Trade Corp.
FYP	Five-year plan
GATT	General Agreement on Tariffs and Trade
GHAF	General Headquarters of the Armed Forces
GLF	Great Leap Forward movement
GM	General Motors Corp.
HAM	Honda of America Manufacturing Inc.
IE	Industrial engineering
JIT	Just-in-time
JUSE	Japanese Union of Scientists and Engineers
MACHIMPEX	Machinery Import and Export Corp., China
MIT	Massachusetts Institute of Technology
MITI	Ministry of International Trade and Industry, Japan
MMS	Ministry of the Material Supply, China
MMUC	Mazda Motor Manufacturing (USA) Corp.
MNC	Multinational corporation
MOFERT/ MOFTEC	Ministry of Foreign Economic Relations and Trade, China (Ministry of Foreign Trade and

	Economic Cooperation)
NIC	Newly Industrialized Countries
NORINCO	Northern Industrial Corporation, China
NTB	Non-Tariff Barrier
NUMMI	New United Motor Manufacturing Inc., USA
PRC	People's Republic of China
QC	Quality control
R&D	Research and development
SAW	Second Auto Works, China
SEC	State Economic Commission, China
SEZ	Special Economic Zones, China
SPC	State Planning Commission, China
SQC	Statistical quality control
TMC	Toyota Motor Corp.
TQC	Total quality control
TSW	Toyoda Spinning and Weaving
VA	Value analysis
VE	Value engineering
VER	Voluntary Export Constraint
VW	Volkswagen Corp.

Preface

Since 1949, both political actors and academic analysts have assumed that the force of nationalism will be in continuous decline, whereas political and economic integration is the wave of the future. Yet the end of the Cold War has encouraged balkanization of the world as well as a mounting demand for cultural nationalism. Even where eventual political integration is taken for granted, nationalist aspirations have re-asserted themselves. Meanwhile, the world economy is being integrated by global corporations whose capital, technology and firm organization are making those same national boundaries more and more porous. This book deals with the seeming contradiction between rising nationalism and globalism.

It is now possible for cultural identity to express itself through political boundaries, yet be a part of the global economy at the same time. It appears that political and economic boundaries need not necessarily converge any more. To illustrate this point, I have selected three countries, the United States, Japan, and the People's Republic of China, for a comparative study. In these societies, the relationship between government and economy, the ways in which inter-firm organizational relationships have evolved, and the manner in which their national economies are regulated are all very different. Yet these patently divergent societies have all been affected by the globalization process and are converging in economic organization. I have chosen to study the automobile industry, an industry which has made significant contributions to the national economies of these countries and which has played an important role in both creating and maintaining the advanced industrial societies.

This book is the product of generous help from several people. My special thanks goes first of all to Dr. Ishwer C. Ojha. Some time ago, he challenged me to experiment with a conceptual approach to international economy.   Additionally, he provided me with advice and criticisms needed for completing this work. Without his support, this book would have been impossible.

I am also indebted to Mrs. Helen D. Ojha, along with the rest of the Ojha family, for putting me up during the months when I devoted my time to revising the manuscript and finishing this book.

In Beijing, I owe my appreciation to a number of Chinese friends and acquaintances, too numerous to name here, for arranging interviews and factory visits, as well as for spending their time in providing me with some insight in the workings of the Chinese automobile industry.

I want, lastly, to thank all those individuals who, in more ways than one, have lent me valuable support.

Without doubt, I am solely responsible for any deficiencies in the book.

GLOBALIZATION OF THE AUTOMOBILE INDUSTRY

Chapter One

Globalization and Management of National Economies: The Relations between Manufacturers and Suppliers

At the end of the twentieth century, the globalizing trend of the world economy is beginning to affect government management of national economies. National governments in both advanced and emerging economies are turning increasingly to markets for economic management and retreating from insulation against international market forces. In this transition from protection-oriented, mercantilist and command national economies to global market forces, all nations have ambivalent and sometimes contradictory policies.[1] Thus, the United States holds onto managed trade through quotas, retaliation, and strategic trade policies. At the same time, it seeks to enhance national competitiveness by creating advanced factor endowments[2] and infrastructure (Barnet and Cavanagh 1994), such as the project on information highways. The second largest economy, Japan, publicly rejects managed trade but maintains voluntary export restraints. The People's Republic of China is also in a period of transition from the command economy. It is trying to create market mechanisms to attract foreign investment and establish linkages with the global economy.

But why are national governments changing their ways of managing their economies? An important explanation lies in the effect of global market forces on the policy choices of the government authorities. Nowadays, neither market demand nor corporate operations confine themselves to the territorial borders of nation-states. To survive in a global marketplace, companies must compete globally. Moreover, they must forge strategic alliances with former business rivals to succeed. Gone are the days when a corporation could act as a lone ranger in pursuit of global growth, as the Ford Motor Company did early in this century (Barnet and Cavanagh 1994).

To add as much value as possible in each chain of corporate business, wherever it is located (Porter 1986; Michalet 1991), firms need strategic alliances, because self-help or reliance on internal resources alone no longer suffices for competing simultaneously across many functions, multiple cultures, and many regulatory boundaries. Firms need not only to pool skills and human resources, improve understanding of diverse national tastes, and share risks and costs in R&D and production, ignoring their differences in national identities (Lei 1989; Gugler 1992), but they need also to cross policy barriers and take advantage of policy incentives (Barnet and Cavanagh 1994) established and maintained by government regulations.

In this shift towards competitiveness through strategic alliances, corporations have built up a worldwide network economy[3] by promoting production and trade within the competing "global value chains" (Porter 1986) as well as among their alliances and sourcing partnerships. Corporations have additionally replaced bilateral "multi-domestic" deals of the 1960s and 1970s with multi-lateral strategy in investment and trade. Unlike multi-domestic operations, in which a corporation keeps its R&D in the home country (Kindleberger 1977) while duplicating other functions for targeted foreign national markets, a global firm executes each functional activity and competence at any given location for the global market, attending to diverse national preferences from the stage of product design onwards (Lynch 1990).

In the developed economies, globalization is driven by strategic alliances. But it also involves cross-border linkages broader yet more subtle than strategic alliances, reflected in the increasing porousness of the boundaries demarcating manufacturer-supplier relations that are traditionally defined by informal rules, customs and national regulations. As they change interfirm organizational linkages domestically to support these strategic alliances (Lei 1989; Kotabe and Murray 1990; Nonaka 1991), global corporations are also forming partnerships with a few economies at lower stages of development that offer competitive functional performance and/or strategic market access. By extending the life cycles of the standardized products to the latter economies, they aim not only to delay the decline in profit rates (Vernon 1966; 1977), as in the previous decades, but also to recover sunken costs on the technologies that must be phased out in globalization.

Globalization thus reflects an altered basis of corporate and national competitiveness as well as of international investment and commerce. Instead of the traditional comparative advantages in the physical resources located within territorial borders, competitiveness depends increasingly on such strategic inputs as the skills, know-how, and knowledge of a nation's labor force, its information infrastructure, picky consumers, and competitive suppliers at home (Porter 1990; Drucker 1993), as well as the existence and strength of global linkages. This means that those corporations which possess technology and access to worldwide capital and major consumer markets have come to influence the levels at which nations produce and trade, which in turn determines the welfare levels of the nation-states (Michalet 1991; Stopford and Strange 1991; Strange 1992).

Since the locational advantage derivable from physical resources has become less and less important for competitiveness, national governments need to find alternative ways of maintaining sovereign control of economic boundaries to provide and improve national living standards (Stopford and Strange 1991; Strange 1992). This pressure, along with the opportunities for moving up the manufacturing ladder which structural change in the advanced economies has opened up for the emerging economies, has prompted the national governments outside the "Triad"[4] to drop their hostility towards international capital and technology. They begin to create business-friendly environments, agreeing to change manufacturer-supplier linkages, to meet global corporations' requirements for performance. In exchange, governments seek cooperation in raising the local content of the production.

Globalization, however, has also imposed costs on societies. Structural change, in particular, has left behind closed plants and laid-off staff, thereby dividing the foreign and domestic sectors of the national economies and raising bitter political debate. Some of these debates, such as those on the identity of a product or corporation or the strategies for obtaining or regaining competitiveness, assume a nationalist theme. Others, like the debate on whether the boundaries between corporate competition and cooperation should be redrawn, touch on the basic philosophical beliefs of a society. Both point to the imperfection of market competition as grounds for policy action from the national political authorities. National governments have therefore continued to maintain national economic boundaries, both to improve competitiveness and to meet the demands of national security and of domestic politics, which make it imperative to keep a certain level of employment. Yet they have had to incorporate global linkages into national economic policy making.

While global linkages have affected the policy choices of the national governments, they have not affected all to the same degree. This is because all national economies do not have the same levels of global linkages. The emerging economies that depend on the capital, technology, and marketing prowess of the global corporations to introduce new products, modernize the manufacturing capabilities, and upgrade participation in world trade have generally had to take up the junior position in a partnership. This compares with inter-corporate strategic alliances in the advanced economies which arise among firms of equal strength on the basis of complementarity in skills, competencies, and market access. They are brought together by a competitive strategy for developing better products in a faster and/or a more efficient way (Nueno and Oosterveld 1988; Lei 1989; Baranson 1990).

Globalization, of course, is an evolution of the world economy throughout the twentieth century accompanied by the evolution of the economic theories explaining international trade. In classical theory, trade began anywhere within a nation through voluntary swapping of goods between any two parties. The exchange was supposed to improve the well-being of both parties, regardless of the underlying efficiency in production, provided that the value which each assigned to the two products varied. Ricardo, who pioneered the study of political economy, applied the analysis to international transactions. He explained trade in terms of the differences in the productivity of labor between two countries. By the 1930s, two Swedish economists had developed the Heckscher-Ohlin theorem,[5] which argued that trade stemmed from national differences in resources. Some twenty years later, the neo-classical economists singled out technology, which was implied in the Ricardian theory, as a key determinant of trade. They also identified the comparative advantage of nations in their factor endowments as the foundation of not only trade but also different production techniques which each could most profitably utilize.

In both the classical and neo-classical worlds, trade was bilateral. The actors of the world economy were primarily nation-states. Initially, trade followed flag under the gunboat policy. The role of the nation-states in inter-national trade continued after the 1950s when newly independent countries sought trade and finance as sovereign participants in the world economy. Trade was also supposed to be complementary in both classical and neo-classical theories, given different physical endowments of each country. In reality, however, the majority of trade during this period occurred in the same industry. Evidence reveals that intra-industry trade is explainable by intra-corporate transactions supporting the multinational investment of the firms.[6]

Corporations, therefore, were the leading force transforming the world from a bilateral to a multinational system of trade and production. As this statement indicates, corporations were engaged in not only the exchange of goods, as were the nation-states, but also in direct investment for production in foreign countries (DFI). When it first started, DFI had invariably been aimed at exploiting the comparative advantage of the recipient societies in primary resources. But in the new industries which became the engines of growth during the late nineteenth and early twentieth centuries and for which trade first began among the countries in the Northern hemisphere, DFI was made to exploit the strategic advantage of mass production technology and managerial hierarchy, build marketing and after-sale service networks, establish trading and information-gathering posts, and expand sales and market access. In the inter-war years, corporations responded to the mercantilist warfare of the nation-states with further investment wherever possible, while sharing R&D outputs and/or working out cartel arrangements with competitors to maintain the respective shares of the world market (Chandler 1986).

A full transition to multinational trade and investment did not occur, however, until after WWII, when multinational corporations (MNCs) redrew the international division of labor by switching their investment from primary to manufacturing industries. To a great extent, the decision for the switch was forced on the MNCs by the postwar movement of nationalization in the newly independent nations that were eager to develop their own technological and industrial bases. Yet, the favorable environment for the transition was created with the establishment of a multilateral trade regime under the General Agreement on Tariffs and Trade (GATT). Specifically, GATT was set up to encourage an expansion of trade through tariff reduction. This was aimed at preventing a repetition of the beggar-thy-neighbor policies of the 1930s which might have brought down the capitalist world economy now in Cold War confrontation with the communists (Gilpin 1987; Leonard 1988).

Sectorial reduction of tariff led by the hegemonic economy, the United States, indeed opened up markets for products from the recovering as well as the developing nations. When firms in Europe and Japan rebuilt their capabilities and began to challenge the competitive position of corporations in America, the latter started to cut costs by relocating part of production to those capitalist developing nations that sought to upgrade their economic activities by sourcing products for the MNCs with the cheap labor which the latter had in abundance. Meanwhile, the international conflicts that began to emerge from intra-industry trade were managed from sector to sector with bilateral quotas and other non-tariff barriers (NTBs), all introduced without directly violating the GATT rules.

As the world changed to a multinational economy, the organizational form of the multinational businesses also changed. Until the 1950s, North-South investment remained concentrated in the primary sector of the recipient countries. The MNCs set up subsidiaries with 100 percent of ownership to control prices to improve profit rates, particularly through transfer pricing of the intermediate inputs for supply across the territorial borders of the nation-states. But the total control of the primary resources by foreign capital caused resentment in the newly independent developing economies. In order to use their factor endowments or comparative advantages in international trade to form linkages with the world economy, the new nation-states first tried to regulate the foreign subsidiaries. When they failed to bring about the desired change, the regulatory policies escalated to national appropriation. This was epitomized by the nationalization of the oil business in Iran in the late 1940s and early 1950s, which culminated in the formation of OPEC in 1958. The Iranian revolution eventually failed because national ownership alone could not give it access to the world economy. It still faced the barrier of the MNCs' control over the world distribution system. But nationalization of oil business by Iran, as well as other episodes of nationalization in the newly independent economies, provided grounds for both the developing countries and MNCs to consider joint ventures instead of wholly owned subsidiaries when they set up manufacturing deals in the multinational system of production and trade.

In establishing a joint venture, a host country typically took a 51:49 split of equity shares with an investing MNC. To solicit cooperation from the latter, the national government would make concessions on tariffs and other policies designed to suppress the cost of labor employed for sourcing for the world economy. All in all, joint ventures gave the host country greater opportunities than outright nationalization for climbing up the ladder of industrialization in the "flying geese" model of economic development. This was because the arrangement allowed it to participate in a part of the manufacturing activities in the new international division of labor that resulted from an extension of the life cycle of an MNC's products.[7] On its part, the MNC got to delay the decline of the profit rate on its standardized products, particularly if they were made to supply not merely the host and home but also the world markets (Vernon 1966; 1977).

A second structural change was well on its way while the MNCs shifted DFI from the primary to manufacturing sectors of the world economy. With economic recovery towards the end of the 1950s, Japan and the industrial nations in Europe reverted their currencies to convertibility, portending the financial deregulation of the 1960s.[8] Financial liberalization made it possible to borrow internationally at different locations. Further deregulation in the 1970s and 1980s witnessed the growing mobility of financial capital as well as the rising frequency of transnational deals, while equity markets and national banks became greatly integrated. Fueling this process of globalization were rapid advances of information technology that not only permitted instantaneous transfer of funds across three financial capitals of the world, New York, London and Tokyo, but also supplied new tools for implementing transactions of monumental size.

Integration today is such that intervention of any central bank alone is no longer adequate for regulating the flow of capital across its national borders or managing its exchange and interest rates crisis. One of the best examples of late was the New York stock market crash of October 1987.

Financial globalization has in turn energized globalization of production. Capital deregularization had first happened in the early 1960s, about the same time the MNCs began to move their investment from primary resources to manufacturing. Since product life cycles remained relatively stable until the late 1970s, the key determinants of the corporate competitive advantage in these days were the location of production and access to the national markets. For this reason, the MNCs, particularly the early movers from the United States, found the comparative advantages of countries in the Southern hemisphere compatible with their competitive strategy. They competed by relocating labor-intensive production of standardized products to those economies that had abundant and low-cost labor, as well as stable policies friendly to the interests of multinational business. Financial deregulation which allowed corporations to raise capital at several locations in the world with both the banks and equity markets further facilitated the relocation strategy.

But this cozy pace of rivalry disappeared during the late 1960s and the 1970s when the Japanese firms joined the competitive game. Instead of settling on low-cost sourcing like the firms in America, the Japanese corporations dedicated themselves to the relentless pursuit of quality, cost reduction, product reliability, and variety, a feat which they achieved by perfecting product design and manufacturing processes with intra- and inter-corporate teamwork (Kumpe and Bolwijin 1988). The competitive strategy of the Japanese firms met the needs of changing market demands in the affluent societies, which moved away from mass consumption to niche demands from the late 1970s onwards as consumers with access to revolutionary information technology learned about the products that could satisfy them in price as well as quality, service, and uniqueness in design.

The result is a change in the nature of competition among firms. Increasingly, locational advantage gives way to competition in technology. Instead of competing for cheap labor sites, the new competition now focuses on R&D, both incremental innovation and fundamental R&D that is designed to generate completely new products as well as ever-flexible production processes. Correspondingly, some Japanese and European corporations have revised their concept of the locational advantage. While they incorporate the comparative advantage of the factor endowments of each country in their competitive strategy, these corporations often find it necessary to integrate such critical activity as component sourcing to maximize the competitive niche that may be generated from innovation in both products and manufacturing processes (Kotabe and Murray 1990).

Superiority in product design and manufacturing processes, in particular, underlined the competitiveness of the Japanese corporations. Indeed, they had achieved both by installing a multifunctional approach to jobs in a revolutionary system of lean production (Womack, Jones, and Roos 1992) that was supported by a rotational career system. The Japanese manufacturers minimized costs and wastes with just-in-time manufacturing, which they realized with the support of just-in-time supplies introduced by parts and components makers on the basis of long-term institutionalized teamwork (Cusumano 1985). More importantly, the Japanese manufacturers used their collaborative relations with suppliers to speed up the product development pace to respond flexibly to the rapid shifts in the demands in the world's most affluent and dynamic markets. The competitive niche of the Japanese corporations thus forced the MNCs based elsewhere in the world to shift their competitive strategy towards both products and production processes, especially by duplicating the Japanese corporations' method of collaborative competition.

Corporations must participate in both types of innovation because the winners of the game get to define the norms of technology and standards of interface, both critical for introducing new products in the future. The experience gained this way has also become critical for developing a competitive edge. Additionally, firms must constantly innovate, because new generations of products can come out every few months instead of years. The design of their products must also make allowances for diverse national preferences to meet niche demands in all the major markets in the world (Lynch 1990). In other words, corporations must learn to deal with the challenges that come from multipal directions and multipal dimensions, battling with current as well as potential rivals at any stage of a global value-chain and striving for competitiveness in every functional aspect of corporate activities (Michalet 1991).

At the root of the changed nature of competition, finally, is a shift in the basis of competitiveness for high-tech production and trade. It has shifted from the physical resources within national economic boundaries to advanced factor inputs of which no single corporation of any nationality has the complete stock. Neither is any one corporation capable of monopolizing every niche market. To obtain strategic factor inputs and needed market access, corporations have had to enter into strategic alliances with their former competitors. Since much of the strategic endowments can be created only with the assistance of national policy, national governments are also redesigning their policies to reshape the firms' and thus the countries' competitive advantages.

It has been stated that trade followed foreign policy until the 1950s. In an important way, this was because the competitive edge which a corporation was seeking over its rivals depended on the traditional comparative advantage embedded in the national boundaries of the recipients of DFI. Corporations relied on the power of the home state to improve their bargaining position versus the governments of the recipient countries. In exchange, corporations yielded to the security concerns and foreign policy decisions of the home government because of the latter's role in guarding the physical resources of the home nation and in safeguarding the well-being of its citizens. The competitiveness of the corporations at this time depended on the competitiveness of the nations, which rested in turn on the national military strength. During the Cold War, national security interests took supremacy because the ideological and political legitimacy of the countries in the capitalist world economy faced a challenge from the competing communist system. Besides the race in the defense capabilities, multilateral production and trade were promoted under GATT, permitting the nations to manage their economic conflicts sector by sector with the escape mechanism of bilateral NTBs.

But corollary growth far exceeded the expectations of the architects of the postwar political and economic order. By transferring technology abroad and opening up its market, the hegemonic power, the United States, and its MNCs provided the conduit for realizing the "flying geese" model of economic development, lifting first Europe and Japan and then other newly industrialized economies, with some of the latter, particularly those in East Asia, helping in turn to lift the growth of the countries next door. But the success of the Asian economies was owed not only to the expansionary strategy of the American MNCs, but also to the instruments and acceptance of the industrial policy that was pioneered by Japan's "developmental state" (Johnson 1982).[9]

Inevitably, the competitiveness of Japanese corporations, with their ability to pursue technological innovation forcefully, expand market share, and swiftly shift to the upper niches of the consumer market, as well as the legend of the nurturing effect of the Japanese government, provoked responses from the United States and Europe. In the realm of public policy, one of the first problems during much of the 1980s concerned how to resolve the dilemma confronting the government of the declining hegemony. It was clear by this time that some policy action had to be taken to bring the American corporations back on the track of the technological competition. The U.S. government saw the need to stop them from losing more industrial sectors to Japanese firms and to match Japan in technology policy. On the other hand, the U.S. government was faced with much opposition from various social interests, especially those from the "sunset" industries. Even among the firms in the "sunrise" industries, there were differences over who should receive what support to what degree. Ultimately, the policy dilemma reflected its roots in a fundamental belief in the optimal benefit of individualistic competition which microeconomics and its derivative trade theories had rationalized and which the legislative and executive branches of the government bureaucracies had followed faithfully.

It was to resolve this dilemma that a leading economist at the Massachusetts Institute of Technology repudiated the myth that international trade was spontaneous and atomistic. A look at the history of the world economy since the end of WWII, particularly that of the industries leading growth and expansion, and one would agree that postwar trade had been strategic.[10] Why, then, would not international trade theory adjust to this reality? Why would not the government engage in strategic trade, fostering international exchanges by those industries that generated a bigger share of rent and greater spillover effect on the domestic economy? Why not support the industries that provided higher value-added businesses at home and higher wages for citizens?

Indeed, the birth of the strategic trade theory had trailed after a revival of mercantilism or neo-mercantilism in the major markets elsewhere in the world that carried with it a determination to promote and guard high-tech production and trade. In Europe, it was marked by twelve nations' adoption of the national champion programs. Their objective was to force consolidation in the priority industries and provide needed assistance, so that national corporations could work together on R&D projects, share risks and costs, and improve efficiency to the extent they could compete with rivals in Japan and the United States. When this national approach to neo-mercantilism failed to bring about the desired end, a pan-European effort was launched in its stead (Sharp 1991; Sandholtz 1992). Firms in North America responded by urging their national governments to match up with both the national and regional programs in Europe to cushion their transition to globalism (Stevens 1990; Bressand 1990; Whalley 1992).

Meanwhile, a debate had evolved in the United States on just how the government could apply the strategic trade policy without violating the principles of equal access and equal opportunity embedded in the spirit of individualistic competition. Instead of letting the government target or direct corporate actions as the theory suggests, some academicians argued for strengthening market institutions to force home-based corporations to compete and innovate vigorously. Thus, antitrust legislation should continue rather than being dismantled. On its part, the government could focus on mobilizing support for creating an advanced infrastructure and an educational system that is capable of supplying the advanced human capital needed to build the competitive advantage of firms as well as the country (Porter 1990; Porter and Montgomery 1991).

Others disagree. They propose altering antitrust regulation so that home based corporations could collaborate with their suppliers in competition with their foreign-based counterparts. Here, a redefinition of competition is ventured. Instead of taking place everywhere and with every party, competition is suggested as requiring collaboration between a firm and its suppliers insofar as innovation requires scale, teamwork, and corollary cross-fertilization. Market can be left alone to compete after the structural relations are redesigned with the revision of the antitrust rules (Teece 1986; 1989; 1991). Still others argue for a broader approach to collaborative competition. Not only must industries drop the adversity characteristic of Anglo-American capitalism and shift toward the cooperative capitalism of Japan and continental Europe, but financial and educational institutions, as well as linkages among the research institutions, must also be reformed for the nation to create the technology and industries of the twenty-first century (Thurow 1992).

Regardless of their differences, the emerging theories of international trade and business organizations converge on treating technology as a territorial instead of a universal asset. A legacy of the classical paradigm of international political economy, the territorial perspective of competition in innovation received a boost from changing world politics when the Cold War ended. For the first time since WWII, national governments themselves can unabashedly engage in economic confrontations. For the first time since then, the possibility has opened for shifting some of the budget from national defense towards improving certain social institutions so as to help home-based corporations to compete with their opponents.

They seek to obtain and maintain as much higher grade of the economic activities and higher salaried jobs at home as they can. To this end, national governments are ready to use a whole range of policies both to protect and promote innovative products and processes, and to guard them jealously as sovereign properties. This means those countries which wish to build linkages with global value chains have had to compete to provide them with favorable investment climate, especially if the former want to maximize the spillover effect from DFI, whether by bargaining for training or by raising the domestic content supplied by local small and medium-sized businesses (Stevens 1990; Stopford and Strange 1991; Strange 1992).

This territorial view of the technological competition, of course, conflicts with the corporations' demands for new policies that are capable of accommodating their needs to cross national and regional economic boundaries to access the supply of advanced factor inputs as well as markets (Gilpin 1987; Stopford and Strange 1991; Strange 1989; 1992). Corporations, after all, must reduce costs and risks of innovation by pooling advanced resources. They must also learn to exploit new ideas and new technologies from any location and any function. Similarly, they must pursue a new locational strategy that entails moving R&D facilities from the home country to the neighborhoods of the consumers, including the domestic turf of the competitors, so as to understand diverse national tastes and monitor trends in consumption to get on the bandwagon of the next generation of R&D. Ultimately, corporations that compete globally must build networks of alliances with former as well as with current opponents, no matter in which countries they are based (Lei 1989; Gugler 1992), so as to position themselves in all the major markets before the doors of the regional blocs are shut. While they continue to look for sourcing sites to compete in costs, corporations are selecting them according to the criteria of maximizing values in each aspect of the global value chain instead of according to the nationalist ideology at home.

As a result of globalization, corporations have become players in the international political economy in their own rights. With the network economy in place, a global corporation begins to develop empathy with its strategic allies and sourcing partners. It also begins to share more interests with colleagues, associates, and consumers in different societies of the same global value chain rather than with declining sectors in the homeland (Michalet 1991; Stopford and Strange 1991; Strange 1989, 1992). This is partly explainable by the domestic structural change which the corporation has had to introduce not only to improve the competitive advantage of its global value chain versus those of its rivals but also to maintain the balance of power between it and its strategic allies. To this effect, the global corporation has had to divest the technologically unrelated assets acquired during the earlier decades as well as to intensify investment in R&D. An inexhaustive laundry list of the structural change which it has had to undertake to restore and strengthen the core business includes redesigning relations with suppliers, developing long-term teamwork with the latter, adopting a multi-disciplinary and multi-functional approach to business, technological competition as well as knowledge creation, and, as a corollary, shifting to consensual rather than hierarchical decision-making (Lei 1989; Kotabe and Murray 1990; Nonaka 1991). With their business networks engulfing much of international production and trade, global corporations are increasingly becoming key agents in determining the nations' positions in the restructured division of labor in the world.

While the power of the world economy has shifted to the global corporations, the ability of the nations to pursue policies of their own choice has become dependent on their respective bargaining clout versus the globalizing economy. The weaker a country is as a partner, hypothesizes this book, the graver the pressure comes for it to bear the costs of the policy adjustments required of global competition. In other words, the weak partners of global linkages are less able than their stronger counterparts to bargain terms for joining and maintaining linkages with global corporations. They must therefore exercise greater restraint in exhibiting ambivalence and contradictions in policy.

Interfirm organizational linkages between manufacturers and their domestic suppliers make up one aspect of national economies under severe pressure for adjustment in the process of globalization. They therefore provide one area in which national governments can display their policy ambivalence and contradictions. The tension surrounding this aspect of the national economic boundary arises from the fact that all societies have to deal with the problems of inputs supplied in their economies, no matter at what stages of development. Because they have evolved historically under specific conditions of national economic development and the characteristics of the individual cultures, the structural linkages in different societies necessarily differ from one another in fundamental ways. Yet how the supplies are sourced in an economy determines where technological learning takes place, where R&D is located, and how technological development is organized. This in turn determines the competitiveness of corporations and nation-states. For this reason, structural change has become an integral part of the overall strategy for achieving competitiveness with global linkages.

Auto manufacturing is one of the industries which corporations and nations have opened up for global linkages to achieve competitiveness. As the most important aspect of the Industrial Revolution, it has also been the key contributor to employment and national income as well as to the ideal types of structural relations in two largest economies in the world, Anglo-Saxon individualistic capitalism in the United States, and group-oriented cooperative capitalism in Japan (Thurow 1992). Additionally, the auto industry has gone through several transformations to date, giving birth to two historically competitive systems--mass production and lean production. Because of its unique position in the two national economies, auto industry's globalization and structural change have caused much trauma and controversy, particularly in the United States, which has had to shed a mass production method of its own creation and converge with Japan on lean manufacturing. The processes of change propelled by the industry's globalizing trend have thus brought much tension to bilateral economic relations, just when the Japanese auto industry is going through maturity and experiencing its own pains of structural adjustment to deal with the new challenges of global competition.

In China, auto manufacturing provides only a small fraction of employment and national income. But it has been chosen as a "pillar industry"[11] for development to represent the maturing of the industrial revolution in the world's most populous emerging economy. China, however, depends on global linkages to develop auto manufacturing, despite its preference for having a national industry. The state enterprises in this industry have thus come under severe pressure to adjust their structural relationships, giving it good cause for ambivalence and contradictions towards the global linkages. For historical and symbolic reasons, therefore, auto manufacturing, more than any other industry in China, is where a comparative case study may fruitfully be conducted on how economies with different levels of global linkages actually respond to the political and economic demands of such relationships.

Chapter Two of this book will look at the American response to the pressure of globalization. It begins with a review of the origin of structural linkages in America and traces through their change, particularly the auto industry's transition to globalization. It is well documented that after the transformation from family to corporate capitalism was completed in the 1920s, hierarchically organized corporate America, the main contributor to growth and employment, expanded for decades by fine tuning functional specialization for competition in a largely insulated domestic market place (Chandler 1962; 1964; 1977; 1990). While building up internal R&D, they also compromised the competitive threat with vertical integration, which shifted much of product design and process development capabilities from the suppliers to the manufacturers (Williamson 1970; 1975; 1986).

In the U.S. automobile industry, a few assemblers divided up the domestic market into segments. They made comfortable profits by selling a few car models in each and sitting on stable life cycles and secure price markups. From time to time, the assemblers introduced cosmetic changes in product design and styling, which they buffed up with marketing and advertising. More importantly, they got away with fat and easy profits by manipulating short-term atomistic price competition among their parts and components vendors. The profits were so fat and easy, in fact, the American auto makers did not mind imports chipping them away a bit beginning in the late 1950s. It was not until after the foreign brands had taken away more than one quarter of the American market following two oil shocks that they started to look around for ways to revitalize their past competitiveness (Abernathy 1981; Clark 1983; Helper 1990).

With its market power, however, the United States was able to bargain time for American auto builders to make improvements, particularly by soliciting voluntary export restraints from Japanese car makers. Initially, the American assemblers sought to obtain this objective by pouring money and technology into it. But continued problems in quality and costs compelled them to look beyond procedural changes (Schonberger and Gilbert 1983) and at the critical impact of structural relations on competitiveness in products and manufacturing processes (Deming 1986). They had to move away from antagonistic and uncertain relations with their vendors and build long-term teamwork, directing the vendors to compete in product design and process superiority like the Japanese, who had now transplanted production to this country, lengthening the contract period, and adjusting the criteria of vendor selection as well as working together to improve quality and cost competitiveness (Helper 1991; 1992; Cusumano and Takeishi 1991).

As the structural recession and the pain of structural change persist, the American government has also begun to force Japan to share the costs of globalization. It is mandating that Japanese transplants raise the content of the cars built in North America, especially by transferring to this side of the Pacific joint design and product development activities which provide higher grades of jobs and better opportunity for the American suppliers to develop and maintain technological competitiveness through advanced teamwork. Additionally, it is putting pressure on Japanese auto makers to open up the exclusive supplies market with their Japanese subcontractors by importing more parts from the American suppliers for auto assembly in Japan.

While identified as a market barrier for international trade today, the collaborative relationship between Japanese manufacturers and suppliers emerged initially as a mechanism for crossing the entry barrier for new industries and developing domestic capabilities in a "big spurt" strategy (Gerschenkron 1962) to catch up with the world's most powerful countries. Chapter Three of this book will trace the historical evolution of structural relations in Japan, parallel to the study for the United States in Chapter Two, in order to shed light on the nature of the Japanese response to the political and economic pressures of globalization.

In Japan's transition to a capitalist economy, the state intervened to pool the nation's resources, including scarce entrepreneurial talents in the merchant class and the skills and knowledge of the traditional elite, the samurai. With the development of business ideology, Japan was able to link risk-taking entrepreneuriship with creation of modern industries and institutions necessary for making Japan a great power. This helped to legitimize profit-making and raise the status of business career (Takahashi 1969). Thanks to nationalism, the largest identification circle also became drawn (Ishida 1984). It unified the energy of different segments of the population and channeled it towards collaborative competition in entrepreneurial enterprises. The government introduced incentives to solicit collaboration from businesses (Roberts 1973) while adopting "voice"[12] or consultative decision making to guide them in risk-taking. Together with mutual trust based on personal connection and reputation, loyalty and personal commitment--the ethical code of behavior which the former elite had transferred to the new objective of sharing and managing business risks--it provided the basic contractual framework for managing teamwork between firms (Hirschmeier 1965; Fraser 1988).

In the automobile industry, teamwork was adapted by Toyota as early as the 1930s to support its self-help approach to market entry and technological development in competition with Nissan which had followed a strategy of technology transfer (Cusumano 1985). Toyota enlarged its corporate identification circle by first including the parts makers in its neighborhood of Nagoya as members of the Toyota group. It offered long-term contracts to those who collaborated in quality improvement and product specialization. It also used its market power to discipline them when it saw fit. The assembler formalized supplier cooperative associations, started initially by the parts makers, as a voice mechanism to guide and support competition among the suppliers and as a forum for them to discuss problems, share information and find solutions. These contrasted with the market competition which Nissan was pursuing, like most other Japanese manufacturing houses of the day (Adachi, Ono, and Odaka 1983; Cusumano 1985; Smitka 1991).

Toyota continued with the teamwork approach to competitiveness, both in-house and with the suppliers in its group, when it shifted from truck to small car production from the early 1950s onwards. It implemented procedural improvements according to the suggestions of certain American experts (Deming 1986) while integrating them with the fundamental changes it was introducing in the production process to develop a system capable of handling production on a smaller scale yet in greater variety than built into the imported manufacturing process, one that could genuinely meet the requirements of domestic consumer markets (Cusumano 1985; Ono 1988).

The superiority of the Toyota system for technological development and building market share subsequently forced its chief competitor, Nissan, to convert to teamwork, duplicating some of the Toyota techniques while repairing and stabilizing relations with suppliers (Wada 1976). Thus, auto parts makers grew with assemblers in the postwar period of rapid economic expansion, improving their scale and accumulating expertise as well as building up proprietary technology, all the while working with assemblers to improve product designs and production processes in competition with other

Japanese auto manufacturing groups and, eventually, with manufacturers overseas (Asanuma 1989; Smitka 1991).

But the collaborative competition that was supported by mutual trust, obligation and loyalty within each auto-making group, along with large stakes in joint expansion, raised market barrier for Honda Motors, forcing it to rely on in-house R&D, constant product innovation, and international sales to enter the auto industry in the late 1960s (Sakiya 1982). With globalization, however, this vertically integrated competitive strategy, a deviant of the Japanese type, has been increasingly followed by other Japanese auto makers, including Toyota, the creator of Japan's teamwork approach to competitiveness. Both the political pressure of global linkages and the sky-rocketing costs of technological competition are making it difficult for the Japanese to maintain their traditionally exclusive relationships.

Auto assemblers and suppliers alike are redrawing the boundaries of their identification circles or business groups to manage change. The powerful subcontracting houses are expanding cross-supplies and diversifying sales to non-Japanese assemblers while forging strategic alliances with world-class suppliers of other nationalities to support the competition in technology. These in turn are putting pressure on the Japanese auto assemblers to integrate R&D to develop products of their own unique design and protect their proprietary technology. At the same time, Japanese assemblers are bending to the pressure of global linkages to buy more parts and components from the non-Japanese suppliers.

Unlike the previous two chapters which look at how the processes of globalization have affected the two largest economies in the world, Chapter Four of this book examines how the global linkages between auto makers in the Triad and an emerging economy like China have taken shape, how these global linkages have worked, and what policy responses they have provoked. This, again, requires a visit to the origin of the historically ideal structural relations in the country, as well as the techniques of national economic management which had created and maintained such relations before China opened up to the world economy in the early 1980s.

From 1949 to 1980, China managed its command economy by periodically shifting the locus of policy making between the center and the provincial governments on the one hand and between the center and the production units on the other (Schurman 1968a). When flexibility in policy implementation was needed for the policy of the center to suit local conditions, the central planners in Beijing would decentralize decision-making power to the provinces and/or factories (Schurmann 1960). But when decentralization led to "cellularized" local production and trade, contrary to the objective of developing interregional specialization of production, economy of scale, and comparative advantages of resources (Donnithorne 1964;

1972), they would take back the policy-making autonomy (Reynolds 1978), resulting in cyclical shifts in reforms (Nathan 1976; Winckler 1973).

The development of China's auto industry and the structural relations resulting from it reflect the effect of these policy shifts. Initially, auto manufacturing became one of the major industries which China used to create basic capacities in the national economy. Without the ability to develop by itself, China had borrowed a "comprehensive" or a fully vertically integrated, system of production from the Soviet Union during the 1950s. The central planners also set up fixed relations between the manufacturers and their matching suppliers to support entry, balance demand and production and guarantee 80 percent of the inputs supplies needed in China's "three 80s" supplies system.[13] When they decentralized policy-making in the late 1950s and early 1970s to encourage the development of the local industries in the spirit of "self-reliance," the local authorities duplicated the entry and industrial management techniques of the central bureaucracy. As a result, a total of about one hundred and thirty "small and comprehensive" and "medium and comprehensive" auto makers joined two centrally managed volume producers.[14] By 1979, they had fixed matching relations with more than two thousand direct suppliers.[15]

After reforms began in the early 1980s, China turned to partnerships with the Triad to add new products as well as upgrade skills and technology in auto manufacturing. Its transition to large-scale import-substitution car production since the late 1980s, in particular, has forced it to reconsider how to achieve policy adjustments in the economy. The central government continues to depend on shifting center-periphery relations to correct unintended development of reforms as well as to push new policies. But nowadays it must consider the consequences of balancing its policy objectives with flexibility in implementation in the periphery.

Policy adjustments cannot be totally autarkic as long as China's national economy is increasingly being linked with the global economy. China has had to minimize the destabilizing effects on the interests of the foreign investors and heed their demands when it amends the joint venture laws so as to prevent the amendment from driving them away. It has also had to introduce some changes in domestic economic system to maintain and expand global linkages. In this context, China is beginning to deal with the problem of product quality, a key purchasing condition of the joint venture auto builders, in the joint efforts to raise the domestic content of vehicle assembly, a second-stage development of import substitution production. It has also had to continue with decentralization to attract foreign investment to the automotive supplies sector so as to introduce the modernization needed before Chinese vendors can replace imported knock down kits with domestically sourced parts and components.

The concluding chapter of this book will compare and evaluate the responses of the United States, Japan, and China to the pressure of the globalizing economy. The automotive corporations in the United States and Japan have turned to global alliances to access niche markets, and pool resources as well as share R&D costs and risks to compete in technology, diffusing the best practices along the way. In comparison, China has switched from economic autarky to partnerships with global market forces to acquire the technology, technical know-how, and managerial expertise it needs for moving up the ladder of manufacturing and, possibly, developing new comparative advantages in international trade. All have faced the problems of changing and reengineering domestic manufacturer-supplier relations after establishing global linkages. All have had to deal with the pains that structural change has incurred in their societies. The different contributions which each of them makes or different strength which each brings to global linkages, however, have determined the ability of each to influence the terms of the global linkages.

The United States, with the highest purchasing power in the world, great capital mobilization capability, and world-ranking technological capacity, has been able to establish the terms of market penetration as well as the level of the linkages it wants from its global business relationships. In many cases of interest clashes, it has also been able to retaliate against its partners or allies. Its punitive behavior has certainly extracted concessions from the Japanese auto makers. A recent example includes the promise of Toyota and Mazda to escalate the restraints they have been exercising in vehicle exports to include establishing voluntary targets for purchasing American components.[16]

On their part, the Japanese are often able to set the standards of market competition in the world, as contributors to the capital and product and process technologies to the global linkages. The Japanese auto assemblers have been able to uphold their selection criteria while agreeing to increasing the American vendors' role in product development for transplant operation in the United States and opening up the "captive" market in their *keiretsu* groups for foreign supplied parts to be assembled back home. The transplant assemblers have sought to ally with those American vendors who are able to make special contributions in proprietary technology and who have demonstrated consistency in out-performing Japanese suppliers.

Compared to the United States and Japan, China has entered into global linkages as the weaker of two partners. One of its key bargaining chips versus global corporations is access to the rapidly expanding domestic market. Because of its technological weakness, China can not change at will the terms of market entry and ongoing relationships with global corporations. When conflicts arise in joint ventures, the central government has had to accommodate the interests of the foreign partners in order to keep them in the country instead of retaliating against them as may an advanced economy, such as the United States. It has also consistently improved the terms of foreign investment instead of retreating from the world economy in anticipation of future clashes. Additionally, the central planners have allowed the provinces and enterprises to keep their independence to maintain existing Sino-foreign partnerships and attract more foreign investors, particularly into the automotive supplies sector. Meanwhile, both the central and local governments have turned to reorganizing relations between the auto makers and their suppliers to resolve fundamentally the issue of imports versus development of the domestic capabilities.

Thus, globalization has added a new dimension--global linkages-- to the policy-making considerations of participating national economies. Just how much a national economy must adapt to the demands of international market forces and introduce the changes required at home and how much it is able to protect the domestic sick or "sunset" sectors and cushion the impact of structural change depends on how much strength it possesses, at least in terms of technology, capital, and worldwide marketing capabilities.

Through conceptual case studies, this book illustrates that all societies face the same problems when they open up. Yet all have the potential to become competitive in the globalizing world economy while the international division of labor is being reformulated. This book argues that it is those economies which are able to take advantage of the opening up to introduce necessary changes and those which are able to work with the constraints of their systems and turn them into advantages that will eventually succeed in competing in the world.

NOTES

1. The latest examples find expression in the struggle of the European car industry. See "Too Late for Champions," *Economist* (5 Feb. 1994): 19 and "Europe's Car Makers," *Economist* (5 Feb. 1994): 20-22.

2. The term was first raised by Porter (1990).

3. The conception of the network economy in the world may be driven home by a map of strategic alliances among the rival microelectronic giants (Gugler 1992).

4. The term "Triad" includes the United States, Japan, and Europe, and the newly industrialized countries which depend substantially on the markets in

these advanced economies for growth, as the concept is advanced by Kenichi Ohmae (1985).

5. See D. Ricardo, *The Principles of Political Economy and Taxation* (Cambridge: Cambridge University Press, 1981), particularly Chapter 7. The first edition of his masterpiece came out in 1817. The theory of the two Swedish authors, advanced in 1919 and 1933 respectively, is cited in any textbook of international trade.

6. An indication of the intra-industry trade that is contributed by the intrafirm transactions is reflected in the fact that more than eighty percept of the payments which the U.S. MNCs receive as royalties comes from their affiliates overseas (Stopford and Strange 1991, 17).

7. With the success of the first period of export-oriented growth, the host countries, particularly what later became known as the newly industrialized economies in East Asia, could also launch the second stage of import substitution production and demand that an escalation of the domestic content from DFI support the upgrading of the technological level of the export processing activities. For a good description of the second stage import-substitution program which Taiwan initiated to support its attempt to upgrade export processing activities, see R. I. Wu, "Economic Development Strategies and the Role of DFI in Taiwan," in C. F. Lee and S. C. Hu, Eds. *Taiwan's Foreign Investment Exports and Financial Analysis* (Greenwich, CT: JAI Press Inc., 1989), 65-89. Compare this with the upgrading strategy of South Korea as discussed by P. W. Kuznets, "Government and Economic Strategy in Contemporary South Korea," *Pacific Affairs* 58, no. 1 (Spring 1985): 44-67. The importance of the backward linkage effect which the national government must try to foster from DFI to develop national base of technology was first pointed out by A. O. Hirschman, in *The Strategy of Economic Development* (New Haven: Yale University Press, 1958). For the definition of the backward linkage effect, see p.100. For the rationale, see particularly chapters 6 and 10.

8. The changes in the financial sector that led to globalization of the world economy included the birth of the Euro-currency and Euro-bond markets in the 1960s, and deregulation that took American dollars off gold and changed from a fixed to a flexible exchange rate regime during the Nineteen Seventies, as well as further deregulation in the 1980s, particularly in the Anglo-Saxon economies, which permitted a greater number of financial institutions to participate in various kinds of international deals. See R.C. Smith, *Global Financial Services* (New York: Harper Business, 1990), 65-83 in particular.

9. For a few examples of how the Asian developmental states use industrial policy and the institutional requirements for its successful application, consult B. Balassa, "The Lessons of East Asian Development: An Overview," *Economic Development and Cultural Change* 36, no. 3 (April 1988): S273-S290; C. I. Bradford, Jr., "Trade and Structural Change: NICs and Next Tier NICs as Transitional Economies," *World Development* 15, no. 3 (1987): 299-316; J. Browett, "The Newly Industrializing Countries and Radical Theories of Development," *World Development* 13, no. 7 (1985): 789-803; P. W. Kuznets, "An East Asian Model of Economic Development: Japan, Taiwan, and South Korea," *Economic Development and Cultural Change* 36, no. 3 (April 1988): S11-S43; C. Y. Lin, "East Asia and Latin America as Contrasting Models,"

Economic Development and Cultural Change 36, no. 3 (April 1988): S153-S197; and G. Ranis, "The Role of Institutions in Transition Growth: The East Asian Newly Industrializing Countries," *World Development* 17, no. 9 (1989): 1443-1453.

10. Instead of taking place among firms and/or countries with mutually complementary resources and in a perfectly competitive market, MIT economist Krugman proposed, that international trade had been driven by economy of scale, cumulative know-how, and innovation in a world oligopoly. See P. R. Krugman, "Introduction: New Thinking abut Trade Policy," in P. R. Krugman, Ed., *Strategic Trade Policy and the New International Economics* (Cambridge, MA: MIT Press, 1987): 1-22.

11. "China to Learn Foreign Experience in Market Economy: Jiang," *Xinhua General News Service* (12 May 1993); T. Walker, "Ford Agrees to Dollars 90m Parts Venture in China," *Financial Times* (23 March 1993): 30.

12. The concept of voice was raised by Hirschman. Helper then examined it in her discussion of comparative business decision making and management of the structural relations between the United States and Japan (Helper 1990).

13. That is, the government guaranteed only eighty percept of the inputs for the enterprises, so that the latter must figure out how to make up for the rest of the 20 percept on their own (Maruyama 1980).

14. Among the medium-sized assemblers were Beijing Auto Works manufacturing the BJ 212 Jeep; Nanjing Auto Works, manufacturing a model of 2.5-ton truck; Shanghai Auto Works, manufacturing sedans; and Jinan Auto Works, producing eight-ton Yellow River trucks. Later, Beijing No. 2 Auto Works joined to assemble BJ130 light trucks. Some of the assemblers, such as the Beijing and Nanjing Auto Works, were converted from repair to craft assembly in 1958 during China's Great Leap Forward. The information on Beijing No.2 Autowork is based on Author's Interview with Erniu Xuan (Beijing, January 1992). Otherwise, see Xue (1988, 43-44, 47).

15. According to one Chinese insider, the total number of assemblers was reduced to thrity-seven by 1983, then rose to about eighty in 1985, and to 116 in 1986. They were scattered in twenty-two local administrative regions and fell under the control of eight ministries (Xue 1988, 11, 48-52, 58). Among the 130 assemblers, forty were still engaged in some scale of vehicle assembly in 1993, with the rest probably in fitting of special-purpose vehicles and buses or production of components. S. Vines, "Industry Tastes Life in Fast Lane," *South China Morning Post* (23 March 1993): 3.

16. W. Dawjubs and N. Dunne, "On the Verge of Trading Insults," *Financial Times* (7 March 1994): 16.

Chapter Two

Globalization, Firm Organization, and Interfirm Market Relations in the U.S. Automobile Industry

Until the 1970s, large hierarchically organized American corporations enjoyed a leading position in the world economy. Back home, they had been the chief contributors to economic growth and employment. Abroad, their multinational operations fueled a historically unprecedented expansion of world production and trade. Corporate America did not have to worry about competitive threat, because no one could challenge the hegemony of the United States after WWII. Europe had just moved from postwar reconstruction to recovery. Japan remained focused on restructuring, reorganization and technological catching up. The capitalist developing nations, today known as the newly industrialized economies, depended on American investment and technology to link up with the world economy and upgrade their manufacturing capabilities.

Mass production, a technological contribution of the auto industry, had led to American dominance in many of the world's industries. Besides providing plenty of jobs in the United States, auto builders also paid one of the highest manufacturing wages. During the 1950s and 1960s, the American public provided a vast pool of captive consumers to the Big Three auto manufacturers. Although imports crept in from the latter 1950s onwards, they were limited in market share and kept off the main part of the Big Three's business. Besides, GM and Ford had taken counter measures to reestablish production in Europe upon its transition to recovery. The two largest American auto assemblers provided not only their production technology, but also their method of organizing the interfirm relations to the rest of the world. Thus, they produced and prospered within economically secure national boundaries as well as expanded, intruded and sometimes even imposed their intrafirm and interfirm relations on the other national economies.

During these decades, American auto builders also institutionalized adversarial relations with their domestic suppliers. As productivity built into the functionally specialized mass production system plateaued, they sought to increase profitability by forcing price reductions on suppliers. To this end, assemblers re-installed bidding to create a competitive market structure in automotive supplies and manipulated business uncertainty among the parts and components makers. The competition in price, however, had not only eroded many of the suppliers' capabilities to improve product design and production processes and shifted control to the assemblers, but also bred distrust among them (Shapiro 1985; Helper 1990; Womack, Jones, and Roos 1991).

Amid such growth and structural change in American industries in the postwar decades, two competing perspectives evolved in investigating the causal relationship between the structure of American enterprise and technological development. One looked at the interaction between the changing market environment and strategic decisions within a firm. This may be termed an intrafirm perspective. The other was the interfirm perspective, which reviewed the evolution of the linkages that a manufacturer had with its suppliers and examined the effect of these linkages on the corporate effort at and capacity for innovation. The historical approach was a favorite with the intrafirm perspective of investigation. A descriptive model of American enterprise thus emerged and its elaboration proliferated. The same evolutionary processes of market forces underlay some authors' attempts to provide a theory for the descriptive model. Earlier works of the interfirm perspective borrowed the analytical approach and tools of the intrafirm perspective. On this basis, comparative studies of the manufacturing techniques of different societies sprang up during the 1980s to offer prescriptive remedies to American enterprise on how to stop the erosion of competitiveness which had begun since the 1970s.

To be sure, most of the descriptive writings on American industries focus on the impact of corporate structural change on innovation, the reasons for the change, and its outcome. They investigate these issues by combining two perspectives of analysis. For example, they attribute the change in the interfirm structural relations to not only the market environment at large but also to strategic reorganization within a firm. Similarly, they point out how an understanding of interfirm linkages can help to pinpoint the sources of product innovation in an industry as well as trace obstacles to corporate innovation to their origin. Because it has built its analysis within the context of a domestic market environment, however, the descriptive model of inquiry is inadequate for generating explanations and serving as a decision aid for achieving competitiveness in a globalizing world economy. Still, it provides much insight about the evolution of American corporations as well as the tradition of the individualistic competition which, to this date, they struggle to maintain.

With publications spanning four decades, Chandler (1962; 1964; 1977; 1990) has set up the relationship between market[1] and managers as the principal framework within which to investigate change in corporate America. He focuses his inquiry on identifying reasons for the decline of the invisible hand of the market forces and the rise of the corporate managers' visible hand in shaping market forces following the managerial revolution in the United States.

He has found, for instance, that managerial corporations that came to be administered by professional managers at the turn of the nineteenth century were able to capture the benefit of the emerging railroad and telegraph systems more effectively than single-product and single-service family shops, thanks partly to growing structural differentiation in these corporations. This in turn contributed to the further development of their functionally specialized and multilayered corporate structure (Chandler 1962). As early as the 1860s, a connection appeared between the scale of an American enterprise and innovation. Firms typically grew in size and transformed themselves structurally not only because they demanded new products and services and spearheaded their diffusion, but also because they were committed to creating them internally, when they were not available in the market place. To gain better control of their production and capture a good share of the emerging national market when a rising number of cities and industries was becoming integrated by the national railroad networks, corporations in the "most vibrant businesses" towards the end of the nineteenth century had also vertically integrated upstream activities of wholesaling and retailing as well as downstream sourcing (Chandler 1964, 9-10).

In his more recent works, Chandler (1977; 1990) has elaborated further on his earlier analysis. He notes that after the managerial revolution had changed the market environment, adding functionally organized operating units became the way in which American industrial firms competed and expanded: A modern manufacturing enterprise first made throughput-based specific investment to obtain economy of scale in production. It then integrated other functions, ranging from specialized marketing and supplies to R&D, to capture the benefits of economy of scope as well as reduce transaction costs. Yet it was ultimately "the existence of this (managerial) hierarchy," with the middle and top managers supervising and coordinating the activities of the independent operating units, that made "the activities and operations of the whole enterprise more than the sum of its operating units" (Chandler 1990, 15).

This was because under a managerial hierarchy, compared to the market, the competition had shifted from production costs alone to an emphasis on "functional and strategic effectiveness" that was aimed at seizing larger market shares with a higher profit margin. After they had sunk in specific investment, corporations sought to improve coordination of the activities of their functional departments by running the finance department more effectively to redirect the internal cash flow speedily in response to changes in technology and market demands. By becoming the first to work out the bugs in the production processes and improve the designs of their products and by getting a head start in learning to anticipate and meet customer needs as well as distributing goods and services, these enterprises had gained the first mover advantage in the market. This allowed them to erect barriers in the market by forcing new entrants to compete on their terms. As a result, the large and vertically integrated corporations that had established positions in a concentrated market[2] controlled innovation in the national economy. In this manner, managerial hierarchy came to establish a toehold in the major sectors of the American industry, spearheading economic expansion while themselves growing within the nation as well as overseas.

Chandler's descriptive theory supplied an explanation to Galbraith's observation (1980) that large corporations were becoming a permanent phenomenon in the postwar national economy in America, accompanied by a growing labor movement that had risen to counter the force of capital. Similarly, it provided a laboratory for testing and validating Schumpeter's pioneering hypothesis that innovation had changed from the random initiatives of individual entrepreneurs to the organized activities of large corporations. Some theorists of neo-classical microeconomics went about testing this hypothesis by investigating corporate behavioral patterns in the postwar decades, sometimes with the help of the analytical techniques of psychology (Kamien and Schwartz 1982).[3]

They started by identifying innovation[4] as an act of self-interested entrepreneurship or an outcome of rational decision making. Then these theorists looked for the motivations driving the decisions of the large American corporations of relatively equal size, relatively equal functional and strategic effectiveness, and relatively equal technological capabilities. The question was what caused them to continue with innovation rather than collapsing into technological stagnation after they had already divided up the market. The theorists concentrated on finding out the structural mechanisms that generated the right amount and mixture of incentives for inducing optimal technological effort from the firms. They had two suppositions to work with. If the cost of not engaging in innovation or of not placing enough effort in it was high, then a firm would be more likely to identify with innovation. Similarly, if the cost of capital for financing innovation and the risk and uncertainty for such investment were comparatively low, then it would be more inclined to allocating more resources to innovation.

Charting a continuous range of market structure in a national economy, these economists found oligopoly superior both to perfectly competitive structure and to monopoly for motivating innovation. Their explanation was twofold. First, the firms in a concentrated market were better positioned than those in a perfectly competitive market for raising the needed capital. For one thing, the former could earn a higher level of profit. This was because they faced a more visible demand curve in the product market and, thus, could set their price less competitively or with a higher premium. Higher profit margins could in turn translate into better ratings in the capital market than those obtainable by firms in a perfectly competitive industry. Additionally, higher profit margins allowed the firms to accumulate internal resources for corporate R&D.

Second, the oligopolies were more able to inhibit rapid imitation than firms in a perfectly competitive industry, thereby protecting the level of payoff accruable from R&D. This provided added incentives for innovation. Conversely, the oligopolies were less likely than a monopoly to develop X-inefficiency,[5] whereby the corporate management would be reluctant to commit to any undertaking that could upset the level of profit which might comfortably be earned from an existing product. If, however, there was no threat perception to their market share and profit margins, then oligopoly firms could behave like monopolies and not engage in innovation, even though they had greater resource allocation capabilities. This points to the level of threat as a critical variable for inducing innovation. In other words, if the threat perception in terms of both market share and profit level remained high, then the opportunity cost of not engaging in innovation would be high. It was precisely this threat perception which prevented the oligopoly firms from sliding into price competition and which kept their commitment to R&D. The threat perception would be high, particularly if a challenger tried to enter the industry with substitutes which would threaten to eliminate the profit of the established firms.

The threat perception escalated, indeed, as U.S. corporations began to face increasing global competition both at home and abroad from the 1970s onwards. The situation in the automobile industry was particularly alarming, since it remained one of the largest job providers in the national economy as well as the symbol of the economic power of the United States. This forced economic theorists to evaluate and identify the nature of the threat and the organizational responses to it as well as the subsequent decline of the American automobile industry both in the United States and overseas. Analysts also undertook to identify the general decline of the industrial and manufacturing centers in America that were affected by the developments in the auto industry. Thus, the debate on the necessary organizational changes in both intra- and interfirm relationships began to take shape.

Williamson (1970; 1975; 1986) pioneered the comparative study of the efficiency of the managerial hierarchy in managing innovation versus that of market in an attempt to explain the organizational change both within the American corporations and between them. Unlike many economists who treated innovation as an undifferentiated whole (Kamien and Schwartz 1982), Williamson conceptualized it as a decomposable process of several stages of creative activity, including invention, R&D and production, as well as distribution. He matched each stage of the activity with an efficient structure of enterprise according to the life cycle of business organization,[6] with each having a correspondingly efficient firm size. He then imposed two alternative structures for managing R&D, namely, market and managerial hierarchy, on the continuous scale of the organization. On this basis, he proceeded to investigate how and why managerial hierarchy had come to replace market as the agent for promoting and appropriating innovation.

In his earlier volumes, Williamson (1970; 1975) focused on resolving a central dilemma of dynamic growth in the processes of the American industrial revolution: On one hand, the improvement of a product or the addition of a new one required innovation at several technologically separable stages of production, particularly that of inputs supply such as components manufacturing. On the other, the American suppliers that had historically risen, together with the final assemblers, on functional specialization and technological economy of scale had gained their first mover advantage in the intermediate inputs market. They consequently obtained a powerful bargaining position versus the assemblers. This power relationship not infrequently threatened to discourage suppliers from dovetailing their objective of maximizing efficiency scale, profit level, and managerial stability with the assemblers' interests in innovation and profit maximization in the final product market.

Williamson re-framed the analytical question raised by many neo-classical micro economists (Kamien and Schwartz 1982). Instead of How could a modern American corporation be brought to see its enlightened self-interests in innovation in a single undifferentiated product market? the question became How could a supplier be brought to identify with the competitive needs of a final assembler? The corollary question became which management structure could lower the costs of transferring the output of innovation from a supplier to the assembler. It was to neutralize the bargaining power of the suppliers and minimize the costs of interfirm transfer of product technology that major assemblers began to integrate R&D vertically.

Later, Williamson (1986) went on to construct a topology of six transactional environment influencing the terms of interfirm technology transfer, depending on how specific the asset investment in innovation and production turned out to be, how frequently the interfirm transactions occurred, what bargaining position a supplier could gain with an assembler by controlling product innovation and how crucial it was for the assembler to secure control of such activity to remain competitive in the final product market. He hypothesized six transactional outcomes within two alternative regimes of R&D management.

According to his analysis, market could efficiently determine the location of innovation in at least four of six transactional situations.[7] This applied when a product was bought only infrequently, whether it was a standard piece of equipment (situation No. 1), a customized one (situation No. 2) or concerned construction of a new plant (situation No. 3). Procurement should still be favored over integration, if it involved standard materials, even if the transaction was repetitive (situation No. 4). But if the investment was specific for a product which the assembler must use all the time, whether it involved "customized materials" (situation No. 5) or parts or components (situation No. 6), then the assembler should internalize the activity. The rule of thumb, therefore, was that the more "idiosyncratic" the asset investment and the more "recurrent" the transaction proved to be for the assembler, the more likely that managerial hierarchy would replace market in managing R&D.

Williamson found support for his theory of innovation management from Chandler's (1990) analysis of corporate America's purchasing strategy. Chandler agreed that frequency of transaction would be a necessary condition for corporate America to take over the control of the supplies from the market. He also identified a strategic decision to maximize cost efficiency and profit as the key reason driving the change in the governance structure. This explained why a firm would prefer purchasing to integration when multiple sources of supply were available or when internalization could not directly improve the scale efficiency in assembly. Under either circumstance, maintaining a competitive market structure seemed to make more sense. This, of course, would force market competition on the suppliers, which would surely serve to strengthen the firm or the assembler's bargaining position.

When the power for managing innovation shifted from market to the managerial hierarchy, however, the pattern of R&D changed. With internalization, cost minimization for corporate profit maximization came to dominate purchasing. Since their job had been reduced to pushing functional specialization to exploit the scale and scope efficiencies built into the system of mass production, particularly after corporate America had added headquarters on top of functional departments to strengthen financial control and coordinate development, managers had begun to respond to the commands of financial targets and sought after those areas of R&D that promised to expand quarterly sales and therefore raise quarterly departmental profit rates (Chandler 1962; 1977; 1990). This meant that the type of innovation which looked costly or less profitable in the short run and which could threaten the career advancement of departmental managers was more likely to be shoved under the rug than to be promoted. Just how financially riskier innovation might be fostered and how managers could be brought to take more risks remained subjects into which Williamson's theory of innovation management did not venture.

This human side of the functional and strategic competition of American enterprise had long received attention from Drucker (1967) who saw corporate America as a social institution (Drucker 1946) as much as an economic organization. From Drucker's perspective, a corporation could be successful only if its chief executive officer had a vision about its future competitive position. He must be a trend setter in introducing change in the market and technology instead of a trend follower. Similarly, he had to assume responsibility for motivating departmental managers to give their best efforts for long-term corporate gains instead of settling on a secure path and slaving for short-term profits.

For the most part, however, the debate revolved around what had exactly caused market to surrender the control of the intra-industry trade to the hierarchy. A few economists conducted quantitative tests to support different arguments. Lustgarten (1975), for example, tried to explain the change in terms of Galbraith's theory (1980) of countervailing power. In effect, he supported Stigler's hypothesis (1951) that make-or-buy decisions were determined by a firm's scale of production as the industry climbed down the learning curve. One had only to observe the ratio of a corporation's demand for an input to its total supply in the market to note the change. Perry (1978) differed with the learning-curve hypothesis. He saw vertical integration as resulting from the manufacturer's decision to maximize profits. This explained why corporations would sometimes integrate supplies partially instead of all the way. His contention found an echo in Carlton (1979) when the latter attributed the change of power to the failure of market in providing certainty in inputs supply and, hence, its failure in reducing costs and improving corporate profits in production.

Micro-economic studies like these, however, ended up giving more attention to the discussion of the advantages of managerial hierarchy over market in managing risks, costs, and uncertainty than directly linking the analysis of the structural change with innovation.[8] This neglect appeared to have resulted from their focus on testing out the hypothesis of microeconomics theories by using increasingly sophisticated statistical and econometric tools.

In comparison, Williamson's transaction cost theory provided a greater insight into the dynamics of the American enterprise. Monterverde and Teece (1982) applied his theory to analyze make-or-buy decisions of the American auto industry. They found that in the case of the design and production skills that were particular to a specific assembler in developing new components, the components suppliers could increase their bargaining power if the auto assembler should shift research and development responsibilities to the latter. For this reason, it became essential for the assembler to invest in firm-specific R&D to gain its bargaining advantage versus the parts and components makers. This hierarchical relationship allowed the assemblers not only to effectively capture externalities from the R&D and reduce contractual costs, but also to protect its proprietary interests.

Grossman and Hart (1985), on the other hand, concluded through mathematical modeling that integration driven by transaction cost considerations could damage entrepreneurship, even though it could reduce purchasing costs in the short run in the theory. Yet Williamson and his supporters did not take into account this effect of the hierarchical relationship between the assemblers and their suppliers, because they had devoted their attention to comparing the costs of the deals made through market and hierarchical relationships.

Hierarchy, finally, could downgrade a firm's investment in R&D for product innovation if the activity threatened to disrupt the firm's profit objectives. But the micro-economic theories, the transaction cost theory, and the descriptive analysis of Chandler could not adequately address this consequence of the intrafirm hierarchical relationships. Indeed, microeconomics theories argued that oligopoly would establish a dynamic equilibrium which would disallow firms to ignore R&D, whereas the transaction costs theory and Chandler's analysis assumed that the existence of market and hierarchy as alternative governance structures would suffice to neutralize the tendency of firms to protect short-term profits at the expense of product innovation. In contrast, Drucker (1967) believes that the conceptual and behavioral changes of top management could bring back commitment to corporate competitiveness. On the other hand, Abernathy, along with his colleagues (1978; 1981; 1983), tried to locate the sources of risk aversion in the hierarchy and suggest ways in which the entrepreneurial instinct of managers could triumph over their aversion to risk. Unlike Schumpeter, who had emphasized the role of the managers in innovation, Abernathy and his colleagues stressed technology as the main variable for this activity. This resulted in redefining the term innovation, and differentiating "epochal" (Clark 1983) or radical product innovation from incremental innovation, thereby changing innovation from a static into a dynamic process.

Abernathy (1978) began by investigating the history of the American automobile industry. He found that hierarchy was very effective in capturing the cost benefit of standardization. But it also discouraged radical product innovation, which would ultimately lead to the decline of the industry, a point which Thomson (1954) had already noted at a time when standardization was considered essential to mass production, mass marketing, and to seizing and maintaining market shares.[9]

After reviewing the rise and decline of productivity levels in the auto industry, Abernathy concluded that reversing product life cycles by implementing a staggered strategy of standardization among product divisions would allow radical product innovation typical of the early stage of the life cycle of the auto industry to continue well into the later stage, when economy of scale had already been built in. Abernathy also suggested that the auto firms reduce the level of integration which saved costs yet had at the same time obstructed innovation.

In a policy paper in 1981, he blamed hierarchy for taking away the competitive threat and turning R&D into a defensive strategy. This supported the hypothesis that threat perception was crucial for stimulating competition in technology (Kamien and Schwartz 1982). With threat, the operational departments would have to face preferences in segmented consumer markets instead of feeling protected from their pressure. They would have to deal with challenges from both the intrafirm and interfirm competitors. Under the threat of corporate competition, managers would no longer be able to behave in a predictable manner. They would have to consider rivals' decisions and performance and seek long-term profits through R&D. It was in affecting change like this rather than influencing competitive environment with antitrust regulations that Abernathy saw an important role for government policy.

Later, Abernathy, Clark, and Kantrow (1983) argued that the aging American auto industry could be revitalized only if the auto makers would pay attention to the preferences of the market. It would be the only way for the auto industry to realize "dematurity," or restoring the industry's life cycle back to its youthful and more dynamic stage. The more radical the market revision of preferences, the greater the pressure would be on managers to move away from imitating competitors towards searching for their own niches, as they learned to master "differential excellence in manufacturing," the new source of competitiveness. Similarly, the more the firms pursued dematurity in product design, the greater the effect would be on innovative activities, fostering the rebirth of both the auto makers and their suppliers. Clark (1983) emphasized additionally the need for the corporations to revive their "entrepreneurial thrust" in order to take advantage of the radical shift in the demand to compete in "epochal" innovation. But he did not specify how firms were supposed to realize this strategy.

Until the firms could find a radical solution, Hayes and Wheelwright's matrix analysis (1979a; 1979b) of product/process life cycles provided a stopgap. They suggested that managers shift to compete innovatively by improving the coordination of their marketing and manufacturing strategies. This might be one way of carrying out the staggered strategy which Abernathy (1978) had recommended for realizing dematurity. But their analysis also highlighted the difficulties which American firms were experiencing in re-shaping their internal resources and reorganizing skills and organizational competencies to meet renewed challenges in both process and product technologies.

Abernathy and his colleagues thus provided a new typology of innovation based on the analysis of productivity. They saw epochal innovation as more effectively pulled by market, thanks to its ability to generate entrepreneurial competition, contrasting with hierarchical coordination and control, which only resulted in incremental improvement. But to trigger epochal innovation as well as raise productivity, power needed to be decentralized. Decision-making control had to be removed from the chief financial officers at the corporate headquarters and returned to those managers who would take risks in product and process strategy (Hayes and Abernathy 1980).

The problem was that responsiveness to market alone may not work for innovation and productivity. For one thing, declining demand for automotive products had to a great extent been responsible for weakening the capital goods industry by the 1980s (Arnett and Smith 1974; Mateyka et al. 1982). The same may have been true for components supplies. It was therefore very difficult for suppliers to find the necessary funding for technological upgrading to deliver products based on radical innovation. As long as price remained the critical competitive criterion, components vendors found it difficult to introduce innovative products. The auto assemblers found themselves in a similar situation after decades of cost reduction and incremental product change introduced through application of on-the-shelf technologies (Rubenstein and Ettlie 1978). To bypass these hurdles, some suggested that firms replace integration of components manufacturing with long-term contracts and internalize, instead, the design and development of critical equipment as Japanese and European firms did. It was possible that by following this strategy firms and suppliers could both become more innovative (Hayes and Abernathy 1980). On the other hand, others argued that a more sophisticated linkage was needed to stimulate innovation on both sides so as to jointly revive the American auto industry (Kumpe and Bolwijin 1988; Vanderwerf 1990).

In his writings, Abernathy identified improvement in productivity as the solution to reversing the loss of corporate competitiveness. He also emphasized technology as the key to improving productivity. However, Abernathy did not explain why a major vertical shift in decision making power leading to decentralization might be necessary for productivity to increase. Deming (1986), on the other hand, stood Abernathy's proposition, Chandler's analysis, and Williamson's transaction cost theories on their heads. For Deming, producing a defect-free product rather than technology was the primary answer to reestablishing American competitiveness. He argued for building quality into a production system already in place and urged firms to redesign horizontal linkages with the suppliers by abandoning competitive bidding in favor of single sourcing.

By supporting single sourcing, Deming de-emphasized the traditional argument that competition was necessary for technological development. In his comparative analysis of the Japanese and American production systems, Deming argued that market competition had impeded innovation in the United States. Sourcing by one supplier was more effective for meeting the quality objectives. But to make single sourcing work, corporations must replace the "arms-length" strategy that was used for depressing inputs prices in spot deals as well as cushioning demand fluctuations with "arms-around" strategy which would foster cooperative relationships with vendors. This was because quality control, a critical ingredient for process improvement and product R&D, required long-term commitment from both suppliers and manufacturers. Only single sourcing could provide such commitment.

Deming, like Drucker (1967), identified visionary leadership as the key to systemic change within a firm. But unlike Drucker, who equated vision with instincts about future trends in technology, Deming singled out long-term commitment to business that was unaffected by the results of quarterly earnings reports as the prerequisite for change. Like Drucker, Deming also emphasized the importance of developing and nurturing human capital for corporate competitiveness. While the former saw the best effort of each employee within the vertical structure as sufficient, Deming argued for improving the knowledge effort with teamwork to achieve quality. Deming therefore called for dismantling functional barriers within the hierarchy. For him, teamwork must be first instituted within the firm before it could be extended to suppliers.

By suggesting revision of structural linkages, Deming provided a new schema for analyzing change in American enterprise. He identified a number of indicators for measuring the change. First, whether purchasing was made on the basis of minimizing initial price or quality and total cost control. Second, whether the manufacturer played suppliers against each other or worked with them. Third, whether the firm constantly changed suppliers or built up long-term partnerships with them, and finally, whether multiple or single sourcing was the basis of inter-firm transaction (Deming 1986; Aguayo 1990).

Deming's proposition for transforming structural linkages received widespread support among business analysts. In light of Japan's success, most of them favored discarding spots deals except for the highly standardized items. But Deming's recommendation that single sourcing replace competitive bidding ran into resistance. There was widespread fear that single sourcing in the United States might not work in the same manner as in Japan. For example, American suppliers might take advantage of the transition to single sourcing to go after profit maximization instead of innovation. They might also hold manufacturers hostage in bargaining. Therefore, most analysts urged firms to seek a protective strategy with diversification, particularly for strategic components (Krafjic 1983; Schonberger and Gilbert 1983; Burt and Soukup 1985).

The resistance to single sourcing, of course, is rooted in the belief system which microeconomics theories have strengthened. This has in turned influenced the American regulatory policy that promotes market competition for innovation (Jorde and Teece 1989; Teece 1991). In the face of the ideological commitment to competition, it may be necessary to clarify what single sourcing is. Single sourcing should refer to a strategic approach to purchasing that extends buying beyond acquisition of a part or component to that of additional values which a supplier could bring with its engineering and process capabilities. By saving on costs for the firm in the long run and boosting profits for the suppliers, this approach should produce mutual benefits and a "win-win" outcome to both parties of the transaction (Newman 1988). Single sourcing may also provide more innovative parts and components for a firm, as the vendors learn about the firm's intent and long-term commitment through sizable multi-year contracts which make it possible for the vendors to invest in production and R&D upgrading. With the information provided by the firm, they can understand how their components fit into the overall scheme of the final product, find out problems, and correct them (Aguayo 1990).

Additionally, single sourcing may be a process for weeding out mediocre suppliers by providing those suppliers that prove more competitive in quality and value-added contents with opportunities to grow and prosper. This contrasts with bidding that breeds mediocrity by putting pressure on the firm to withhold its full support for the vendors when temporary setbacks in the market place occur (Leednors and Blenkhorn 1988). After building up a stable base of suppliers, a firm can direct them to focus competition on quality, engineering capabilities and efficiency rather than price alone. But building up partnership this way requires that the firm reward the winners with sizable orders on the basis of their past performance. Indeed, Japanese corporations have employed this strategy of competition with their structural partnerships to generate superior products as well as superior manufacturing systems (Garvin 1988; McMillan 1990).

In response to their historical belief systems and the critical debate in microeconomics analysis, American corporations have demonstrated ambivalence towards the decline of their autonomy as a result of global competition and the weakening viability of national boundaries. Indeed, in the automobile industry, corporations had lost about one fourth of the most dynamic small car segment of the domestic market to Japanese producers by the 1980s (Table 2.1). To stop further erosion of their position as well as to protect their remaining dominance in the domestic market, the American auto makers decided to measure up in competitiveness. They have tried to duplicate the world's best practices to compete in the global economy. On the other hand, they have yet to commit to partnership with suppliers to build a truly competitive just-in-time (JIT) system of lean production which can provide gains for both parties.[10] In most cases, the survival of individual corporations, particularly in economic bad times, continues to take priority over the principle of reciprocity that is required of inter-corporate teamwork (Womack and Jones 1994).

To cushion the transition to lean production, the American auto companies have tried to shift part of the burden of domestic structural change onto the Japanese companies. While advocating free trade, they have asked for and received support from the American government to extract voluntary export restraints from Japanese auto makers. In the 1990s, they have further enlisted help from both the executive and congressional branches of the United States government to broaden bilateral trade with Japan to boost American automotive exports.

While the debate over which governance structure to use for inter-corporate transactions remains unresolved, American corporations have rapidly adopted JIT inventory control. For the auto companies, this means forcing vendors to bear at least part of the burden of adjustment while the auto companies struggle to manage the risks they face in the period of structural change. In the event, many American manufacturers choose to support only those suppliers who are willing and able to share the risks of change (Schonberger and Gilbert 1983). But this has made the position of suppliers even more tenuous in the absence of single sourcing, limited competition, and long-term contractual relations.

As it turns out, JIT inventory control introduced this way can not serve the objective of improving quality and provide a stable production system. Such a system can be achieved only by changing the nature of the production process through a complete reorganization not only of worker-management relations, but also of the role of workers in a production process (Zipkin 1991). In other words, systematic improvement in a production process that has JIT as an integral component necessitates a partnership with suppliers. It requires that innovative suppliers correspondingly change the goal of their business strategy from the size of sales to the amount of value they can add to the assemblers' products. They must become experts in the components they supply. They must also pay attention to how their components are used in an end product so as to add value to it. Finally, suppliers must select the firms with which they want to form long-term partnerships. They need to diversify as well as exercise discrimination in order to keep their commitment to innovation (Jackson 1985; More 1986; Gross 1989; Anderson and Narus 1991; Porter 1991).

Whether they are for maintaining bidding or switching to single sourcing, all the theorists agree that corporate purchasing functions must change (Schonberger and Gilbert 1983; Garvin 1984, 1988; Burt and Soukup 1985; Leedners and Blenkhorn 1988; Newman 1988; Burt 1989). Purchasing is now recognized as central not only to minimizing defects but also to competing in quality. At least in this respect, the Japanese model has influenced significantly the way with which American corporations change and improve their business processes. Thus, purchasing has become linked to engineering, and the pricing of components has come to be coordinated with that of vendors' engineering capabilities (Garvin 1984, 1988).

The buyers have now to assume the responsibility for evaluating the performance of suppliers to make sure that the latter meet quality, price, delivery and service requirements of firms in implementing JIT systems (Schonberger and Gilbert 1983). To do their job properly, however, the buyers must be technically competent, so that they can provide critical suppliers for work in design and product development as well as production processes. But most corporations do not have such buyers. It is therefore suggested that they seek assistance from outside consultants for a transitional period (Newman 1988; Burt 1989). But in the long run, firms are advised to

Table 2.1
Market Share of New Cars Sold in the United States (1982-1991) (,000) [1]

Car Sales	'86 units	%	'85[3] units	%	'84 unit	%	'83 units	%	'82 units	%
Total	11,490 (+4.1)	100.0	11,042 (+6.3)	100.0	10,391 (+13.2)	100.0	9,177 (+15)	100.0	7,978	100.0
Big 3	7,845 (-2.3)	68.2	8,032[6] (+3.7)	71.9	7,744[7] (+16.3)	74.5	6,660[8] (+17.6)	72.6	5,665[9]	71.0
Import	3,248 (+14.5)	28.3	2,838 (+16.3)	25.7	2,440 (+2.4)	23.5	2,383 (+7.3)	25.4	2,221	27.8
Japan[12] Makes	2,386 (+12.6)	20.8	2,219 (+16.4)	20.1	1,906 (-0.5)	18.3	1,916[11] (+6.3)	20.9	1,802	22.6
Euro. Makes	693 (+16.2)	6.0	620[13] (+14.2)	5.6	534 (+11.4)	5.1	467	5.1	419	5.3
Transplant:										
Japan Makes U.S. Blt.	295 (+58.9)	2.6 (+39.0)	186[14]	1.7	134 (+165.0)	1.3	50	0.5	--	--
Euro. Makes U.S. Blt	74 (-4.7)	0.6	77.5[15] (+5.0)	0.7	74 (-13.2)	0.7	85 (-6.7)	0.9	91	1.1
Japan[16] Derived	2,681 (+11.6)	23.3	2,404 (+17.8)	21.8	2,040 (+3.8)	19.6	1,966 (+9.1)	21.4	1,802	22.6

Car Sales	'91[2] units	%	'90 units	%	'89 units	%	'88 units	%	'87 units	%
Total	8,176 (-12.0)	100.0	9,296[4] (-4.3)	100.0	9,713 (-8.3)	100.0	10,595 (-3.6)	100.0	10,225 (-11)	100.0
Big 3	--	--	5,782 (-8.2)	62.2	6,296[5] (-8.9)	64.2	6,910 (+5.7)	65.2	6,537 (-16.7)	63.9
Import	2,104 (-14.2)	25.7	2,453 (-9.1)	26.4	2,698 (-12.1)	27.8	3,069 (-2.4)	29.0	3,144 (-3.2)	30.7
Japan Makes	1,821[10] (-4.4)	22.3	1,721 (-10.0)	18.5	1,911 (-9.1)	19.7	2,103 (-3.2)	19.8	2,173 (-8.9)	21.2
Euro. Makes	339 (-26.0)	4.1	503 (-16.0)	5.5	490 (-13.8)	5.0	569 (-11.7)	5.4	645 (-6.9)	6.3
Transplant:										
Japan Makes U.S. Blt	1,124 (+6.0)	13.8	1,061 (36.2)	11.4	779 (+31.6)	8.0	591 (+22.5)	5.6	482 (+63.5)	4.7
Euro. Makes U.S. Blt	--		--		--		25 (-59.2)	0.2	61 (-17.4)	0.6
Japan Derived	2,945 (-5.3)	36.0	2,781 (+3.4)	30.0	2,690 (-0.2)	27.7	2,694 (+1.5)	25.4	2,655 (-1.0)	26.0

Notes

1. Unless otherwise footnoted, see annual issues of *Automotive News, Market Data Book, 1984 through 1992.* The figures are rounded to the thousands and percentages to one decimal point. All the units mentioned in the footnotes refer to those in the thousands.

2. From Jan. to Dec. of the year. The same holds for 1990. See K. Done, "'Pots and Kettles' Clash into Auto War," *Financial Times* (28 January 1992): 3, with source of data being *Automotive News.*

39

3. From January 1 to December 31, 1985. The same holds for 1984. Figures and percentages are based on *Automotive News* (13 January 1986): 46.

4. For 1986 through 1990, see *Automotive News: Market Data Book*, 1991. The total imports include those of Korea's Hyundai and the European makes include those of Yugo.

5. This aggregate conforms to that in the 1990 issue of *Automotive News, Market Data Book*, but differs from that in the table of five-year sales figures in the 1991 issue of the same publication.

6. This aggregate differs from that in the 1987 issue of *Automotive News, Market Data Book*. The latter contains a mistake in the total sales figure for Ford.

7. Including more than 123 units by American Motors for 1985 and over 190 units for the same builder in 1984. *Automotive News* (13 January 1986): 46.

8. Includes more than 193 units of sales made by American Motors. *Automotive News, Market Data Book*, 1984.

9. Includes more than 112 units of sales made by American Motors. *Automotive News, Market Data Book*, 1984.

10. Derived from the table as presented in K. Done, "'Pots and Kettles' Clash into Auto War." Subtracting the Japanese makes as defined by Done (totaling 2,472 units, which includes the U.S.- built units) from the Japanese derived gives 473 units as the ones built by the Japanese auto makers that are sold under the Big three's badges. Add this to the imports from Japan (subtracting the 1,124 units built in the U.S.) and we get 1,821 units as listed here.

11. Includes less than 12 and more than 13 units of Sapporo/Conquest for 1983 and 1982 respectively. *Automotive News, Market Data Book*, 1984.

12. Refers to cars made in Japan, including those sold under the Big 3's badges. Note that this definition of "Japan make" differs from that of Done in the *Financial Times* (28 January 1992): 3. The latter includes units made in the Japanese transplant but excludes those made in Japan for sale by the Big Three under their nameplates.

13. Includes fewer than four units of Yugo. *Automotive News* (13 January 1986): 46.

14. The 1984 figure is for Honda only. The 1985 figure incudes Honda and Nissan. *Automotive News* (13 January 1986): 46.

15. Volkswagen. *Automotive News* (13, January 1986): 46.

16. The term is borrowed from K. Done, in the *Financial Times* (28 January 1992): 3. Here, it refers to Japan makes (import) plus units made in the Japanese transplants.

follow the Japanese example in instituting firm-specific training by institutionalizing job rotation across functional departments (Burt and Soukup 1985).

An engineering approach to purchasing will necessarily mean that purchasing managers are no longer treated as performing a clerical function in a corporation. It also means that both firms and suppliers will have to discriminate among companies they will select as new business partners in order to create and manage cooperation between them (More 1986). Purchasing managers must also persuade suppliers to identify with the firms' technological objectives and future products in designing their business strategy. Through the process of "reverse marketing," firms can improve their competitiveness by relying on the vendors to voluntarily suggest ways to improve their quality, cost, service, and product delivery. Thus, purchasing becomes conceptually linked to marketing, too (Leedner and Blenkhorn 1988; Anderson and Narus 1991).

As an initial step towards a collaborative relationship, firms and their suppliers can begin with joint value analysis. Suppliers should treat the exercise as a process whereby they can redesign components with the necessary information provided by the firms instead of using such an analysis as a tool for cutting corners and lowering profits to become competitive in bidding. On their part, firms should accept the the idea that the purpose of this joint effort is for vendors to improve their profits while reducing costs for the manufacturers (Newman 1988). Similar cooperation may also be extended to equipment procurement so that firms can utilize new equipment and advanced processes more effectively (More 1986).

If anything, the foregoing analysis points to the ways in which the Japanese model has impacted and, in some cases, influenced American corporations in intrafirm organization as well as interfirm structural relations. But to properly evaluate whether national economic boundaries have maintained their autonomy or have become porous, it is necessary to examine the other side of the coin or how the Japanese model has fared after arriving in the United States. In the 1980s, Japanese auto makers set up transplant production in America in answer to the growing pressure of managed trade and voluntary export restraints. An important point of investigation, therefore, is whether the Japanese intrafirm and interfirm relations have become Americanized or whether the transplants have been successful in pursuing Japanese methods across national boundaries.

To assess the impact of the Japanese transplants on the American suppliers critically, one must first develop a classification scheme. Conceptually, there may be three types of the Japanese auto firms in the United States: transplant assemblers, transplant manufacturers and joint venture transplants. It is hard, however, to distinguish between the first two types because of the difficulty in ascertaining the sources of the parts and components, the main criterion for differentiating these plants from each other. The paucity of data on the sale and imports of the automotive parts also renders it impossible to trace the transaction to the original supplies sourced. Thus, this study uses fifty percent of the domestic content as the cut-off point to distinguish a transplant assembler and manufacturer. fifty percent is also adequate for exploring how the global economy is imposing itself across national boundaries. In fact, in their effort to reduce the political and trade tensions with this economy, all the Japanese transplants passed the fifty percent threshold of domestic content by 1989. Lastly, the joint venture transplants, like the transplant manufacturers, purchase from both associate transplant suppliers and traditional American vendors. A comparison of the sourcing behavior between the two types of transplants may therefore help in examining the structural impact of the Japanese auto firms.

This study sets up three indicators for comparing the purchasing and supply management behavior of a selected number of transplants. They consist of: 1) the criteria for selecting a traditional American vendor as supplier; 2) the characteristics of the selection process used by the transplant, including the role of bidding and other purchasing techniques in final selection; and 3) the nature of relations which the transplants seek to develop with the American vendors.

Honda of America Manufacturing Inc. (HAM) started its car production in the United States in 1982 (Shook 1988).[11] By 1987, sixty-two percent of the parts used in the transplant at Marysville, Ohio, were of domestic content. A portion of these came from traditional American vendors, whereas the rest came from the joint ventures formed between HAM and transplant suppliers or between the traditional American vendors and the Japanese suppliers. In early 1992, HAM reported the split between the two sources as two-thirds to one-third.[12] Critical components like engines and transmissions are still made in-house.

HAM insists that it acquires only the best available or "one hundred percent good" parts, no matter from which corporation of which national origin the supplies come. It insists that bidding candidates understand and meet its quality standards. It is also important for the transplant that suppliers see they are selling the automotive parts not only to HAM, but also to the consumers of Honda automobiles. The transplant insists that just-in-time be a total commitment from prospective American vendors. It requires additionally that the suppliers commit to developing an in-house design and engineering capacity. As experience shows, the American vendors of Honda of America have had to invest in R&D and tooling and production changes, shorten lead times, and convert to the metric system as well as commit to total improvement in quality control. More recently, the capacity for design and engineering has become the key factor in determining whether an American vendor will get an order to supply critical parts and components through the newly introduced "design-in" process.

After the initial bidding, the candidate suppliers have to undergo a scrutinizing interview with HAM. They must demonstrate initiative and curiosity about HAM's operation during this process and allow inspection of their facilities by the transplant's research group under a program entitled "Quality Assurance Visits." If the research group finds any shortcomings as a result of such visits, the suppliers must correct it within a specified period of time. Upon passing this examination, the candidates will be required to provide sample parts for Honda to study and test. Only after this series of screenings and evaluations will HAM ask the surviving candidates for price quotations. They must disclose the price/cost breakdowns for everything that goes into a specific part, from the cost of the raw materials to those of fabrication, packaging and transportation, so that Honda can make sure that the suppliers meet its cost as well as its quality targets.

While it requires vendors to share information on detailed costs, Honda seeks to help them to identify problems of quality and efficiency. It helps suppliers to correct these problems by dispatching its engineers to the vendors' plants. Sometimes it renders assistance through its major Japanese suppliers. In 1988, Honda further decided to establish an R&D facility and a new production-engineering center to support localization of up to seventy-five percent of production in the United States in an effort to pacify nationalist sentiment in this economy as well as to turn America into a sourcing base for certain automotive parts for exports back to the East Asia.[13] To help it select new vendors and enter into new partnerships, Honda of America extends the vendor selection process not only downstream to vendor management but also upstream to thorough combing of the pool of vendors available in this country and constant monitoring of the progress they have made in quality and technology.

Finally, HAM encourages American vendors to diversify their sales so as to raise their economy of scale and reduce costs. At the same time, however, it demands that vendors give special attention to Honda, their principal customer. To encourage vendors to seek continuous improvement, HAM has also introduced a monthly grading system. If they fail to meet its standards, the vendors may get penalized. But, generally, HAM emphasizes the inducement rather than penalty function of the grading system. It gives out awards for excellence and effort in quality, delivery, and cost improvement, as well as a special award on its "Vendor Appreciation Day" each spring.

The vendor evaluation process may be tough on the suppliers, but the rewards are manifold. First, the vendors get a reputation for quality by supplying to Honda. Second, they get stability in business orders as long as they can match any new suppliers that happen to offer more competitive products at a better price. The best of the suppliers may also have a chance to become sole suppliers, just as some Japanese parts transplants of HAM do.

HAM's experience in vendor selection and supply management, including both the criteria which it puts out for purchasing and the way it uses bidding in the selection process, is shared by other Japanese transplant auto assemblers. One of such transplant is Mazda Motor Manufacturing (U.S.A.) Corp. (MMUC). MMUC, unlike Honda, is a joint venture transplant. It commenced car manufacturing at Flat Rock, Michigan, after Ford, Mazda's minority owner since 1979, agreed to buy 60 percent of its outputs under the nameplate Probe so that the economy of scale in production could be achieved (at 200,000 units annually) (Hill 1989; Oshima 1989).[14]

Like Honda of America, MMUC insists that its vendors commit to *kaizen* or "never-ending improvement" in quality and 100 percent customer satisfaction, which it believes suppliers can realize only by constantly reducing defects and strengthening their in-house design and engineering capabilities. MMUC also insists that American vendors shorten the lead time for product development for its locally designed parts, as the Japanese transplant begins to transfer vehicle design activity to this country. To help American vendors cultivate such capabilities, MMUC has urged them to redesign their corporate structure. On one occasion during the late 1980s, MMUC's chairman suggested that those suppliers interested in participating in joint product design should switch from functional to multi-disciplinary approaches to jobs, from compartmentalization to multi-functional teamwork, and from hierarchical command to a more consultative process in in-house communication in order to manage their product development projects more effectively (Nobuto 1989).

Mazda (U.S.A.) did have help from Ford regarding American suppliers, so it could begin selection with a list of candidates and proceed more directly to price quotation. On the other hand, the transplant may have taken on the suppliers recommended by Ford out of obligation to its joint venture partner. As with Honda of America, bidding is a complex process of evaluation that is designed to make sure that the joint venture transplant's costs and quality targets are met. Those who pass this screening get to go through prototype evaluation tests and quality control inspection by MMUC's executives.

In 1989, the transplant organized three supplier workshops to work closely with satellite firms on quality control, purchasing and design, as the pressure on localization of car design began to mount. This was in addition to the routine assistance that Mazda (U.S.A.) was already providing to suppliers, such as sending teams of people from its purchasing, quality control, production engineering, and R&D

departments to help suppliers to improve production processes, inventory control, and quality assurance programs, as well as to teach suppliers to get their own suppliers to improve product quality as well. By rendering assistance like this, MMUC aims ultimately to turn American vendors into partners who can genuinely contribute to parts development and thus to the design, engineering, and production of new vehicle models in much the same way as Mazda's Japanese suppliers back in Japan.

Additionally, MMUC has also mobilized Mazda's major parts transplants to teach competitive practices to American vendors, Ford's parts divisions included. To be sure, the joint venture transplant has benefited from the experience that the major parts transplants have already gained from tutoring American vendors in quality, cost, delivery and safety. Large Japanese parts transplants like Nippon Denso have transferred their technology partly by allowing the American vendors to enter their facilities at any time. In return, they demand a long-term commitment from the American vendors and expect them to share both profits and losses. Like MMUC, some of the parts transplants also plan to set up their own supplier associations with American vendors.

Nippon Denso has taken Mazda's urge to coach American vendors to become competitive in quality, cost, delivery and safety in the same vein. The parts transplant evidently does so not only because it has an obligation to fulfill towards MMUC, one of its long-term minority customers, but also because it understands the obligation which Mazda owes to the Ford Motor Company, its joint venture partner. This explains why Nippon Denso is willing to transfer its technology and know-how to Ford's parts divisions, even though it has the full knowledge that the latter is a potential competitor in such products as heaters, condensers, and evaporators. But collaboration like this is sure to give the American vendors an additional impression of how much mutual trust, commitment and loyalty exist between the two Japanese automotive enterprises despite certain differences.

It is interesting to compare HAM and MMUC with two transplants of Toyota, Japan's largest car producer. Since 1983, Toyota has established two ventures in this country. One, NUMMI (New United Motor Manufacturing Inc.), is a joint venture with GM. The other, a transplant facility at Georgetown, Kentucky, was established in 1987 (Krafcik 1986).[15] According to a 1983 agreement, GM contributed to NUMMI its former facilities at Fremont, California, while Toyota contributed vehicle design and plant management techniques. Toyota management at NUMMI shares with its counterpart at the other two transplants an expectation of "one hundred percent conformance to specifications" from American vendors. It also insists that the vendors commit to just-in-time delivery and *kaizen*.

As a joint venture partner at NUMMI, Toyota began from a starting point similar to Mazda's in the vendor selection process. It took on a good number of GM's internal parts suppliers, as well as some independents previously used by America's largest producer, to train them to become competitive performers. This provides one probable explanation why Toyota's management at NUMMI let the American vendors bid on pre-established specs for contracts that lasted from six months to a year at least through the first model year in 1986, a practice that was not dissimilar to the way that the American car companies used to conduct their relationship with their vendors. To the surprise of some American trainees at NUMMI,[16] Toyota preferred bidding and multiple sourcing when it made sense.

With NUMMI serving as a demonstration facility for GM, Toyota was able to apply many of its own purchasing techniques to the joint venture, for instance, transferring target pricing techniques across the Pacific. Toyota has taught NUMMI's purchasing managers to emphasize other targets besides price in vendor selection and to expect all suppliers to lower their price continuously over the life of the vehicle model, based on the assumption of a learning curve as well as commitment to *kaizen*, including measures of cost reduction, and incremental innovation. NUMMI conducts value analysis and value engineering (VA/VE) with suppliers to help to find ways to cut inventory and waste as well as improve process designs to cut costs genuinely.

Additionally, the management at NUMMI organizes multi-functional teams among the staff from the purchasing, quality control, and other departments to make quarterly visits to suppliers, so that problems can be detected and corrected promptly. This contrasts with the traditional approach whereby the assembler would make a stopover at supplier plants only when problems occurred. NUMMI also encourages the suppliers to dispatch representatives to the joint venture transplant for extended periods, so that information on problems can more quickly be transmitted to the suppliers' plants.

NUMMI has designed a quality report system to resolve the problem of defects. The system rates the suppliers quarterly in quality, delivery, service and overall performance. In rating the suppliers, NUMMI, like Honda of America, prefers to emphasize motivating the current vendors to implement continuous improvement and problem-solving rather than to switch suppliers on the basis of competitive price bids. The real objective is to improve the current suppliers to the extent that they either match the best in the market in both cost and quality, or they deliver better performance. To help vendors to solve problems in product quality and production processes, Toyota, like Mazda (USA), also mobilizes experts from the members of its network of suppliers, if help is requested.[17]

Obviously, teamwork is considered essential for building quality cars at NUMMI, as it is in HAM and MMUC. To build teamwork, NUMMI has established a supplier council modeled on Toyota's suppliers' association in Japan, to encourage cooperation from its American vendors, including in-house suppliers departments, and independents. Regularly scheduled meetings of this organization direct the suppliers' work to improve quality and meet the targets set by NUMMI. These meetings, and perhaps other activities in the council serve in effect as a regular forum for the suppliers to discuss problems, find ways to solve them, examine their performance, review progress towards fulfillment of the annual goals as they are built in the target price, share information on the best practices, and introduce new policies.

At NUMMI, Toyota has introduced long-term partnership to its American suppliers, too. Once it takes on a vendor, NUMMI typically commits itself to working with the vendor and giving it an opportunity to learn to supply according to the requirements of the lean production system. Further, NUMMI relies on either a dual supplier strategy or sole sourcing for certain mechanically complex and pre-assembled system items. According to a former manager at the joint venture, some of GM's parts divisions have become long-term suppliers by giving special attention to its orders. They started by assigning specially selected workers to work on the parts supplied to NUMMI while the rest worked on those supplied to GM's own assembly plants (Krafcik 1986).

As sole owner, Toyota seems to run its own manufacturing plant in Kentucky more in the Japanese style. It obviously enforces more stringent rules in vendor selection. This is reflected in the fact that the Georgetown transplant has carried over only some of the vendors from NUMMI. Besides demands for quality and costs, Toyota expects that the candidate suppliers will possess design and engineering capabilities. Toyota is putting more and more emphasis on such capabilities as it localizes vehicle design activities in this country. Like other Japanese transplant manufacturers, Toyota looks at a candidate for the ability to add significant value to the relationship. It generally gives contracts to those who can supply custom-designed parts of high quality and who keep up with the technological innovations necessary for designing a new car model. Because of the emphasis on technological capability, Toyota sees the commitment to collaboration and information sharing with the transplant as crucial for vendor selection. This is one way for Toyota to work with suppliers for at least four years, the normal market time for a new model and the time needed for recouping the costs on R&D.

Toyota treats those vendors who deliver innovative and quality parts as long-term partners. To help the suppliers to resolve the problems in design and engineering and to teach them partnership, it has also opened up a technical center at Ann Arbor, Michigan. It intends to use the center to prepare the American suppliers for "design-in" activities in support of the transplant's decision to shift more and more engineering job to this country. In early 1992, Toyota

Table 2.2
Linkage Characteristics of Japanese Auto Transplants

Purchasing Criteria	Vendor Selection	Linkage Management
Ensure 100% quality and conformance to specs. Understand auto-maker's expectations & needs; commit to meet them Buy from the best globally (TM)* Commit to *kaizen*: •improve ceaselessly; •develop R&D capacity; •upgrade parts, reduce defects & improve producion process (JV)**	Evaluate at length & proceed in steps: •tour and inspect candidate's facilities and QC programs; •demand timely correction of problems found during inspection; •request prototype for test and study; •demand information sharing Adopt target pricing Combine target pricing w/ bidding for short-term conract (JV) **	Transfer teamwork & teach commitment: •render assistance; •regularize exchange of visits (JV);** •establish performance rating system; •induce learning and improvement before punishment Extend spot transactions to long-term contractual relations if targets are met Introduce small numbers in sourcing; but use multiple sourcing if rational (JV)**

*   Case of TM or transplant manufacturer
* *   Case of JV or joint venture

also began to explore the possibility of hiring independent engineering companies that were not Japanese in origin to provide assistance to the American vendors.

Table 2.2 summarizes the supplier management techniques which the Japanese auto transplants have transferred to this economy. As expected, the two types of transplants, transplant manufacturers and joint venture transplants, now apply similar purchasing criteria as well as vendor selection and supplier management techniques. Additionally, some of the policies which the transplant manufacturers have been able to follow from the beginning are compared with those which the joint ventures have sought to introduce to tackle the particular problems they face. For instance, all transplants reviewed here have adopted target pricing in vendor selection. But Toyota at NUMMI has implemented target pricing together with short-term bidding. But the initial differences which the two types of transplants have shown in that their purchasing may decrease over time if the joint ventures begin to act like fully owned Japanese transplant manufacturers, aiming to compete globally and thus hunting for the best suppliers in the world.

One consequence of this technology transfer, of course, is structural change in the supplies market associated with the transplant production. Teamwork, as well as the transition from spot deals to model year contracting length, must have reduced the number of the vendors still operating in the market. This is likely, particularly with both the transplant auto builders and major Japanese parts transplants adopting a partnership strategy with the American vendors. Indeed, the trend may strengthen in the 1990s when all the auto transplants begin to enforce more stringent rules on quality, design and engineering capabilities while localizing product design and introducing new vehicle models.

The question is what impact developments like this have on the interfirm organizational boundaries between American auto assemblers and their vendors. Table 2.3 provides a guide for recounting such impact, partly in comparison with the transplants' policy measures summarized in Table 2.2. It summarizes the changes which American auto makers had introduced by the late 1980s and early 1990s, as well as the direction in which they may be moving, if they follow the advice of the industry experts.[18]

The Big Three, for example, are replacing commodity-like parts with integrated system components as the new purchasing criteria. They expect total packaged services from the vendors. Besides the tougher performance expectations for quality, costs, and delivery, this means anything from product concept, product design and engineering, to prototyping, all the way down to the production of the final parts. Thanks to their growing interest in system components, American assemblers are also substituting R&D capacity for price as a key determinant in vendor selection. Under the influence of the joint venture transplants who have improved performance with technology transfer, the Big Three are similarly giving preference to

Table 2.3

Characteristics of Linkage Relations, American Auto Makers and Vendors, Post-1980s

Purchasing Criteria	Selction	Linkage Interface	Number/Tier
Supply system components instead of "commodity" parts	Give order preferably to those with system capabilities	Adopt JIT system: • JIT delivery; • JIT supply backed by JIT manufacturing*	Fewer direct suppliers Smaller number of captive parts divisions
Possess "world-class" capability in quality, costs, service, delivery and quickness in product change*	Apply no-bid or single sourcing to suppliers of advanced components and processes Adopt joint value analysis/joint value engineering in bidding	Switch to collaborative relations: • joint product design and development; • share profits derived from joint cost reduction, etc.	More well-defined tiers: • 1st-tier market concentrates on providing system components; • alliances to co-supply systems and total services; • 2nd-tier suppliers may supply sub-assemblies
Have R & D capacity in: • design, engineering, development, and related managerial expertise and know-how	Adopt target pricing and multi-year contracting	Reorganize internal parts division into system inputs based on specialty supplier like	

50

Purchasing Criteria	Selction	Linkage Interface	Number/Tier
Have ability to manage next-tier sub-contractors	Negotiate price adjustment per changing prices of materials	large independents	
		Suppliers' response: •use M&A to acquire	
Have ability to support assemblers in global investment	Demand disclosure of detailed information on price/cost breakdowns, production process steps and related operational strategy	R&D capacity; •form supplier alliances to supply higher value-added system products •commit to long-term partnership by building ties w/ one assembler while developing business with others	
	Open internal parts suppliers to bidding and reward competitive ones with model-year-length contract and global sourcirg	Exchange information	
		Adopt multi-year contracting for strategic components & expertise	

* For "Lean Production" model yet to be implemented fully.

Sources

R. Lamming, The Structures in the North American Automotive Components Industry (Cambridge, MA: MIT IMVP/MEMA, 21 Oct. 1988); R. Lamming, The Post-Japanese Model for International Automotive Components Automotive Components Industry: The Next "Best Practice" for Suppliers (Cambridge, MA: MIT IMVP International Policy Forum, May 1989); A. M. Sheriff, The Fragmentation of the World Motor Vehicle Market and Its Potential Impact on the Supplier Industry (Cambridge, MA, MIT IMVP/MEMA Seminar, 20 Oct. 1988): 17-22; D. L. Marler, The Post-Japanese Mode of Automotive Component supply: Selected North American Case Studies (Cambridge, MA: MIT IMVP International Policy Forum, May 1989); C. F. Sabel, et al, Collaborative Manufacturing: New Supplier Relations in the Automobile Industry and the Redefinition of the Industrial Corporation (Cambridge, MA: MIT IMVP International Policy Forum, May 1989); Nishiguchi Toshihiro, Reforming Automotive Purchasing Organizations in North America: Lessons for Europe (Cambridge, MA: MIT IMVP International Policy Forum, May 1989); R. Cohen, "GM Cost Cutter Sharpens His Ax," New York Times (9 June 1992), Section D, 1, 9; S. Helper, How Much Has Really Changed between U.S. Makers and their Suppliers, Sloan Management Review 32, no. 4 (Summer 1991); S. Helper, Strategy and Irreversibility in Supplier Relations, Business History Review (1992); AIM Newsletter 3, no.2 (May 1988).

those suppliers who have the ability to reduce costs annually and manage procurement of subassemblies from other subcontractors, as they shift to source more and more parts outside.[19] Finally, those suppliers that have either succeeded or are striving for the most improvement stand a better chance to do business with the American auto assemblers, especially if they are able to provide support for the latter's expansion into other regional markets in the world.

Following the transplants, American auto assemblers have instituted changes in the vendor selection process to encourage suppliers to accept the new purchasing criteria. Since the early 1980s, they have been using competitive bidding in a different way. Previously, an assembler would put out a bid after having developed a design spec. The strategy induced suppliers to win the deal with the lowest of their three offers. But upon meeting the assembler's target rates in quality, delivery and reliability, suppliers would proceed to make upward adjustments in the agreed price. With the changes in purchasing criteria, however, competitive bidding begins to take account of the suppliers' contribution in joint development.

In place of the rock-bottom pricing characteristic of traditional bidding, systemic capability is assuming critical importance in an assembler's decision with whom to place an order. This explains why an American auto maker should begin to experiment with no-bid sourcing or provide a multi-year supply contract to a vendor who has the expertise in a particular product and process technology and who intends to become the auto maker's technological partner. Where bidding applies, the assembler now also applies joint value analysis or joint value engineering, just like the transplants, to ensure that neither quality nor price is neglected in the process (Marler 1989).

The Big Three have also begun to build target pricing into the bidding process. More and more, they are tying contract placement, particularly multi-year contracting or contract renewal, to a supplier's record in meeting their cost/price targets. A new routine in vendor selection and performance monitoring that may have important influence in contract placement involves the suppliers' disclosure of detailed information on their production processes. Like the transplants, the Big Three require that the suppliers share information on the cost of each production step, and of production scheduling. Additionally, they demand that the suppliers submit statistical control charts (Helper 1991; 1992).

Finally, pricing management has changed, corresponding to the change in assemblers' bidding strategy. Instead of allowing annual price increases for some of the contracts already placed, American auto assemblers now seek to work out the necessary adjustment with suppliers to compensate for the cost inflation which the latter may be experiencing as a result of an increase in materials costs.

In vendor selection, however, the American auto makers continue to face serious structural constraints from the captive supply sector. The problem is especially acute for GM, the most vertically integrated of the Big Three. As late as 1989, GM reportedly still purchased some eighty percent of its parts from internal parts suppliers. This compared with Ford, the next most vertically integrated assembler in America, which had managed to shift about fifty percent of its parts production outside by the same year. To make its internal parts divisions competitive versus the independents, GM initially poured investment into technological upgrading. But after spending $5 billion on fancy industrial hardware for nearly a decade, GM had ended up as the most costly of the Big Three, unable to obtain the desired results. At this point, the largest auto maker in the United States conceded that compartmentalization within the hierarchy must be corrected. For instance, it could cut the lead time in product development and put a stop on cost escalation by bringing the captive parts divisions into the design process. This should at least allow it to impose the competitive performance requirements on the latter, just as it does with external suppliers (Koerner 1989; Lamming 1989).[20]

Increasing outsourcing could be another solution. But the strategy proves difficult under the pressure of the United Auto Worker's union (UAW). Partly because of this pressure, GM reverted to the strategy of disintegration at one point and sought instead to turn its parts divisions into first-tier suppliers through a policy of consolidation and rationalization on the basis of technological specialization. Ten in-house parts suppliers were consequently formed, with small business units within each assuming the responsibility for developing a specialty in supplying a given system or subassembly in competition with the independents, ideally through cooperation with other specialty units when flexible response for specific tasks was required. To compensate for the policy reversal, GM established a "Target for Excellence" program. It copied the experience of NUMMI, dispatching multi-functional teams from GM's purchasing, product engineering, manufacturing and quality control departments to assess the performance of its suppliers.[21]

The persistent problems of inefficiency and cost disadvantages,[22] finally, have forced GM to return to bidding. By opening up its contracts with the captive parts divisions and forcing them to sell on the open market, GM hopes to get them to compete with the independents. In a period of three years by the mid-1990s, the assembler plans to achieve a fifty percent improvement in productivity among its internal parts suppliers. GM, of course, has the successful experience of its European division to draw on. There, it has learned that when an assembler dispatches its engineers to help the suppliers redesign their production processes, it can dramatically enhance the latter's efficiency and productivity. The major difference in transferring this experience across the Atlantic is that in the United States, GM targets the internal parts makers for assistance whereas in Europe where production is less vertically integrated, it has achieved success largely with external providers.[23]

In turning to GM Europe for help to transform the internal parts suppliers, however, GM has essentially conceded to its failure in making NUMMI's approach work outside the transplant. Indeed, it considers GM Europe's shock therapy as crucial for jump starting the change that it desperately wants.[24] To encourage the commitment to the change, GM promises model-year long contract to those divisions which succeed. It has also begun to look at the past performance of the internal suppliers in cost/price reduction before determining whether to give them a green light for supplying GM's global operation.[25]

While more and more parts are outsourced, with factors other than price alone assuming importance in transactional decisions, managing relations with current suppliers has become a key issue for the American auto assemblers. This began with JIT delivery, which meant shifting the responsibility for quality and production control to the suppliers as it first started, along with an increased role for suppliers in design, engineering, and sometimes even styling. As a reflection of this power decentralization, the Big Three now seek transactions with those suppliers who possess technological leadership in product and process technologies. This marks a first step away from linkage animosity and towards regularized interaction on the basis of long-term supply contracts, joint efforts at quality assurance, and early involvement of suppliers in vehicle design.

However, the JIT delivery system has not produced the desired result wherever it is adopted. In a number of studies, experts affiliated with the International Motor Vehicle Program, at the Massachusetts Institute of Technology, find that American auto assemblers continue to experience problems in defects and product design despite JIT delivery.[26] They blame it on the auto makers' failure to demand not only JIT delivery but also JIT manufacturing from vendors, which is crucial for tracing rejects to their origin and eliminating wastes as well as excess in-process inventory. More often than not, the parts are delivered to the assemblers on a small lot basis without the necessary development of JIT manufacturing.[27] For their part, some of the in-house parts divisions that remained protected from order switching had reportedly experienced serious problems in defects and in-stock inventory by the late 1980s. But if assemblers combine tough demands on both aspects of the JIT system with a commitment to stabilizing delivery schedules with the

suppliers and provision of other types of assistance, they may help the
suppliers to achieve small-lot production while building flexibility in
the production system at the same time. This will not only facilitate
fast design change, now a key area of competition, but also ease the
difficulties for the assemblers in moving towards the lean production
required for competition in the decades ahead.

Thus, auto assemblers in the United States are switching towards
increased collaboration or teamwork in auto manufacturing. While
large suppliers with proprietary engineering capabilities, innovative
products and processes, research capacity, and a commitment to
continued cost reduction are actively sought out by the Big Three for
technological "sharing" agreements, some independents are
delivering innovative parts and/or processes on their own for sale to
the auto makers.[28] Corresponding to this transition to partnership,
the Big Three are also beginning to share with suppliers profits that
are derived from cost reduction (Nishiguchi 1993).

With their tough demands for innovative inputs, quality, and
productivity, the assemblers have shaken up the entire supply
industry. This has put a heavy burden on suppliers to upgrade their
technological capacity. Suppliers who possess greater financial
resources can seek mergers and acquisitions to acquire such capacity.
Other parts manufacturers who formerly supplied single function
commodity parts are turning to a strategy of coalition to take
advantage of one another's technological strength and synergy in
design, engineering, and research to jointly supply integrated system
products and complete service.[29] Some of them have subsequently
assumed the responsibility for coordinating joint activities with
contractual arrangements.

Additionally, suppliers are establishing design and engineering
centers in the Detroit area to compete with the Japanese parts
transplants. As some innovative independents have found out,
building long-term dedicated relations with an auto maker proves
essential for establishing a market position. This is because it allows
them to test and rapidly commercialize innovative products and
processes. To offset potentially excessive dependency on the principal
assembler, innovative suppliers are also trying to develop and
maintain sales with other assemblers, the other two of the Big Three
and the Japanese auto transplants, as well as other industrial
customers. But they make sure that diversification would not
sacrifice dedicated service to the principal customer--standard practice
between a Japanese auto maker and its parts suppliers.[30]

Routinized exchange of information is still another aspect of
improved teamwork between the American auto assemblers and
suppliers (Table 2.3). More and more American vendors are
introducing statistical process control as well as providing charts to
the auto assemblers. As required, they are also supplying information

on production scheduling, the breakdown of the steps in their operating process and the cost of each step. Surely, such information helps the assemblers to understand the suppliers' production process better and to set tough but fair quality and price targets. It is also crucial for providing the assemblers with the ability to help suppliers to meet these targets. Thus, the assemblers encourage the suppliers to send their engineers for lengthy residence at the former's plants in order to understand and resolve the technical and engineering problems which their parts may be causing in the actual process of auto assembly. The assemblers are also providing more and more technical information to the suppliers.

Table 2.4 relies on the survey result of Helper and Sako (1994) to

Table 2.4
Comparison of Changing Structural Relations
in the U.S. Auto Industry, 1984-1993

Year	Share Information w/Assembler*	Trust Assembler for Fair Treatment	Assistance from Assembler**
1984	38%	36%	--
1989	--	49%	34%
1993	80%	41%	53%

*   Detailed information about the suppliers' production process.
* *   Offering assistance to the current suppliers to match a new entrant in lower unit price at the same product quality.

Source: S. Helper and M. Sako, *Supplier Relations in the Auto Industry: A Limited Japanese-U.S. Convergence*. Paper Presented at International Motor Vehicle Program (IMVP) Researchers' Meeting (Cambridge, Mass.: January 1994): 5.

illustrate the changing nature of interfirm organizational relations between American auto makers and their suppliers after a decade of structural change in competition with the Japanese transplants. The data indicate that the American vendors have indeed increased the information shared with the Big Three. This however, is not matched by an improvement in trust. In other words, suppliers do not trust assemblers any more now than they did traditionally, even though they are providing more proprietary information about their operations to assemblers. One reason, as implied in Table 2.3, may be that the suppliers resent having to assume so much of the burden of structural adjustment while the auto makers themselves fall short of reciprocating with the necessary commitment. This is despite the fact that assemblers have learned to take more initiatives over the years in helping current suppliers to become more competitive than new entrants in the market. A recent study, however, goes further and blames the continuing mutual distrust on the persistent fear of the auto assemblers for rising transaction costs, if they should commit to developing mutually dependent synergetic partnerships with their suppliers (Helper and Levine 1993).

Table 2.5
Comparison of Inter-Corporate Information Sharing,
Type of Information Exchanged between Suppliers and Assemblers,
1990*

Ranking	Big Three	Japanese Transplant
Shared Most	production capacity; QC Program (95.2)	process steps breakdown (100)
Second	statistical process control data (90.5)	OC Program (91.3)
Third	equipment used (85.7)	production capacity 87.0
Fourth	general cost breakdown (66.7)	general cost breakdown (65.2)
Fifth	process steps break-down; inventory level (57.1)	equipment used (56.5)
Sixth	cost of each process step (14.3)	inventory level (52.2)
Seventh	--	cost of each process step (13.0)

* Type of information which the auto makers have obtained about the suppliers. The percentage as bracketed represents the answer which the Big Three, five Japanese transplants and six joint venture transplants have made respectively to the relevant survey questions.

Source: Michael A. Cusumano and Akira Takeishi, "Supplier Relations and Management: A Survey of Japanese, Japanese-Transplant, and U.S. Auto Plants," *Strategic Management Journal* 12 (1991): 576.

Table 2.5 uses a comparison of the types of information exchanged across organizational boundaries to inquire further about the disparity between the increased information sharing on the one hand and lack of trust between American auto makers and their suppliers on the other. From the breakdown of the information exchanged, one notices that the American auto makers seem to know just half as much about each step of suppliers' production processes as the Japanese transplants (fifty-seven percent vs. one hundred percent). While this difference lends support to Helper and Sako's finding that American suppliers continue to distrust the Big Three, it also shows a possible connection between this distrust and the Big Three's failure to shake the habit of relying on arms-length techniques in dealing with their suppliers. This explains why statistical process control data should play such an important role for the American assemblers in information gathering (Helper 1991; 1992). Conversely, it explains why the Big Three have provided much less assistance to the suppliers than the Japanese transplants in terms of specific sugges-

Table 2.6
Comparison of Sourcing,
by Number of Suppliers per Part in %, 1990

Number of Supplier	Big Three	Japanese Transplants
1	59.1	83.3
2	13.6	16.7
3	13.6	--
4	13.6	--
5	4.6	--
>5	4.6	--
Total	100.0	100.0
Mean	1.8	1.2

Source: Cusumano and Takeishi, "Supplier Relations and Management: A Survey of Japanese, Japanese-Transplant and U.S. Auto Plants," *Strategic Management Journal* 12 (1991): 569.

tions on how they may improve their competitiveness. For instance, how should suppliers improve product quality? What changes should they introduce in their production process and how can they improve inventory control? In what way should product design be altered? Finally, what alternative materials should the suppliers adopt (Cusumano and Takeishi 1991, 576)?

But increased information sharing, along with the more regularized interaction which the Big Three have introduced to their American vendors, has led to fewer suppliers with whom they maintain an on-going relationship. Table 2.6 provides evidence that the American auto makers are converging with the Japanese transplants in the number of the vendors they use for parts and components supplies.

For example, the Big Three had come to rely on one vendor only for as much as fifty-nine percent of their supplies in 1990. They used two suppliers for the next fourteen percent of their outsourced parts for the same year. If this trend continues, then the Big Three should depend on sole sourcing and a two-supplier strategy for at least seventy-three percent of their components and parts. This is despite the fact that some fifty percent of the Big Three's major suppliers remain their captive parts divisions (Cusumano and Takeishi 1991).[31] Many vendors in the market, of course, are weeded out in this process of structural concentration. Ford Motor Company, for example, has seen its wire harness suppliers reduced from twenty-seven in 1970 to four in the early 1990s (Helper and Levine 1993).

One implication of the Big Three's switch to a smaller number of suppliers for outsourcing is the growing stability of their relationship,

Table 2.7
Comparison of Inter-Corporate Contractual Relations,
1990 (Part I)

Indicators of Contractual Relations, Average by Year	Big Three	Japanese Transplants
Length of Contract	1.7	2.5
Length of Parts Transaction	3.2	1.6
Length of Model Life Cycle	3.6	1.7

Source: Cusumano and Takeishi, "Supplier Relations and Management: A Survey of Japanese, Japanese-Transplant, and U.S. Auto Plants," *Strategic Management Journal* 12 (1991): 571.

which should find expression in a lengthened contractual relationship between the two parties. In Table 2.7 and Table 2.8, one can see that the typical contract which the Big Three give out has increased from one year to an average of one point seven years, even though the length remains shorter than that of the contracts which the Japanese transplants give out. But these tables also suggest that the stability of the interfirm relationship derives from contract renewal instead of multi-year contracting. Indeed, Table 2.8 tells us that as much as eighty-two percent of the contracts remain annual in duration. But if one compares the average length of the contract with the average length of the parts transaction, which is about the same as the average length of the model life-cycle (Table 2.7), one gets the impression that the Big Three have more or less used the same suppliers for the same parts, as long as the life cycle of the product model continues to last. Instead of dropping a current supplier every time a new vendor comes along with a lower bid, as in the past, an

Table 2.8
Comparison of Inter-Corporate Contractual Relations,
1990 (Part II)

Contract Length by Year	Big Three (%)	Japanese Transplants (%)
1	81.8	50.0
4	4.6	50.0
5	13.6	--
Total	100.0	100.0
Average	1.7	2.5

Source: Cusumano and Takeishi, "Supplier Relations and Management: A Survey of Japanese, Japanese-Transplant, and U.S. Auto Plants," *Strategic Management Journal* 12 (1991): 571.

American auto maker may now be using contract renewal as an instrument to induce collaborative behavior from vendors. Similarly, assemblers can take advantage of the opportunity to check on how well the individual vendors are performing in fulfilling cost, price, and quality targets. This analysis is consistent with the data in Table 2.4 which show that American auto assemblers are offering more assistance to those current vendors who supply quality products, so that they match up with or beat the new entrant in unit price (Helper and Sako 1993). Finally, as indicated in Table 2.9, the Big Three are converging with the Japanese transplants in the criteria with which they select vendors and manage supplier relationships. Indeed, the American auto makers have become almost as quality conscious as the Japanese transplants. The two groups of assemblers also attach a similar degree of importance to the delivery record of suppliers, as well as their design, engineering, and R&D capabilities. The Japanese transplants, however, place more emphasis on a supplier's ability to meet the target prices. To a great extent, this should explain why the transplants are able to reduce their annual costs while the American auto makers have consistently witnessed an upward adjustment in the costs of the parts they procure annually. The Big Three, on the other hand, pay much more attention than the Japanese transplants to past business ties as well as to

Table 2.9
Comparison of Vendor Selection Criteria, 1990

Ranking by Importance*	Big Three	Japanese Transplants
Most important	quality (4.8)	quality (5.0)
Second	delivery; design and engineering (4.6)	target-pricing performance; delivery; design and engineering (4.7)
Third	manufacturing; past business ties (4.4)	initial price bid; cost reduction (4.4)
Fourth	initial price bid; target pricing performance; cost reduction; R&D capability (4.1)	R&D capability (4.2)
Fifth	financial affiliation (3.8)	past business ties (3.1)
Sixth	--	financial affiliation (1.9)

* Ranked according to a 5-point mean score as bracketed in the next two columns. 5 is the most important whereas 1 is the least important.

Source: Cusumano and Takeishi, "Supplier Relations and Management: A Survey of Japanese, Japanese-Transplant, and U.S. Auto Plants," *Strategic Management Journal* 12 (1991): 572.

the financial affiliation of American suppliers in the vendor selection process, reflecting the pressure they are facing in having to ensure the survival of the captive parts divisions. Lastly, the importance of the initial bid has decreased substantially for the American auto makers after they have adopted target pricing.

Until recently, American auto makers relied largely on internal R&D for new product and process technologies because of vertical integration, a legacy of past competitive policies. They did not give suppliers any say in design and engineering. As a result, suppliers had to bid to process each part and on the basis of short-term contracts according to the blueprints of the assemblers. By forcing a competitive market structure on the suppliers, the strategy also had a negative impact on technological development. Those suppliers who cut corners in the manufacturing process under severe price competition lost an opportunity to improve technological learning. For their part, the American assemblers lost much of their ability to adopt innovations developed outside their own R&D establishments. In fact, they were more worried about collaboration with suppliers, fearing it might give the suppliers a chance to use the proprietary information on one assembler's innovation to get a better deal from its rivals, than they were interested in thinking how they could use the suppliers strategically to generate competitive products and process technology.[32]

By the 1980s, however, this type of inter-corporate relationship had to change. The industry came to identify technology as the most important variable for change. The Japanese competition and their type of inter-corporate relationship, of course, provided another catalyst for the change. The globalization of the economy and competitive pressure from the porousness of the national economic boundaries made it impossible for the American auto makers to continue with a vertically integrated model of innovation. First, they had to realize that both the suppliers and assemblers must simultaneously invest in technology to move to computer aided design and computer aided manufacturing. This was followed by a recognition of the need to replace organizational rigidity with teamwork to remove the barriers against necessary change. Organizational structural change, indeed, has been the hardest task for the American automotive companies to accomplish. For instance, job rotation has still not made inroads into these corporations. Long-term commitment to interfirm relations is also still lacking. Furthermore, intrafirm competition as well as interfirm distrust continue to make it difficult for all to implement structural re-engineering. Without a fundamental inter-firm process redesign, however, technology alone may not be sufficient to provide American auto corporations with a competitive edge.

Like their American counterparts, the Japanese auto assemblers also carry out internal R&D. But unlike the Americans, they depend on suppliers for much of the industry's innovation. Japanese suppliers are responsible for designing and engineering their own products as well as for quality control. In exchange for the value-added services provided to the assemblers, the suppliers receive long-term contracts. Over the years, this strategy has encouraged mutual loyalty and trust across the interfirm organizational boundaries. When they transfer production to the United States, the Japanese transplants have forced their American suppliers to develop the same type of interfirm relationship. But in this process of change, they have also tried to provide guidance as well as assistance to American vendors. This compares to the American auto makers who, at least initially, left it to the vendors themselves to improve their competitiveness.

When they begin to develop relationships with external suppliers and reduce their commitment to internal supply sources, however, the American auto makers are also modifying vertical integration into some form of horizontal integration. Their structural relations with suppliers have consequently altered. The trend is gaining momentum, as both assemblers and suppliers seek to form alliances with automotive corporations of other nationalities to compete globally.

With global linkages growing and globalization continuing to make progress, national and regional markets begin to compete with one another. Nowadays, not any single national market is able to dominate the world any more. When GM tries to increase the market share for its Opel model, for example, it has had to make European suppliers competitive by guiding them to change as the Japanese have guided the American vendors. In fact, competitive pressure is forcing all the auto makers in the world to adopt the best production processes and product innovation irrespective of the sources of such creative outputs. Globalization is forcing not only Americans but also Europeans and Japanese to change. No one is immune from such pressure. No one, indeed, can afford to rely on a parochial system of production to compete in the future.

NOTES

1. "Market" here derives from Drucker's definition of "free enterprise." It refers to the belief and a corollary operating environment, that a privately owned and independently managed corporation produces goods for profit and sells them in a competitive market at prices that are determined by supply and demand. The government's function here is restricted to "setting the frame

within which business is to be conducted rather than ... running business enterprises" (Drucker 1946, 3-4).

2. A concentrated market is one dominated by oligopolies or a few large firms of relatively equal size and technological strength.

3. Note that the following three paragraphs on the works of the theorists of the industrial organization are based on the analysis of Kamien and Schwartz (1982).

4. Many of the theorists of industrial organization implicitly define corporate innovation as encompassing the whole range of such creatively destructive activities, from basic research-related invention to R&D undertaken for commercializing innovative product as well as process innovation (Kamien and Schwartz 1982, 2, 49).

5. For the concept of X-inefficiency, see H. Leibenstein, "*Beyond Economic Man: A New Foundation for Microeconomics*," Chapter 3, particularly pp.37-47. Leibenstein attributes X-inefficiency to a lack of managerial commitment to cost reduction through incremental improvement of the production process, particularly in the developing economies where the enterprises are often state monopolists. As it is applied to western economies such as that of the United States, one may credit its ability to reap windfall gains as a "fast second" in the market with a monopoly 's laxity in technological innovation.

6. Note, however, that Williamson provided the definition of the life cycle of an economic organization in his later work (Williamson 1986, 199-203). Even so, one could see the evolution of the thought as early as his book in 1970. For the discussion in this and the next two paragraphs, refer also to Williamson (1970, chaps. 7, 10, 11; 1975, chaps. 3, 5, 8).

7. The asset investment made by a supplier may not be directly specific to the product(s) of an assembler. Or it may be partially specific. In both cases, the transactions between the two parties may be either occasional or recurrent. In all four situations, observers Williamson, market will clear the deal (Williamson 1986). For the six situations, see particularly the figures on pp.112-117. For "internalization", see p.86 in the same volume.

8. Technological diffusion and its resulting positive externalities for the society seemed to receive more interest than development of technology. Carlton, for example, noted that new production techniques were more likely to get diffused under the hierarchy than market. Prior to integration, he found, suppliers were discouraged from adopting these techniques, because they the dominant buyer squeezed them in prices and they faced uncertainty in sales (Carlton 1979).

9. Large hierarchical auto manufacturers rode high over their smaller counterparts because the former were able to spearhead standardization internally. They were especially aggressive in pushing those areas of standardization that granted them cost economies and bargaining position versus the remaining suppliers (Thomson 1954).

10. Here, the gains should mean not only profit sharing, but also a mutual commitment that is consciously maintained in the down cycle of the economy when losses are incurred.

11. Unless otherwise noted, the story of Honda's operation in the United States in this chapter is based on Shook (1988). Refer particularly to pp.117-118, 172-177.

12. D. Heath, "Can US Firms Compete with Japanese Keiretsu" *Louisville Courier Journal* (4 February 1992).

13. Rehder, "Japanese Transplants: A New Model for Detroit," *Business Horizon* (January-February, 1988): 52-61.

14. Unless otherwise noted, information on Mazda is based on Hill (1989) and Oshima (1989).

15. Unless otherwise noted, the account of Toyota's experience at NUMMI and Georgetown, Kentucky, is based on Krafcik (1986). Refer particularly to pp. 20-30.

16. Ibid.

17. They may redesign the vendor's production system through reworking industrial engineering, plant layouts, and scheduling, as well as quality control. An example is the case of an American wire harness supplier that was selling 10 percent of its products to NUMMI. One suspects the Japanese party that helped this American company was Nippon Denso (Nishiguchi 1987, 6-7; 1989a, 4).

18. Including the measures which experts suggest should characterize the trends in the industry as it continues the processes of globalization, dubbed as the "post-Japanese" system of production. The term and the underlying concept is first raised in the International Motor Vehicle Program at Massachusetts Institute of Technology (Lamming 1989).

19. In a "classical" parts supplies system for engine production of the late 1960s, for example, only some of the carburetors and electrical parts were sourced by independents. In comparison, the outsourced parts in engine building in the mid-1980s increased to include the aluminum head, some of the processes for the camshaft, form and machine valves, cast iron and aluminum blocks, pistons, the water pump, oil pump, fuel injection system, and so on (Smith 1986, Exhib. 3 and Exhib. 4). Those interested in the degree of vertical integration in critical components in the Big Three as of the late 1980s may also find another useful source in Andrea, Everett and Luria (1988).

20. For the percentage quoted, see Koerner (1989, 16) and Lamming (1989, 8, 13-14). The discussion on the reforms which GM tried by the late 1980s is based on Koerner unless otherwise noted.

21. For consolidation and rationalization, see Sabel, Kern, and Herrigel (1989). Refer particularly to pp.14-16, 19.

22. One study explains why a vertically integrated American auto maker like GM continues to suffer from inefficiency and thus become the most costly producer, unable to recoup the heavy investment in technology. He finds says that "More often than not, the North American competition for a contract between in-house captive component divisions and independent suppliers is apt to be nominal: if it occurred, it did so for the sake of external information gathering and comparative cost analysis drawing on the market. At the end of the supplier selection process, however, captive suppliers tacitly know that no matter what happens a contract will be awarded to them because there is little incentive whatsoever for the auto maker to sever its own component divisions.

For better or worse, such tacit understanding and practice might have relieved the captive suppliers of the tension normally associated with open market competition" (Nishiguchi, 1993, 9). This compares with the typical competitive pressure felt by the Japanese suppliers, for whom "even though the likelihood of obtaining a contract is relatively high, the on-going pressure before and after, and for that matter, throughout the duration of the contract (which usually lasts for a car product cycle) is also relatively high. This pressure may be compounded with the competition, against which a supplier's overall performance indicators (including price, quality, delivery, technological improvements, and supplier suggestions) will be continually measured. Unlike all-or-nothing decision making, sometimes readily apparent in the North American business culture, the Japanese sourcing practice dictates that based on auto makers' periodic monitoring and feedback the suppliers that consistently exhibit the results of their continuous improvement will progressively obtain increased orders and responsibilities whereas poor performers' orders and responsibilities will decline unless their performance improves within a designated time period" (Ibid.).

23. R. Cohen, "GM Cost Cutter Sharpens His Ax," *New York Times* (2 June 1992), D 1, and D. P. Levin, "Cost Cutter Lifts Ax over G.M. Plants," *New York Times* (2 March 1993), D 4.

24. Compared to NUMMI, which takes a gradual approach to working with suppliers, the method first introduced at GM Europe and later in the United States typically begins with the assembler's dispatch of process engineers to the suppliers' plants. These engineers go about process re-design as soon as they arrive, not infrequently destroying the old facilities without giving the suppliers any underlying reason for the change. It is known that they do not have the same commitment to teaching the suppliers the fundamentals, since they usually stay at the suppliers' for about a week only.

25. R. Cohen, "GM Cost Cutter Sharpens His Ax," *New York Times* (2 June 1992), D 1, and D. P. Levin, "Cost Cutter Lifts Ax over G.M. Plants," *New York Times* (2 March 1993), D 4.

26. For a comparative study demonstrating synchronized manufacturing as the core of the just-in-time supply systems, see Nishiguchi (1989a) on whom this discussion on the problem with the JIT system will be based, unless otherwise noted.

27. For problems in initial experiments with JIT, see University of Michigan (1989, 33).

28. The increased collaboration was first noted by Sabel, Kern, and Herrigel (1989). The authors also projected a trend in which "the design and production of an automobile requires collaboration of many specialized firms, none of which could complete or even organize the task alone" (1989, 2). Under this system, direct suppliers would specialize in the design and manufacture of system components whereas assemblers would specialize in integrating them. The drive toward the collaborative system would come from both the push of market forces for spreading costs and reducing risks in rapid product innovation, and from the pull of suppliers who wish to increase their autonomy versus the assemblers. An indicator to watch on whether the system has arrived is how much of a percentage of the parts purchased involve

important collaboration with specialist subcontractors who supply design and engineering know-how (Ibid. 3, 12).

29. Vendors, for example, have banged together to supply "door cassettes" that are complete with glass, mechanical and electrical components and trim for direct fitting into the vehicle on the assembly line, instead of continuing to supply discrete parts only (Lamming 1989, 14). The burden which the supply industry faces is reflected in GM's complaints about a shortage of capable independents who can not only source subassemblies at a cheaper cost than in-house divisions and deliver them just-in-time, but can also modify the subassemblies' components to reduce costs and improve performance. In the case of subassemblies based on engineering plastics or microelectronics, capable suppliers include those who design a whole system based on sophisticated product or process technologies which the assembler could not master on short notice (Sabel, Kern, and Herrigel 1989, 3, 14-16, 19).

30. Excel Industries, Inc. (EIC) used the alliance strategy with Ford to commercialize the RIM technology for plastic framed windows successfully. Before turning to EIC for joint production of the part, Ford had tried to apply the technology by itself at a Kentucky plant. But it decided on specialist outsourcing after it failed to get the desired result. When the joint management between Ford and EIC did not work out, the assembler sold the Kentucky facility to EIC in exchange for a five-year supply contract. A year later in 1987, Ford acquired a forty percent stake in Excel, to allow its voice to be heard on the board of directors. EIC subsequently duplicated the Japanese style of diversification strategy (Marler 1989, 2, 8-9, 15).

31. The high dependence of the American Big Three on a small number of suppliers for outsourced parts is supported by observations made in another study (Nishiguchi 1993).

32. According to one study, an important reason that GM seeks to get its in-house parts makers to be competitive is that the assembler wants to retain control of the design and engineering of the integrated system components (Sabel, Kern, and Herrigel 1989, 14-16, 19).

Chapter Three

Globalization, Firm Organization, and Interfirm Market Relations in the Japanese Automobile Industry

Since WWII, the Japanese have re-designed not only industrial production processes, but also total quality control. The world first began to notice this in the form of Japanese automotive and electronics products. Japanese competition has forced the other advanced national economies to investigate seriously and adopt many of the practices which the Japanese have developed. This chapter will therefore first explore how Japan created such practices. It will then evaluate the impact of globalization and the necessity of maintaining global linkages for an export dependent economy like Japan's.

Fundamental characteristics of Japan's distinct cultural and historical roots have influenced its organizational structure and behavior.[1] The homogeneity of Japanese society and its long-term relative isolation provided a great continuity in Japanese social relations and cultural traits. Japanese social relations were based on trust, personal commitment, and informal networking, all of which were critical for maintaining structural linkages in the Japanese hierarchy. The same traits became incorporated into Japanese business transactional agreements and provided an opportunity for creating and improving long-term interfirm relationships (March 1988; Smitka 1990; 1991).

Trust required sharing of responsibility and commitment to reciprocity. In Japanese business interactions, voice came as the counterpart of trust. Voice meant participation in the formulation of plans and policy, irrespective of a firm's location in the hierarchy of the *keiretsu*. Such participation not only provided information exchange but also moderated the coercive power inherent in the hierarchical command structure. Trust and voice thus contributed to long-term stable relationships between those firms which were doing business with each other.[2]

For voice to work, flexibility was necessary. Flexibility refers to a willingness to compromise and a preference for conflict resolution[3] through consensus-building. Since every transaction was a part of an ongoing relationship, and every agreement, oral or written, a promise an honorable business must deliver, all parties to a contract must be willing to make adjustments when they were called for by changing economic circumstances. In a Japanese business relationship, reconciliation was valued more than conflict and confrontation. If a firm should pursue antagonistic behavior, its ability to have business relations with other companies would be damaged. All parties to the conflict were therefore under pressure to compromise. This contributed to the emphasis on the underlying inter-firm relationship rather than the legal documentation of the detailed responsibility of each party (Hanami 1984; Ishida 1984; March 1988).

When Japan was forced to end its isolation, it tried rapidly to establish modern industrial sectors for its own survival as a society. Many of the cultural traits reflected in the hierarchical relationships in feudal Japan became incorporated in the processes of industrialization. To catch up with the West, Japan had to import technology as well as export goods to earn the foreign exchange needed for the technology purchase. Similarly, Japan had to create institutions for pooling capital and investing it in high-risk industries. The Japanese government had initially acted as an entrepreneur to overcome the market barrier for infant industries. But it quickly shifted the entrepreneurial function to the private sector to transform Japan's economy more effectively, reserving for itself the role of setting goals for the nation and selecting its developmental priorities. One of the first problems facing Japan, therefore, was how to find the right people to entrust with the responsibility for starting new industries.[4]

The Japanese government turned to those people whose previous experience could be transferred to tasks in an industrializing age. It selected merchant houses like Mitsui as carriers of industrialization, because the latter had been involved in domestic commerce for centuries. The house of Mitsui had used trust to underwrite market risks while transferring in-house expertise for business diversification throughout the Tokugawa period.[5] Now, it could employ the same strategy to break into international trade, establish modern industries and create linkages in the national economy. The Japanese government employed incentives as well as coercion to push private entrepreneurs into one targeted business after another. While it leveraged the incentives on the entrepreneurs' fulfillment of their expectations, the Japanese government was also careful to choose more than one candidate firm to enter each targeted industry to heat up the competition for entry, expansion, and linkage formation.[6]

In commerce as well, trust had served as an important tool for risk management in the new business of merchant banking. The chairman of the First National Bank, Japan's de facto central bank until the Bank of Japan was established in 1882, had specifically set up a borrower trustworthiness as a loan criterion. This criterion depended more on whether the borrower shared the bank's view of investment than his business experience.[7]

Reputation was an important factor on which decision-makers bet their trust. When the government asked Mitsui and Mitsubishi to enter or diversify into a new business, it in effect was borrowing their name and credibility to support its industrial policy. The evolving business conglomerates, or zaibatsu, on the other hand, used their association with the government to boost their prestige. In times of business crisis, they also used their previous support for the government to extract assistance from the latter, an obligation which the government could not refuse (Roberts 1973). Reputation proved equally crucial for inter-corporate decision-making. When Mitsubishi was searching for a railway company in which to invest to transport the output from one of its coal mines at the turn of the century, it settled on two privately owned and operated firms because they had pioneered the practice of manning their top and middle levels of management with engineers and technically educated people and had become more competitive than the steamship companies running on adjacent routes (Ericson 1988).

The vast ranks of samurai, the former military elite, provided a second group of human resources for Japan to draw on to implement its strategies of industrialization. The samurai had both education and management experience which they had accumulated as the administrators in the Tokugawa government and which could now be tapped for running Japan's industrial enterprises. But the problem was that the status-conscious samurai coveted only government posts after the Meiji leaders took up the management of industrial development. They did not want to deal with the businessmen, the landlords, brewers and particularly the merchants, whom they despised because of their profit-making orientation. The samurai did not want to adopt any business profession which they treated with disdain.

To draw samurai, Japan's best and brightest, into business, it became necessary to make it a respectable profession by elevating its status and prestige. It was for this objective that Fukuzawa Yukichi, an eminent philosopher, and Shibusawa, an official turned business leader, led a series of campaigns to construct a business ideology. As a first step, they tried to provide some legitimacy for the profession. Profits, they argued, could be made in either morally correct or

incorrect ways. If a man made money only for himself and refused to
share it with the country and society, then he should rightly be
despised. But if he made money with "altruism and higher principle
than profit" and used his fortune to set up Japan's industries, then he
deserved respect.   What Japan needed, therefore, was those
businessmen who would act as the "benefactor(s) of the community
and servant(s) ... of the state" (Clark 1979, 29).[8]

The samurai had great potential to become heroes like these, if
they took up careers in business and served the country with as much
honor and self-respect as they had previously served their lord with
swordsmanship. Since times had changed, they had also to stop
relying on inherited status for income and prestige and instead earn
both by taking entrepreneurial risks and bringing intelligent
management to industrial enterprises. Fukuzawa and Shibusawa
practiced what they preached. Whereas Fukuzawa founded Keio
University, the first of Japan's private universities, to train men of
talent and capability for both government and business, Shibusawa
gave up his prestigious and powerful position in the Ministry of
Finance to begin a career as a banker, an industrialist, and a champion
of entire private entrepreneurship.

The government did introduce incentives such as cheap credit
and subsidies as well as institutions like joint stock companies as an
alternative organizational form to the merchant houses for the
samurai to pool their capital and limit risks in setting up businesses
which conservative-minded merchants would shun. But one of the
most important tools for managing market risks remained the
security net supplied by personal connections. When he became the
chairman of the First National Bank, for example, Shibusawa
maintained his contacts in the government as well as his political
clout as a former top official in the Ministry of Finance. He used
them to persuade the government to delay the total withdrawal of
deposits for two years during the banking crisis of 1875 to save the
bank from collapse (Hirschmeier 1965; Horie 1965).

To be sure, the former elite brought mutual loyalty and
commitment, the core of their ethical code of behavior, to modern
business ventures when they switched to professional careers. When
Lord Hachisuka Mochiaki entered banking, for example, he rallied
financial support from his ex-retainers. In return, he staked out
personal assets to keep their trading business afloat, even though they
could not make it profitable. Similarly, when Shibusawa asked a
samurai descendent who had been studying in London to become the
chief technician of Japan's first large-scale private cotton-spinning
mills which Shibasawa had just started, the descendent gave up the
opportunity to obtain his degree and went instead to visit British
factories and learn the most advanced practices with whatever time

he had left before reporting back for duty (Fraser 1988; Hirschmeier 1965).

When the elite joined ranks with businessmen to develop industrial power with a capitalist economy, social status became equalized. With equalization of social status at the top of the society, a new way for managing the vertical organizational relations in Japan began to appear. The hierarchical command of the feudal system became moderated and a voice emerged to compensate for the risks which the entrepreneurs were asked to take. Private entrepreneurs were quick to take measures to pave the way for the change. Mitsubishi and Mitsui, for example, pioneered the hiring of university graduates as professional managers between 1870s and 1890s to monitor shifts in government policy more effectively and maintain close contacts with government officials. When they became just as well-educated as the status-conscious bureaucrats, the zaibatsu managers made it more comfortable for the latter to converse informally with them in their regular evening gatherings (Wray 1989b).

More significantly, a formal institutional mechanism for voice came into being when Shibusawa established an industry association in the banking sector so as to familiarize the samurai bankers with the new trade. The association provided a forum where they met and talked with one another as well as exposed and resolved problems of the new industry, which must have included finding answers to such questions as for what purpose the loans should be made amid capital scarcity, to whom to make the loans, and to what degree risk exposure was permitted. At the same association, the bankers could also chat with the merchants, their customers, pat them on their shoulders, and engender trust with the latter. On this basis, the bankers went on to persuade them to switch from cash to commercial notes in clearing transactions and support their transition with subsidized interests (Hirschmeier 1965; Roberts, 1973).

Internally, the business conglomerates were also learning to use voice to manage their increasingly diversified operation. The Mitsubishi headquarters, for example, shifted much decision-making authority to the managers of subordinate member firms. Mitsubishi's president would sit down with them at strategic planning sessions and listen to their opinions before finalizing a policy. Thus, voice became used to induce cooperation and build consensus within the zaibatsu. It was a step further from relying on trust to regulate inter-branch competitive jealousy within a merchant house and maintain the hierarchical order between the headquarters and branch houses.[9]

It would be wrong to assume that the zaibatsu switched to voice totally in managing hierarchical relationships. Sometimes, it tried to force its authority on the subordinate firms to the neglect of voice in the process. When this happened, however, conflict and resistance emerged to frustrate its policy. Mitsubishi met with strong opposition from within N.Y.K., its shipping affiliate, when it insisted that the latter merge with Sumitomo's shipping arm O.S.K., a long-term rival of N.Y.K. and a yet bigger buyer of the ships from Mitsubishi's Nagasaki shipyard during the 1920s. To carry out its decision, Mitsubishi had to plant several outsiders in N.Y.K.'s top management team. It let a finance man previously in charge of other subsidiaries of the zaibatsu be the shipping affiliate's new president, replacing its outgoing predecessor instead of promoting one from within. Mitsubishi headquarters reinforced its decision by buying back the majority interest from N.Y.K.'s largest shareholder at the same time. But this strategy merely antagonized the internal managers at N.Y.K. The vice president of N.Y.K. turned to Japan's classical strategy of identity and group formation, invoking in-group solidarity among the internal managers, to counter "excessive interference from outside institutions." The internal management team held onto the policy of managing recession through technological upgrading instead of financial contraction as recommended by the new president appointed by headquarters. The deadlock between N.Y.K. and the Mitsubishi headquarters did not become resolved until the Japanese government stepped in with its "scrap-and build" policy to stimulate recovery in the shipping business with expansion and technological upgrading during the Great Depression.[10]

Automobile manufacturing was another industry into whose organizational structure such core values of Japanese society as trust, voice, mutual loyalty, personal commitment, and informal networking were finding their way. But this did not happen until the 1930s, when mass production came on the agenda. Initially, it was the national defense establishment that started this high-risk infant industry. The army had sponsored its Osaka Arsenal and a group of defense contractors to develop a prototype of truck, identified as a strategic weapon since the Russo-Japanese War (1904-1905), and put it to trial production. To manage the risks of truck assembly, the government not only secured a burgeoning market with military procurement but also provided various subsidies and tax incentives, along with tariff protection.[11]

The Osaka Arsenal also worked out an arrangement with Jitsugyo Motor Co., a civilian venture that had independently designed a small passenger car, Datsun, for it to be assembled at the same factory where military trucks were being built. Experimental production like this, however, proved insufficient for handling explosive demand for vehicles after the 1923 earthquake destroyed the trolley-based public transport system in Tokyo. Out of this crisis, parts supply gained more than auto assembly, when demands for automotive parts rose not only from among the producers of three-wheeled vehicles but also Ford and GM, that had set up complete knock-down assembly of cars in Japan in the mid-1920s but had to localize production under Japan's domestic content rule. To learn more about automotive technology and to expand business, Jitsugyo Motor Co., or DAT Motors after the predecessor of Nissan had acquired it in 1926, joined many suppliers in subcontracting parts production with the two multi-nationals (Adachi, Ono, and Odaka 1983; Cusumano 1985; Smitka 1991).

DAT Motors' experience, however, revealed the constraint which the military's hierarchical control had on technological learning in auto manufacturing. Because of vertically integrated production and compartmentalized management, the R&D outputs and manufacturing experience of the arsenal could not be transferred to the civilian sector. As a result, Nippon Industries, the creator of Nissan, and Toyoda Automatic Loom, the creator of Toyota, had to determine their strategy for entry into mass production of trucks after the army washed its hands of the industry in the early 1930s. Diversification was one. But the uncertainty for this strategy was high, because the technology of the product and its production processes were too unfamiliar and complex. A less risky approach was technology transfer. The military authority had put out a risk management package to support entry, provided a candidate could qualify as a government-designated producer capable of making 3,000 vehicles annually while implementing the 100 percent domestic content rule (1936 Law on Automobile Enterprises). For the new entrants, however, the biggest source of market risk at that time lay in the economic power of zaibatsu like Mitsui and Mitsubishi. If they entered the industry, the others might not stand a chance (Yakushiji 1977; Cusumano 1985).[12]

As it turned out, Mitsui and Mitsubishi decided to stay away from auto manufacturing, which opened up an opportunity for others to move into the new industry. In Table 3.1, one can see that two competing strategies were chosen for entry, with Nippon Industries selecting technology transfer, supported by mergers and acquisitions, riding on its reputation as an aggressive "new zaibatsu" with shares traded in the stock market instead of privately owned like the older zaibatsu. It also had a greater inclination than Toyota to seeking expansion by venturing into technology-intensive businesses. Nippon Industries (henceforth Nissan) first bought out DAT Motors' manufacturing facility in Osaka and the manufacturing rights to its Datsun cars. It persuaded the Datsun car's American designer and his two American friends who had designed the Osaka factory to join the new auto manufacturing venture. Nissan then purchased a two-year old turnkey plant from the United States, together with the prototypes for the engines and truck. They arrived in Japan with the accompaniment of U.S. engineers to set the production process up for

Table 3.1

Market Environment, Strategy of Competition and Strucutral Linkages in the Japanese Automobile Industry, A Historical Summary, 1930s-1990s

Period	Mkt Environ.	Toyota		Nissan		Honda	
		Entry	Linkage	Entry	Linkage	Entry	Linkage
1930s: • entry in truck production	National	Self-help	Teamwork	Technology transfer	Competitive		
1950s-mid '60s: • shifting from truck to car production	Transitional, from national to inter-national	Self-help	Teamwork	Technology transfer	Shifting towards teamwork • supported by heavy invest-ment in tech.		
mid '60s-1970s: • beginning of "export"	International-ization		Teamwork		Teamwork • heavy invest-ment in tech.	Self-reliance	Self-reliance • supported by cross-procure-ment
1980s-1990s: • transplantation, and up-scaling in market niches	Globalization		Incorporating self-reliance and re-aligning teamwork		Incorporating self-reliance and re-aligning teamwork		Incorporating teamwork

Nissan and teach it the American way of manufacturing, including process control, the standardized method of mass production and vertical integration.

In comparison, Toyoda Automatic Loom, Inc. (henceforth Toyota) chose to enter the automobile industry through internally supported diversification, backed by its record as an inventor which had sold a patent to the Platt Brothers, one of the world's foremost machinery manufacturers, in 1929. Its diversification strategy combined product innovation on the basis of reverse engineering with the ultimate switch to mass production.[13]   By relying on the best available Japanese experts to copy foreign technology, Toyota was able to reverse engineer even machine tools and assembly plants.   Its goal was to improve the best available foreign products in both performance and price.   This approach involved greater risks than Nissan's, but in the long run it proved more successful.   Toyota was also committed to constantly improving vehicle design, which was possible because it equipped its factories with universal machine tools.   This gave it a certain flexibility which Nissan did not possess because of its dependence on the imported specialized machine tools.

Surely, Toyota followed a "self-help" approach also because of a lack of capital.   Unlike Nissan, it could not afford to import designs and complete production technology from abroad.   It therefore had to rely on finding the right partners at home, the ones who could provide it with theoretical insights, to solve the design problems. Toyota first established a relationship with Tohoku Imperial University.   But, in the beginning, it had to manufacture a lot of parts, including the electrical components, since there was no one outside to produce them.   The electrical components department eventually spun off as Nippon Denso.   From among the cottage enterprises Toyota fostered a group of firms from which it selected parts suppliers, some, from the same neighborhood in Nagoya, had long admired the reputation of Toyota, whereas others had previously supplied parts to the assemblers of three-wheelers and American automobile subsidiaries (Adachi, Ono, and Odaka 1983; Smitka 1991).

The Japanese in the 1920s and 1930s had a lot of skepticism about their ability to manufacture four-wheel automobiles, however.   Until then, they had not been successful in making such an automobile. Auto manufacturing was thus an extremely risky business.   Even capital-rich giants like Mitsui and Mitsubishi refused to get involved, in spite of government pressure.   It was in such an environment that Toyota asked the small manufacturers, its potential subcontractors, to share the risks of entry in an industry about which Toyota itself had little knowledge.   Indeed, Toyota's transition from textile machinery to automobile manufacturing would have been much more difficult were it not for the great reputation and trust which the Toyota family had built up with its potential subcontractors.   Their long-term relations provided some certainty to the suppliers for joining Toyota in the high-risk venture.

From inception, Toyota's main concern centered on improvement of product quality. Since it could not invent new products, Toyota's only hope of competitiveness lay in making better products than the one it had already built through reverse engineering. Japanese products during that time had a bad name in quality control. The situation became so bad that the government had to intervene. Nissan and Isuzu, the third auto maker in the market in the 1930s, were suffering from the same problem. In order to build up its competitive edge in product quality, Toyota decided to create a new type of relationship with suppliers. It sought to turn the emerging linkages with the subcontractors from "arms-length" to a more supportive tie. Once it had selected suppliers, Toyota would provide technical and even financial assistance for reduction of defects and improvement of the manufacturing process. By helping the suppliers to improve their capability and, thus, reduce business risks, Toyota was in effect returning the support which suppliers had given it earlier in setting up the high risk venture. The stability of such relationships became all the more necessary when Toyota began to introduce process control by experimenting with JIT supply. Indeed, the suppliers' cooperation became crucial, because Toyota was outsourcing as much as fifty-five percent of its vehicle production.[14]

It has been noted that Toyota had persuaded the suppliers to join in a highly risky venture on the basis of trust. To further institutionalize their stable relations, Toyota devised its own system of voice or participation. In 1939, Toyota expanded its "concentric circle" of manufacturers by including its small suppliers as corporate branches. It formalized long-term relations with the commitment to working with them for joint prosperity. Toyota introduced a system whereby two suppliers were made to compete for the same part. It would reward the supplier which came out with better quality and efficiency with a larger order. To expedite the implementation of its policy, it directed a group of suppliers in the neighboring Nagoya area to form a Kyoryoki Kai or cooperative association to discuss problems, check out new ideas and help each other out in quality control and production techniques. Additionally, it advised them to adopt a strategy of "specialization by product" which allowed it to trace defects in the specific parts to their source. In this process of transformation, a number of suppliers copied Toyota's strategy of making some machine tools in-house to gain better control of the production processes and the flexibility to change product designs. Toyota formally joined the cooperative in 1943 to control planning and rationing of steel as well as coordinate production, when the group switched to subcontracting parts for the aircraft industry under the government ordinance. Toyota subsequently extended its operation

from Nagoya to the Tokyo and Osaka areas and renamed the body
Kyoho Kai or Supplier Cooperation Association.[15]

By following the strategy of self-help, therefore, Toyota was
motivated to build its relations with suppliers on the basis of trust
and mutual obligation as much as on transactional needs. When it
intervened in the policy of the suppliers, Toyota frequently relied on
voice, a practice which received help from the Supplier Cooperation
Association. Toyota promised repeat deals to those suppliers who
took the necessary risks to change and succeeded in delivering quality.
To a great extent, these supplier management techniques assured the
subcontractors of the reward for as well as the stake in cooperation.

In contrast to Toyota, Nissan did not conduct its R&D beyond
testing product models. It did not simultaneously experiment with
new ideas as Toyota did throughout the war years. But Nissan did
turn to Hitachi, a member of its conglomerate, when it had to
duplicate some of the machine tools. It also depended on Hitachi for
technologically complicated electrical components which Hitachi
manufactured through production licensing (Cusumano 1985).[16]

The main focus of Nissan remained on learning to operate the
imported production process and produce trucks according to the
American prototype. It also relied on imports to get the components
and parts that fitted the standards required of the imported product
design and manufacturing process. To internalize the production of
the parts and meet the domestic content requirement of the 1936 Law
on the Automobile Enterprises, however, it had to work with the
blueprints, specs, and designs purchased from the American
suppliers, subcontract parts from Ford-Japan and GM-Japan, and
eventually take over Ford-Japan and its employees when it packed up
and left in 1939 (Yakushiji 1977).

By relying on the vertically integrated production system
transferred from the United States, Nissan had only to subcontract
simple processing jobs out to the small manufacturers in the adjacent
Tokyo-Yokohama-Kawaguchi areas instead of working with them on
the production of parts. Nissan was familiar with the subcontracted
services and could easily internalize any of the processing steps
involved. For this reason, it treated the suppliers as a cheap sourcing
site and kept them at arms length. Nissan did its best to take
advantage of their ruthless competition to cut down processing fees.
Even so, the assembler repeated deals with some suppliers, as did
Isuzu, on the basis of personal ties as well as the hourly fees they
charged. It was to win this market competition that some
subcontractors sought to reduce labor costs, breaking processing steps
further by handing over some steps to trusted relatives or apprentices,
thereby spinning them off as the next tier of subcontractors (Smitka
1991).

Prior to WWII, therefore, Toyota and Nissan had installed two contrasting systems for auto manufacturing. As members of a de facto duopoly, they were competing fiercely against each other in a protected national market. Parts production received a boost after the auto makers followed the order of the Ministry of Commerce and Industry and converted completely to truck production in 1938 (Adachi, Ono, and Odaka 1983; Yakushiji 1977). Automobile production entered a hiatus after the Pearl Harbor incident in 1941, when both were mobilized to subcontract the production of engines and parts for military aircraft. When the production resumed for trucks and opportunity emerged for the production of small cars after the war ended in August 1945, the auto makers faced the question of whether they could continue to compete in the same fashion as before the war.

First of all, the changing social climate in the immediate post war years rendered it impossible for corporations to force workers to accept continuously lower wages and benefits, particularly since the Japanese people had just been made to sacrifice for a lost war. Second, the entire nation was confronted with the question of how to produce products with quality so as to improve Japan's comparative advantage and earn the foreign exchange needed for financing its reconstruction and growth. In the final analysis, the question was how the business community could persuade the general population to support capitalist industrialization, after the philosophers and statesmen had converted the political and social elite to it three-quarters of a century earlier. For Toyota and Nissan, a more specific question was how to get the people to trust and cooperate with them to build quality products after the manufacturers had just dismissed some of them during the post war recessions.[17] It was for rebuilding a national consensus like this that the Japanese business community began to publicize the quality management flow chart (Deming 1986, 4). It argued that quality improvement provided the only way for a corporation to stay in business. As a corollary, product competitiveness would be the only guarantee of workers' job security.

The Japanese auto makers' concern for product quality was put to the test when the American army placed special procurement orders with them during the Korean War. They also received technical assistance when the world's most demanding customer at the time introduced statistical sampling inspection to Japan. But an even greater impetus to change came from the American experts who arrived with the General Headquarters of the Allied Forces to give advice on Japan's reconstruction in the post war era. Among them was Dr. Deming, a statistician and consultant on production management, whose reputation had already preceded him in professional circles. Shortly upon arrival, he helped to establish a quality control (QC) institution, a QC award, by donating the royalties from the translated version of his book to the Japanese Union of Scientists and Engineers (JUSE). JUSE named the award as the Deming Prize. Deming's teachings on QC methods proved popular, not only because they tied quality inspection to improvement in the entire production process, but also because they encouraged participation from every employee within a firm, ranging from the chief executive officers to the workers on the shop floor, as well as from the production organizations in every stage of manufacturing, particularly the inputs suppliers (Cusumano 1985; Deming 1986).

For Toyota, the question was how it should deal with Deming's advice. It surely could apply some of the procedural changes which Deming was recommending to meet the quality standards of the American army so as to win contracts for supplying special procurement in competition with Nissan. At heart, however, Toyota always preferred working out its own solution, even when it incorporated advanced concepts from external sources. This was consistent with its recent decision to repeat the strategy of self-help in its shift from truck to small car production instead of relying on transfer of technology like Nissan and some new entrants (Table 3.1).

Additionally, Deming's advice was designed to resolve the quality problems generated in an American manufacturing process, which differed from Toyota's. Market conditions in Japan also complicated the problem. Market size was much smaller yet tastes more diverse than the national market in the United States. This forced Toyota to focus its attention during the first post war decade on how to economically produce several types of vehicles in smaller quantity while rapidly introducing changes in model designs. Toyota therefore needed a more comprehensive approach to quality and productivity, which included built-in flexibility. To achieve these objectives, it had to depend on the loyalty and dedication of Taiichi Ono, initially the plant manager of the No. 2 Machine Shop (Cusumano 1985; Ono 1988).[18]

In his autobiography, Ono recalled the abhorrent inefficiency he had witnessed at the Toyota Motor Company upon being transferred from Toyota Spinning and Weaving (TSW) where he had been involved in plant rationalization to reduce costs and improve TSW's export competitiveness versus the world's best firms from England. He was determined to raise Toyota Motor Company's competitiveness just as methodically. From 1945, Ono set about tracing the sources of inefficiency. When he took charge of the No. 2 Machine Shop in 1947, Ono began to introduce some procedural changes to improve productivity while supplying both trucks and designed small cars in-house. Thus, when Deming arrived, Ono had already drawn a cognitive map in his mind about how to improve quality and productivity at Toyota Motor Company. Ono's map agreed with Deming's objective but differed in some fundamental ways in strategy.

As Table 3.2 illustrates, Ono conceptualized the given production system as the rational point to start the change, just as Deming did. But he seemed to differ from Deming in what productivity meant and how it might be raised. For instance, Deming believed quality and productivity could be improved by reducing defects. This could be achieved by applying statistical sampling inspections which could be linked to systematic improvement in the existing manufacturing process. Ono, on the other hand, conceptualized the problems as inherent in Toyota's production process. To obtain quality and productivity, it was necessary to go beyond inspection to reduce waste in labor usage and minimize in-process inventory that hid defects. This required re-engineering the relationship between the machines and their attendants, raising the number of the machines attended by the workers, redesigning the process flow, and enhancing the intelligence of the process by educating the latter.

Like Deming, Ono saw the involvement of each worker on the shop floor instead of control by the functional specialists as essential for system-wide improvement of quality and productivity. Unlike Deming, Ono conceptualized each worker as a part of the production process that had to be redesigned. He trained the machine attendants to become multi-skilled, capable of attending several machines that performed different functions at the same time instead of attending to one machine that executed one function only. He also rearranged the machines according to the jobs that needed to be done instead of according to the processing sequence in production. Ono reset the machines and workshop with devices to allow workers to exercise direct control by sight. With the cooperation of the workers, he was able to reduce the time for die change from hours to minutes so as to add further flexibility to the redesigned production process. When he did apply inspection, Ono linked it to the attack on the production system rather than restricting it to catching defective products. He also standardized job procedures for each worker to finish the exact quantity of assembly jobs just in time, according to the pull of the demand at the next stage of fabrication, instead of pushing as much down the flow as possible, thereby reducing and ultimately eliminating in-process inventory as well as the inventories with the suppliers. When the nation-wide quality control movement deepened, fueling the competition between Toyota and Nissan, Ono and his colleagues pushed the process redesign further while formally introducing quality control throughout the company, institutionalizing quality and productivity as a perpetual job in Toyota, a strategy which Deming (1986) later advised every competitive company to adopt.

In retrospect, Ono gave credit to the long-term commitment and support of Toyota's chief executive officers for making it possible for him to introduce and diffuse process redesign throughout the company (Table 3.2). Corporate commitment proved crucial for providing job security to workers to induce them first to accept then become committed to adapting themselves to implement one process innovation after another. These employees subsequently became valuable assets which Toyota had to keep for its system to operate properly. This "life long" employment, as it was called later, was also consistent with an existing practice of favoring job reassignment over firing when an outdated segment of the business had to give way to something new, a practice which had landed Ono his assignment in automobile manufacturing after Toyota decided to phase out its business in textile machinery. Such a practice was also consistent with Toyota's policy of keeping an old piece of equipment and trying to take advantage of its strength by finding ways of using it together with newer machinery instead of discarding it indiscriminately in favor of more advanced technology.[19]

The most difficult problem in quality control management faced by Toyota, however, was external to its own production system. The parts suppliers did not have the resources or know-how to introduce quality control by themselves. Moreover, it was both confusing and painful for them to change their entire production and management system. Until the mid-1950s, there were also acute shortages of raw materials and machinery. The suppliers therefore needed help in procurement,[20] as well as a long-term commitment to support the change demanded by Toyota. But they had also lost trust in Toyota when the latter broke its own commitment to them during the financial crisis of 1949-1950.

Earlier, Toyota had tried to reestablish trust and voice to overcome the resistance to change within the manufacturing plant. Under Ono, it promoted teamwork to help weak and inexperienced workers. Team leaders had to be supportive of the trainees, coaching them individually if necessary, to create trust and induce cooperation. This obligated workers to remove their own resistance to change.

Similar techniques had to be applied to the suppliers, as well. To achieve the goal of flexible manufacturing, Toyota had to help the suppliers by teaching them the new way of production and delivery. It probably lent and sold them its equipment at discount, like the other auto assemblers at the time, and allowed them to use Toyota's reputation for securing loans.[21] As cooperation between Toyota and its suppliers increased, contractual relations had also to be changed. In the midst of the recession in 1954, Toyota re-committed itself to stable and exclusive relations with its suppliers with repeat contracts. It demanded exclusive commitment from suppliers to protect proprietary production secrets.[22] For their part, the suppliers gained

Table 3.2
Alternative Conceptual Schemes and Strategies
for Process and Quality Improvement,
Historical Practice and Reflective Proposition,
the Japanese Automobile Industry

	Ono	Deming
Starting point:	• Stable system; --"normal" vs. "abnormal";	• Stable system;
Objective:	• Quality and productivity: --quality defined as what consumers want at a given price; --productivity conceptualized as reduction of waste in inputs	• Quality & productivity: --quality defined as what consumers want at a given price;** --productivity conceptual-ized as derivable from reduction of defects
Internal mgt. strategy:	• Redesign of man-machine interface; --Decentralized process con-trol by workers instead of centralized control by func-tionally specialized staffs or by automated machineries; --Hands-on practical solution instead of relying on interm-ediation of statistical tools; --Improvement of job proce-dure linked to constant re-skilling, creation of "flexible" workforce*** & perpetual process improvement	• Perfection of production process; --Decentralized sampling inspection by workers instead of inspection by functionally specialized staffs* --Replacement of competi-tion, trouble shooting with re-skilling & perpet-ual process improvement
Linkage strategy:	• Teamwork with suppliers, based on long-term exclus-ive relations;	• Teamwork with suppliers through shifting from competition to long-term exclusive relations;
Contract mgt. strategy:	• Trust, voice, mutual loyalty and obligation in-house and with suppliers;	• Voice; trust and mutual loyalty in contractual relations

*   Note that the points represent Deming's view in the 1950s instead of the 1980s. They are inferred from the description of the quality control strategies and programs which the Japanese auto makers undertook in the 1950s as described in Cusumano (1985, 323-327) and compared to Deming's writing as published in the 1980s. In his writings in the 1980s, Deming's view differed somewhat. It became more identical with Ono's view. This may reflect the lessons which he drew from decades of the Japanese companies' experience in process improvement.
* *   Suggested in the 1950s by Deming and Feigenbaum, another expert working in Japan who was known to have started promotion of total quality control in GE (Cusumano, 1985), 330.
* * *   The term is borrowed from Blinder, A. S. "Japanese Empire Rests on the Coddled Worker," *Newsday* (8 December 1991), 40.

Sources: Based on the 14 points presented by E. Deming in *Out of the Crisis* (Cambridge, Mass.: MIT Press), 23-24 and Chapters 2, 3 and Appendix; T. Ono, *Toyota Production System: Beyond Large-Scale Production* (Cambridge, Mass.: Productivity Press, 1988), 1, 4-7, 12, 18-20, 22, 24, 33, 35, 37, 40-41; M. Cusumano, *The Japanese Automobile Industry* (Cambridge, Mass.: Harvard University Press, 1985), 323-328, 330-332, 350-351, 362, 372; Yasuhiro Monden, *Toyota Production System: Practical Approach to Production Management* (Norcross, GA: Management Press, Institute of Industrial Engineers, 1983), particularly Chapters 1 and 10 and Appendices 4 and 5 and Toyota Jidosha Kabushiki Kaisha. *Toyota: A History of the First 50 Years* (Toyota City, Japan: Toyota Motor Corp., 1988), 192, 194-195.

----

from repeated orders the opportunity to grow in scale and improve their technological capability. The prospects of growth in the end balanced the sacrifices they had to make to meet the demands made by Toyota (Adachi, Ono, and Odaka 1983; Smitka 1991).

As the cooperative relationship with suppliers continued to evolve, Toyota began to share its proprietary information on design and model changes with them. In return, it asked the suppliers to provide details of the price and cost breakdowns. In this process, the function of the purchasing staff changed from hard bargaining to helping suppliers to reduce costs with value analysis so as to meet the targeted price. Toyota also encouraged suppliers to engage in their own cost-cutting value analysis by offering to split the resulting profits. From the mid-1960s onwards, Toyota began to shift more process steps to suppliers to keep up with the rapid expansion of auto manufacturing.[23]

It also tried to introduce institutional flexibility to support its cooperative relations with suppliers. To accommodate changes in circumstances which long-term contracts could not foresee, it had to leave the terms purposely vague. This allowed the two parties to sit down, talk to each other and reconcile differences whenever circumstances changed. Such an approach to contracting proved helpful, particularly in view of the constant adjustments which both parties had to make to accommodate the requirements of process redesign (Hervey 1982).

The supplier cooperative associations provided additional help in promoting cooperation and production innovation. Indeed, Toyota played an active part in directing the learning activity of these associations. Its engineers went there to give formal instructions and used the occasion to learn suppliers' problems. Through these associations, Toyota also managed to diffuse such techniques as cost accounting, statistical quality control, and industrial engineering to subcontractors more successfully than its competitor Nissan. Toyota monitored the development in these associations closely and constantly reorganized them to deal with the problems of cooperative learning and innovation more effectively. In 1948, Toyota reorganized the association, dividing it into three groups on the basis of their geographical location. After its success in diffusing the best techniques among suppliers, Toyota added two more supplier associations according to the functional services provided by suppliers. By the 1970s, these associations had helped the suppliers to become competitive in both cost and quality (Adachi, Ono, and Odaka 1983; Smitka 1991).

This way, Toyota was able to leave the quality control responsibilities to the suppliers while concentrating on its own product and process innovation. As for the individual suppliers, the recognition which each hoped to receive from Toyota as well as from its fellow member firms encouraged it to compete in raising design capacity to win "all Toyota" QC awards which Toyota introduced after it recalled defective vehicles from the United States in 1969 (Cusumano 1985; Ono 1988).

Toyota also escalated outsourcing around this time, both to meet expanding demand in the final product market and to complete transformation of its in-house production processes. The assembler could shift more and more processes to the subcontractors, because it was successful in teaching the internally generated best practices to them. The processes of change, cooperation, and production transformation, were in turn adopted by the Toyota suppliers not only within themselves but also in relation to the latter's own subcontractors.

The change in the macroeconomics situation as a result of the oil shocks in the 1970s brought about a slower rate of growth and rising demand for variety in the final product market, leading to further reduction of production lot size as well as shortened product life cycle. This translated into a greater need for outsourcing as well as a higher speed of change in the intermediate product market. To accommodate the changing market environment, Toyota's direct suppliers began to install the U-line process, following the example of the parent firm. In the U-line formation, eight machines were arranged in a U-shape at each work station so that eight separate fabrication functions could be performed on a part before it was passed on to the next work station. Earlier versions of this multi-machine layout, as introduced by Ono, had each raised labor productivity first by 100 percent, then by another fifty percent to 100 percent over time.[24]

In order to install this multi-processing system while maintaining control over product design, the suppliers had also to copy Toyota's integration of the production of machine tools but shift or spin off certain parts processing jobs to the next tier of subcontractors. First, the direct suppliers had to break down each of the processes to make it manageable for their subcontractors so that the latter could become specialists in these processes. They had also to copy Toyota's strategy of technological diffusion, which included duplicating suppliers associations to improve product quality and productivity among the next tier of subcontractors. Typically, Toyota's direct suppliers transferred to their subcontractors those functions whose scale economies were relatively low.[25] As a common practice, they were most likely assigned to experienced employees who were developing their own spin-off businesses (Broadbridge 1966; Smitka 1991).

By the latter half of the 1960s, Toyota's suppliers had accumulated enough know-how and expertise in their products and production processes to assume the responsibility for black box product engineering.[26] Similarly, they had begun to manage the product and services supplied by their own subcontractors. To recoup the cost of product innovation, however, the direct suppliers had to supply large-sized orders to other auto makers. But the specialization which the lower-tier subcontractors had developed by this time provided the strategic assets for the direct suppliers to win orders.[27]

By the 1970s and 1980s, Toyota had developed an evaluation system to rate suppliers' cumulative performance and future potential in technology. As technology became a critical factor in determining Toyota's global competitive position, it even began to recruit new suppliers in case the current ones should fail to deliver the needed expertise. On their part, the suppliers understood that the size of the deals they received from Toyota depended on how well they fulfilled the obligation expected of them. They knew that Toyota would not object to their profitability so long as they increased their profits through R&D, value analysis, and value engineering that genuinely improved product design and manufacturing processes. In the second half of the 1970s, Toyota's suppliers began to invest in R&D. This was followed by their decision to introduce the robotics that were designed and manufactured by themselves in the 1980s. As a result, they began to contribute to product innovation. The direct suppliers applied the same techniques to motivate cooperation from their own subcontractors. In some ways, they had greater leeway than the assemblers, because the structure of the lower subcontracting tier remained atomistic.

Competitive strategies like these led to hierarchical relationships in the interfirm arena of the Toyota group. Surely, this hierarchical relationship was formalized by equity share holding and interlocking directorships. But its maintenance and smooth running really depended on such values as long-term commitment, mutual loyalty, and reliance on voice and trust. For this reason, Toyota could allow its suppliers to increase their production efficiency and profits by supplying to its competitors at a higher price without fearing that this might affect their relationship with Toyota. Additionally, Japanese business ethics would not permit conducting business on the basis of profit alone without considering loyalty. It was loyalty, above all, which made it possible for the automobile industry to expand and form its competitive "Alps" structure. [28]

It has so far been established that Toyota fell back on core Japanese values to organize technological learning and develop competitive products and production processes first for Japan's unique domestic market, then for the international market. Toyota's approach started differently from Nissan's, because the latter had entered auto manufacturing with a product prototype and production system imported from the United States. Such historical linkages with the world economy made it easier for Nissan to accept the quality control methods recommended by Deming and his American colleagues, as well as the sampling inspection technique emphasized by the U.S. army. Nissan's decision to repeat the strategy of technology transfer when it switched from truck to small car production in the immediate postwar years reinforced this tendency (Table 3.1), since the production system of its British partner Austin was essentially a revision of the American technology.[29]

In competition with Toyota, Nissan did upgrade and introduce significant improvements intrinsic to its production system, partly with the help of the blueprints supplied by the machine tool builders which the two auto assemblers had been using before they closed the door against mutual visits by the first half of the 1950s. Yet, to a great extent, Nissan dedicated itself to perfecting the imported "push" system to the limit while Toyota was methodically developing the "pull" system. This at least partly explains why for a few years after having picked up the auto industry's first Deming prize, Nissan seemed to have lost its sense of direction for competing in process technology.[30]

Nissan also encountered severe difficulties in diffusing quality control measures to its suppliers. Since it had concentrated on outsourcing only simple processing jobs and in-house manufacturing of parts, Nissan based its relationship with the suppliers mostly on reduction of costs rather than helping them to learn how to design a product and introduce mass production. Consequently, its suppliers neither developed product specialization nor improved their internal capacity for R&D and product design as did Toyota's subcontractors. Further, Nissan did not hesitate to cut back processing jobs during the recession of 1949-1950, because of its hierarchical approach to outsourcing. This increased the distrust between Nissan and its cottage suppliers (Smitka 1991).

Japan's second largest auto maker therefore had to take measures to re-establish trust. In 1954,[31] it formed its suppliers' cooperation association, Takara Kai. Like Toyota, Nissan demanded an exclusive relationship with the members of the association, now that it was switching from hierarchy to partnership. Nissan decided to revamp its purchasing strategy in favor of "guidance and upgrading of the subcontracting firms" (Wada 1976).[32] The timing was not accidental, because in 1954, in the middle of another recession, Toyota had also introduced its new procurement strategy to reassure the suppliers of its commitment to teamwork and long-term cooperative relations.

Nissan was now getting ready for the hard times it faced in factory innovation. In support of this policy, it asked suppliers to commit themselves to sharing the pain of the transformation. Since the fundamental upgrading had to be effectively executed only in an incremental way to avoid unnecessary anxiety and insecurity, Nissan had also to provide frequent and close assistance to the suppliers who made the commitment to teamwork.

To begin with, it introduced some symbolic change. Instead of calling the owner of a cottage supplier an "old man", Nissan now addressed him as "president." Similarly, cottage suppliers were no longer "subcontractors" but "outside order firm(s)," which entitled them to voice and partnership instead of lowly positions in a hierarchy (Wada 1976, 90, 118). In return, the suppliers had to take the necessary risks for change. But the Nissan consultants offered to shoulder the blame in the event of failure to reduce the risks and secure their cooperation.

Nissan also kept prices constant so that suppliers could make greater profits from streamlining their production processes. Similarly, Nissan continued to hire and train college graduates for the subcontractors in the recession year of 1957, even though it had stopped annual hiring for its own assembly operation, to lay the foundation for intra-*keiretsu* relationships between the new trainees who were assigned to the subcontractors and the managers and engineers working at Nissan. The policy proved to be of great importance when some of these trainees assumed senior positions in the subcontracting firms.

After transforming the technological base of the subcontractors and reestablishing trust, Nissan went on to select those suppliers that were more willing to take independent initiatives and possessed requisite technologies and funding capability to support Nissan's export expansion before the opening of the domestic market in 1965.

In exchange for total commitment, sometimes including relocation of the plant sites, Nissan assured them of close teamwork.

Since only one supplier in each product area was selected as a teammate for the second phase of expansion and upgrading, those which were not selected were downgraded to the second-tier position. Meanwhile, Nissan's supplier cooperative association shifted its focus from job standardization, factory rationalization, cost accounting, and quality control in the 1959-1960 period to product-oriented value analysis in the 1960s. In 1963, the assembler re-organized the supplier association into branches to provide technical assistance to one hundred and nine suppliers which were trying to become specialized in product and production processes and which had demonstrated the most reliable records for service and quality. Nissan established a closer relationship with them by synchronizing in-house production with the latter's delivery systems through computerizing the production process.[33]

The mutual loyalty established during the second phase of technological upgrading (1961-1964) allowed Nissan to encourage its suppliers to diversify their clients and thus improve their economy of scale and rate of profit. This enabled Nissan to arrive at a similar level of confidence about the suppliers as Toyota. At the same time, it increased mutual dependence between Nissan and its suppliers. To reduce the fear that long-term contractual relations would lead to performance complacency among suppliers, Nissan had to introduce competition among them. It introduced an evaluation process to determine which supplier would be included in product R&D and which therefore would receive the largest order in any area of parts procurement. Thus, Nissan was converging with Toyota in interfirm relationships, while both intensified their competition in the world market after the 1970s.

A key area where their competition had intensified was product design. The higher the frequency of redesigning the parts, the shorter the product life cycle became. This in turn had driven the assemblers to keep R&D in-house and integrated with production. When Nissan's direct suppliers duplicated this locational strategy, along with hierarchic assistance and supplier management methods, with their own subcontractors, the same "Alps" structure as Toyota's emerged in the Nissan Group (Ikeda 1987; Nishiguchi 1987; Asanuma 1989).

The Japanese automobile industry therefore developed a decentralized "learning by association" method of technological development on the basis of a special relationship between a worker and a product. In such a relationship, improvement in a product results mainly from the worker's constant contact, growing familiarity with, and increasing knowledge about the product. The worker must learn to understand how each part relates to the others and how it fits in the finished product before he can improve the design. In the production of a complex product like an automobile, the workers who build separate parts must also learn to work together to innovate. Furthermore, this approach to technological development requires that not only the assemblers but also the subcontractors pursue long-term cooperation in learning. Innovation has thus become a continuous process of understanding and improving a product, which has led both Toyota and Nissan to institutionalize constant re-skilling and continuous improvement.

As it had evolved from the end of WWII, the non-adversarial relationship between assemblers and suppliers not only helped both parties to solve the problem of defects throughout the entire manufacturing process, but also made it possible for them to adopt total quality control as devised by A.V. Feigenbaum, which required cooperation from all functional departments, ranging from market research, product planning, design and testing to manufacturing. Popularized in 1968 as "company-wide QC" by Ishikawa Ichiro, the first chairman of JUSE, learning by association soon became a necessary process for responding to the constantly changing demands of the international consumers.

Ultimately, what sustains learning by association is an understanding of the mutual stake in cooperation, which is essential for developing technological capacity to compete in a world-wide market. As a start, the assemblers had also to render assistance in value analysis and value engineering to the suppliers to make learning effective. Consequently, Toyota and Nissan staffed their procurement departments with engineers experienced in product and process engineering. They also helped suppliers manage their own R&D risks by letting them keep part of the profit from black box engineering and process improvement. Finally, the suppliers associations in each auto manufacturing group provided the subcontractors with an identity, a place for information sharing as well as a venue for joint development of technology.

The point is that the Japanese automobile manufacturing system underwent significant changes after the Second World War. While American experts like Deming and his colleagues greatly influenced the Japanese automobile manufacturing system, they did not impress the Japanese business culture per se. The contractual system which the Japanese corporations have used in their inter-firm relationships, for example, is embedded in the way that the Japanese generally deal with conflicts and challenges. When Japanese companies are confronted with an external challenge, they typically enlarge the concentric circle of identification for their given organizational identity or "in-group."[34] The corporate entities then try to overcome their opponents by building alliances with technologically, geographically, and historically proximate organizations. Indeed, both Toyota and Nissan followed this strategy by establishing their own groups of supplier cooperative associations.

One advantage of the strategy of developing technology through partnership is that the boundary of the in-group circle can both be enlarged and contracted according to the task at the moment. An individual member of the concentric circle can maintain its in-group identity while pursuing heated competition with other members in the same circle. When a new challenge arises, each can realign with its competitors and team up to solve the problem. Toyota's relationship with Nippon Denso shows that mutual identification, trust and loyalty among members of a *keiretsu* can be activated at any time for dealing with any external challenge, despite mutual assertions of independence. This explains why Japanese auto assemblers do not worry about not having formal control over the second and lower tiers of suppliers. Instead, they leave the responsibility for organizing learning by association among the lower tiers of subcontractors entirely to the direct suppliers.

Because of trust, voice, and teamwork, an assembler can also locate R&D outside while continuing to capture the development efficiency in this activity. Although it was the market power of the assemblers that has forced the suppliers to integrate product R&D, the suppliers nonetheless remain loyal to the assemblers' needs and organize their R&D accordingly.

Toyota, of course, is the principal contributor to this method of technological development. Nissan has, in comparison, followed the technological solution more closely than re-skilling. In fact, Nissan did not turn to learning by association totally until 1982 when it began to lose market share in a big way. But Nissan also had its contributions to the Japanese system of manufacturing. It pioneered the "design-in" strategy of joint product development[35] to compensate for the disadvantage it had versus Toyota, which included a wide geographical dispersion of suppliers and, initially, their weaker technological capabilities.

Unlike Toyota and Nissan, the Japanese automobile manufacturers such as Honda and Suzuki began their auto production in an entirely different economic environment. While Toyota and Nissan had initiated auto manufacturing in the years before the Second World War and evolved in the postwar period to compete in the world economy, Honda started out in a significantly changed competitive market internationally. Of the three major Japanese auto makers, Toyota comes closest to a pure Japanese model. It developed the horizontal strategy of technological development by building its relationships with suppliers on trust and voice, the essential components of Japanese business culture. It also emphasized self-help in technological competition, partly through reverse engineering, but mostly through learning by association leading to perpetual improvement. Nissan over time adopted a good part of the Toyota model to compete with Toyota as well as to survive. In comparison, Honda had to be innovative in finding its own niche in the crowded automobile market when it finally moved to car assembly in the 1960s.

As a late entrant in this highly competitive world, Honda did not possess long-term collaborative relations with automotive parts suppliers as Toyota and Nissan did. This meant it could not begin by copying the horizontal strategy developed by Toyota and had, instead, to depend mainly on its internal capacity not only to generate product and process innovation but also to perform the required R&D to develop the automobile and parts of its own design rapidly. Therefore, Honda had to adopt a vertical or "self-reliance" strategy of technological development by necessity (Table 3.1).

In pursuing this strategy, Honda continued with its history of relying on internal R&D for product innovation which Soichiro Honda, the founder of Honda Motors, had pioneered during the 1920s and 1930s, when he first started building racing cars with imported engines.[36] Soichiro Honda had made significant improvement in Honda's racing car models by installing additional devices and substituting different materials for certain parts. When Honda began to supply piston rings to Toyota, it decided to monitor product quality and manufacturing efficiency through internal R&D rather than through associated learning with Toyota like most other parts makers. But to produce quality piston rings on his own, Soichiro Honda had to spend years trying to learn both the underlying theories and the production techniques. With the same strategy, Honda was able to build automatic machine tools in-house successfully, which improved the company's productivity as well as helped to offset the effect of labor shortages during WWII.

When he entered the motorcycle business after WWII, Soichiro Honda used the same strategy as he had in building racing cars for testing and improving his motor bikes. In 1954, Honda Motor began to use international races to test its engines and improve their designs and performance. This proved helpful in producing superior motorcycles in the mass production phase. Honda also used the technology obtained this way to build a small number of sports cars to establish the image of an auto maker that offered differentiated products with superior engine performance. Honda Motors followed the same strategy when it announced its plan to participate in the Formula I Grand Prix in 1963, followed by Formula II races, and thus prepared itself for jump starting the mass production of compact cars.

Product differentiation was extremely critical for Honda, if it were to succeed as the last of eleven auto producers in an already crowded field in Japan. Soichiro Honda believed that the only way for a late entrant to move ahead was to "(n)ever copy others. Do exactly what the others don't do". To avoid direct competition with Toyota and Nissan, Honda entered the "micro-car" segment of the market. Here, Honda competed with Mazda by rapidly introducing the most advanced designs for its products. In 1967, it equipped its small trucks with front-wheel drive technology before any other Japanese auto maker. It was also the first of the Japanese auto assemblers to adopt the double overhead camshaft type of engine and hatchback designs (Nobeoka 1988, 8, 11).

A successful strategy of product differentiation, of course, required the support of both innovation and intensive R&D. While Toyota and Nissan were slow in responding to the U.S. Clean Air Act of 1970, Honda speedily responded with its engine, the CVCC. In this new product, Honda redesigned the conventional combustion process rather than providing an ad hoc solution to the pollution problem by attaching additional devices. The CVCC was acclaimed as a triumph of the strategy of internal R&D. Indeed, Honda's R&D center was able to launch CVCC in time by swiftly mobilizing seventy percent of its researchers to zero in on the project. But even with all its resources, Honda could not have come up with a revolutionary engine in such a short time, if it had not encouraged its R&D personnel to explore unconventional fields and move beyond incrementalism in thinking (Shimokawa 1978).

Inspite of its serious divergence from the Toyota model, insofar as it maintained an essentially vertical strategy of technological development, Honda did share some aspects of the horizontal strategy. For example, teamwork with suppliers was crucial for developing automobile technology for the Toyota system. For Honda, teamwork was equally crucial for in-house R&D. At Honda's autonomous R&D center, individual researchers were encouraged to collaborate with one another according to the needs of the projects. They sometimes pursued several themes of research simultaneously for a single in-house research project, drawing strength from their different disciplinary backgrounds as well as experience in independent research designs. These researchers met as a team to compare notes and select the winning strategy. Cross-departmental teamwork was also employed for product innovation. It was critical for Honda to create the innovative CVCC engine in time and design the Civic subcompact for export when the demand for small cars was becoming an important segment of the American automobile market. Neither the other Japanese auto makers nor American auto assemblers like GM were ready to compete in this market. The same teamwork enabled the project team to develop the Honda Accord in 1976 (Nobeoka 1988, 203).

At Honda's R&D center, teamwork was necessary for product innovation while voice was used to induce collaboration among researchers and engineers. In this sense, Honda was not hierarchical even within its vertical model of technological competition. The explanation lies in the "paperweight" structure installed by Fujisawa, the vice president of Honda Motors, which emphasized voice and participation in management instead of hierarchy and command. Basing promotion on an engineer or researcher's performance record instead of his position in the hierarchy encouraged each to contribute his best. Because of such flat corporate structure, the researchers not only knew each other through joint research projects but also were motivated to cooperate. Additionally, they had access to the chief executive officers, so that an informal relationship between them and the management evolved. This informality made it possible for researchers to voice their differences with a company policy, drawing the attention of the management and thus finding the best solution to the problem at hand. For instance, the engineers differed from Soichiro Honda's choice of the air-cooled engine as the focus of Honda Motor's product technology and made it known to Fujisawa. Fujisawa subsequently persuaded Soichiro Honda to return control to the engineers so that they could concentrate R&D on the water-cooled engine, the technology of their choice, which in the end improved the competitive position of the company.[37]

Honda, however, did not extend the voice and participation which it cultivated actively in its R&D center to suppliers. Instead, it adopted a hierarchical authority structure in dealing with the latter. When Honda Motors was undergoing the financial crisis of 1953, which occurred as a result of the decline in sales due to engine defects, and which was hurting its mass production of the motorbikes necessary for exploiting its market opportunity, Fujisawa simply told the subcontractors that they would have to deliver parts on schedule at thirty percent payment only and wait to receive the balance. If they did not, then they would not get further business from the assembler. Because Honda had the internal capacity to develop innovative engines and had invested more in its manufacturing facilities between 1952 and 1954 than the joint investment of Toyota and Nissan, Fujisawa's threat carried serious credibility with the suppliers. They agreed to the concessions demanded by Honda, even though they felt dissatisfied.

But occasionally, Honda also relied on voice, trust, and teamwork with the suppliers. In 1953, for example, Soichiro Honda personally visited a parts maker to test a new product to replace the defective carburetors responsible for the problems in Honda Motors' engines. When he sought to improve motorcycle's chains later, it was, similarly, to a close personal friend that he turned. In fact, Honda Motors sought voice and trust to resolve those problem areas in which it did not have internal expertise. Whenever it had to deal with other Japanese suppliers with independent expertise, Honda did employ the main criteria of Japanese business culture.

For instance, Honda had to build trust with the Mitsubishi Bank to raise long-term credit to finance its R&D and expansion in mass production. Fujisawa also had to work hard to build loyalty among dealers to break the marketing barriers created by the exclusive dealership networks of Toyota, Nissan, and other auto assemblers (in other words, even some Japanese companies experience market entry problems in Japan). Honda Motors won them over by not only helping them with marketing know-how, but also giving them support for the difficult tasks of repair, servicing, and trade-in transactions. Such cooperative policies contrasted with the company's adherence to the vertical model of technological development, which made it unnecessary for Honda to form a supplier association like the other Japanese auto makers.

Honda's competitive strategy, based on product innovation and differentiation, rationally led to internationalization of both marketing and production. Initially, it was necessary for it to repay the foreign exchange debt incurred during the early 1950s for importing the manufacturing process as well as to maintain the profit flows needed for supporting the internal R&D. In 1959, five years ahead of Toyota and Nissan, it established a permanent sales subsidiary in Los Angeles. This was also five years before the "liberalization" of the Japanese motor vehicle industry came into force and ten years before Honda started to export cars to the United States.

Honda used the American market to test and commercialize its differentiated products. Between 1972 and 1982, it moved up from practical and economical models to sportier and more sophisticated segments of the automobile market. In 1982, it started its transplant production in Ohio. This helped Honda Motors Co. to deflect the temporary impact of voluntary export restraints and protect its share in the American market. It was its success in the American market that provided the additional resources for Honda to build up its total market share and become the number three car maker in Japan. In the mid-1980s, Honda again led the movement to the upscale market segment when it established a separate brand name, Acura, for its luxury car model and set up a new network of dealerships to sell it in the United States.[38]

To a great extent, voluntary export restraints were responsible for triggering the Japanese auto makers' decision to establish transplant production in the United States. Nissan was the first to respond to the twenty-five percent tariffs on the trucks it had been exporting by setting up a facility in Tennessee. Toyota, concerned with the problem of quality as well as the political forces of the labor unions in the United States, moved much more cautiously. It tried to manage the risk by first entering a joint venture with GM. The Japanese auto assemblers subsequently faced the pressure to source parts and

components for the transplant production from American vendors.
Surely, they could not duplicate the *keiretsu* system of parts supply in
the United States. They were also expected to upgrade American
vendors through learning by association.

It is interesting to compare how Toyota, Nissan, and Honda
responded to the protectionist pressure in the United States and how
each tried to adapt its "traditional" strategy to accommodate the
requirements of an increasingly globalized operation. Of the three,
Honda remained the most detached from suppliers in the Japanese
market. Since it did not have a cooperative association of its
suppliers, the Japanese suppliers did not share teamwork with it to
the same extent as they did with Toyota and Nissan. But Honda also
escaped teamwork with suppliers,[39] because it could cross-purchase
certain parts from the suppliers of other auto making groups which
began to seek expansion from the 1970s onwards by making low
volume sales to minor customers like Honda that would not threaten
their networking relationship with their "parent" assembler. Honda
transplants in the United States, however, had to adopt some of the
Japanese type of relationship with the American vendors. It required
them to make long-term investment in production facilities so as to
implement the JIT manufacturing process and share proprietary
information on the cost breakdown of the products as well as the
steps of the manufacturing process. But it imported the higher value-
added parts, built them in-house, or acquired them from transplant
suppliers who had relocated themselves to Ohio.[40]

To remain an internationally self-reliant company, however,
Honda had to localize its product R&D. By 1987, it had considerably
expanded its R&D facility, Honda Research of America.[41] With
globalization of competition, Honda also began to seek partners in
innovation. As early as 1983, it formed a joint venture with Britain's
Austin Rover to develop a luxury car, Rover Sterling, and its
Japanese equivalent, Honda Legend. To recover the R&D costs and
generate sufficient profits for continued innovation, Honda marketed
Legend worldwide, although it built the vehicle in Japan.[42]

In the United States, Honda designed and produced the Accord
series and exported two of three Accords, the coupe, in 1988, and the
station wagon, in 1991, to Japan and Europe respectively. To build up
global competitiveness, however, Honda has also had to upgrade
teamwork to the design stage with local suppliers. Local American
suppliers, for instance, have had to develop and upgrade their
technological level by investing in internal R&D. Those which
possess design capabilities have a much better chance of transacting
with the Japanese assembler. Thus, Rockwell International has
received a contract for supplying components for 1994 models because
of the assistance it has rendered to Honda in product design. On the

other hand, Solvay Automotive, which did not provide such design support remains a low cost parts subcontractor.[43]

Toyota and Nissan have felt even greater pressure than Honda to increase the domestic content in transplant production. Both rising protectionist pressure and the strength of the yen have forced them to localize the content of their cars, beginning with procurement of lower value-added items from the American vendors (Andrea, Everett, and Luria 1988, 2). Nissan, like Toyota and Honda, has established design and R&D facilities, along with its assembly plants, in the United States. But its experience in working with American engineers since the prewar period has obviously made it easier for Nissan to "Americanize" the management. Nissan also localized part of the work regarding product design and development to American parts makers to develop Altima, 1993 model family sedan, which was supposed to compete with Toyota Camry and Honda Accord. Finally, it established an R&D center in Detroit to take advantage of research infrastructure and human capital, so that it can develop vehicle products locally to satisfy the requirements of the environmental and safety regulations more effectively.[44]

Compared to Nissan and Honda, Toyota has been the most cautious in its overseas ventures. But once it set up the transplant operations in the United States, Toyota tried to take the lead in reducing bilateral conflicts with the United States. By 1992, Toyota overtook Nissan and Honda in expanding parts sourced with the American vendors, which it used in the cars assembled in the transplant or exported to the United States from Japan. Toyota's caution has stemmed from a desire to avoid any risks in quality control. Surely, Toyota has established some trust with GM's parts division, with their joint venture adopting the Toyota system of supply. It is also beginning to implement "design-in" with foreign parts suppliers, particularly for the components of high-tech nature.[45]

In transferring some of the design and R&D tasks abroad and fostering "design-in" teamwork with foreign suppliers, the Japanese auto makers are motivated by a strategic decision to satisfy niche market demands in the globalized economy as well as to achieve product differentiation. Worldwide recession is also forcing the auto makers to change their relationship with the suppliers. Nissan, for one, is cutting back on model variations and standardizing more parts used, such as steering wheels, in different models, instead of custom manufacturing the parts. To manage the R&D risks, recover costs and improve profitability, it is also lengthening the product life cycle from four or five years to as much as ten years. Indeed, Nissan is facing severe competition from Toyota, which has managed to cut costs while introducing numerous new models, although it has also begun to use more common automotive parts.[46]

In the late 1980s, the Japanese auto makers made a major shift in their competitive strategy when they began to move from incremental to radical innovation as well as competition in the area of high technology. In response to mounting protectionist pressure overseas, they also began to switch from concentrating on market share to competing for higher profitability with upscale vehicle models. Thus, Honda avoided overtaking Chrysler to become the third largest auto maker in the United States. In the era of incremental competition, the Japanese auto assemblers had depended on raising the speed of the model changes and increasing the number of vehicle models. They did so by using super computers to improve the computer-aided design process, and by introducing further factory modernization to perfect the system of flexible manufacturing. Ultimately, competition like this allowed them to push product differentiation well ahead of consumer demands. But the auto assemblers can no longer afford to compete in the same manner as they intensify the competition in basic technology in the areas of environment, new materials and advanced electronics.[47]

Structural changes are also happening in the Japanese home market as a result of the globalization of market and technological competition that has dramatically raised the cost of R&D. As new technologies begin to replace outdated ones, the assemblers feel obligated to help the incumbent suppliers develop new areas of expertise before old areas exit. Recently, auto analysts have also started to speculate what the new direction of the Toyota system would be, as the Japanese auto assemblers depend more and more on non-Japanese suppliers for design and innovation.[48]

Both Toyota and Nissan are forming strategic alliances with non-Japanese suppliers in order to meet the demands for innovation in high technology. This in turn will probably reshape their historical ties with the suppliers in their own manufacturing groups. Toyota, for example, is prepared to give the largest order to anyone possessing the most advanced technological capabilities, irrespective of the location and national identity of the supplier. For example, it decided to purchase airbag sensors and controls from an American vendor, TRW Technar Inc., in Irwindale, instead of from Nippon Denso, because TRW had beaten Nippon Denso with a new design and a finished product from conception to production in fourteen months, thereby fulfilling the requirement of developing a new product in two years. This compares favorably with most American firms, which take up to four years to move an innovative product design to the stage of final production.[49]

Toyota, however, did not give its contract to TRW in 1987 until after TRW had first spent more than a year socializing and building trust with the assembler. In exchange for its demonstrated commitment and performance, Toyota also presented TRW with a

Toyota technology and development excellence award, the first one given to a company outside Japan. This was in addition to the long-term contract and technical assistance which it gave to TRW for improving efficiency and productivity. Toyota's treatment of TRW marked a significant departure from the "two-supplier principle" to which it had been adhering since the 1930s, the principle which it had designed to stimulate competition in its manufacturing group yet which also committed Toyota to exclusive purchase from the in-group suppliers.

To introduce innovative electronics components, Japanese assemblers are also pursuing joint R&D or "design-in" with foreign suppliers, while the Japanese suppliers themselves are forming strategic alliances with the foreign makers of electronics parts to compete in the same area of technology. In late 1992, Toyota announced its plan to develop twenty-two electronic components for its cars with Motorola, Texas Instruments, National Semiconductor and five other American suppliers. This was in addition to the twenty-four "design-in" semiconductors already completed. But Toyota also instructed its eight direct suppliers to team up in these joint R&D projects.[50]

Nissan, in comparison, is taking a more direct route than Toyota to compete in the globalized market. It has opened up its *keiretsu* network to foreign suppliers. In 1991, Nissan invited twenty-two foreign parts makers, including the Japanese subsidiaries of two American corporations, Garrett Turbo Inc. and TI Japan Ltd., to join its original network of one hundred and seventy suppliers. This was in addition to three foreign suppliers it had already admitted into the network. In fact, Nissan has offered to let any foreign firm that did more than one billion yen worth of business with it annually have an automatic membership in its supplier cooperative association in a measure to improve communications with the foreign suppliers and build long-term relations with them.[51]

Nissan has also formed a strategic alliance with Germany's Robert Bosch to compete with Toyota and Nippon Denso. In 1992, Bosch acquired a 9.6 percent stake in UNISIA after the latter merged with Japan Electronic Control Systems Co. The alliance promises to combine UNISIA's brake and engine technology with Bosch's engine control electronics, in addition to involving Bosch in developing key electronics systems for Nissan right from the "design-in" phase. Nissan hopes to achieve a competitive edge in key electronics systems with Bosch's advanced technology in electronics parts, particularly the latter's technology in controller area networks which link key auto parts like engine brakes and transmissions with optic fibers and reduce body weight as well as enhance safety. To be sure, Bosch is also licensing fuel ejection technology for use in diesel engines to Nippon Denso. But it refrains from building the partnership further, fearing

Nippon Denso as a powerful competitor. Bosch's alliance with Nissan suppliers, on the other hand, provides an opportunity for it to establish a position in the Japanese market quickly.[52]

Structural readjustment has obviously affected all the Japanese automobile manufacturing groups when the auto assemblers begin to extend the concept of cross-supply beyond traditional boundaries, as was first permitted in the 1970s and maintained through the 1980s. As early as the mid-1980s, the suppliers of Toyota and Nissan sought to expand sales by supplying to a third assembler such as Mazda. Both Toyota's Aisan and Nissan's Nippon Carburetor, for example, were selling carburetors to Mazda. Similarly, Nippon Denso and Nissan's Nihon Radiator competed to supply Mazda radiators while Toyota's Gosai sold Mazda hoses. Nippon Denso also tried to increase its sales to Isuzu by lending assistance to the Isuzu's supplier, Tokyo Radiator Manufacturing Ltd. This contrasted with Nissan's decision to place substantial orders with the suppliers of other assemblers such as Isuzu Motors, thereby becoming the largest customer of Zexel Corp. in which Isuzu maintained a twenty percent stake as of April 1991, and for whom Isuzu had in the past been the principal customer. Severe recession since the early 1990s is also forcing the entire supply industry to consolidate. It is not only heralding mergers and exits among the second and third tiers of subcontractors, but also compelling the surviving larger suppliers to seek new customers and raise the scale economy further by cross-supplying both Toyota and Nissan, which neither allowed in the past. In August 1992, Toyota and Saga Tekkohsho Co., a member of Nissan's *keiretsu* group in which the latter held one third of the stake, sat down to negotiate deals.[53]

There are therefore major indications that the historical ties between the Japanese auto assemblers and their direct suppliers are undergoing transformation at the end of the twentieth century. It is still too early to say whether the change is temporary or permanent. If it is solely a consequence of the severe recession, then the change might be temporary in nature. But if the structural change is the result of the globalization of the economy and an inability of the Japanese to protect their economic boundaries any longer, then the movement may transform interfirm relationships in Japan as it has to some extent in the United States.

Whatever the nature of the structural change, global competition is changing the way that technological development is conducted in Japan's auto industry, compared to the prewar years as well as early the postwar period. The demands for innovative products and processes have forced both Toyota and Nissan to move away from horizontal to vertical models of technological development like Honda's. For instance, both Toyota and Nissan have started in-house research of semiconductor chips by the mid-1980s. Toyota has also

begun in-house research on new materials technology. The trends of
change became dramatically evident when Toyota and Nippon Denso
displayed signs of going their separate ways after maintaining close
ties for fifty years. Thus, Nippon Denso is selling components to any
assembler nowadays, including Toyota's rival Nissan. For its part,
Toyota is integrating the design and engineering of some of its
electronics components to preserve uniqueness and proprietary turf
for the Toyota cars.[54]

Whenever possible, the suppliers are also making an effort to
reduce their dependency on a single assembler. The experience of
Shiroki Corp., a builder of mechanical parts for auto interiors in
which Toyota holds a fourteen percent stake, is a case in point. It has
decided to diversify into development of plants fueled by solar power
and other "environment-friendly" technologies, thereby lessening its
dependence on Toyota, which previously provided it for seventy
percent of its income.[55]

As automotive technology goes high-tech, the auto assemblers'
and suppliers' relationship with government is also changing. They
had a close working relationship with the government in the 1930s as
well as the early postwar period. The 1947 regulation on the
registration of the qualified auto parts proved particularly helpful
when the government licensed selected parts makers as certified
suppliers capable of meeting industry standards, thereby upgrading
the pool of the suppliers with whom the assemblers could initiate
teamwork. At the same time, the government's credit policies helped
to direct capital flow into automobile manufacturing. In the 1950s
and 1960s, however, the Japanese auto makers twice rejected the
government's pressure to adopt the Ford system of mass production.
This initiated a cooling off period in their relations with the Ministry
of International Trade and Industry (MITI).[56]

But now cooperative relations are emerging again. In order to
help assemblers to develop environmentally friendly automotive
converters in competition with the American Big Three consortium
in low-pollution technology, MITI is organizing an R&D consortium
among the ten Japanese auto makers. The Japanese government is
also underwriting much of the risk by having the Japan Key
Technology Center, an affiliate of both MITI and the Ministry of Post
and Telecommunications, take a seventy percent stake in the
organization.[57]

With globalization of the economy drawing up new strategic
alliances both at home and overseas and redefining both national
boundaries and national economic models, the Japanese corporations,
Toyota especially, are trying to preserve as many essential features of
their home-grown model as possible to retain their competitiveness.
Indeed, all national economies in this period of transition are trying
to follow a balancing act between achieving and preserving national

competitiveness on one hand and establishing and maintaining linkages with the global economy on the other. There is no telling yet how these balancing acts will finally change the way that national economic competitiveness is managed.

NOTES

1. The framework of discussion here is based on Takeshi Ishida's analysis of the concentric strategy of in-group formation and its consequent impact on competition and conflict management in the Japanese society (1984). Refer also to an insightful case study supporting Ishida's hypothesis by Tadashi Hanami (1984).

2. Unless otherwise noted, the discussion on trust, voice and their use in Japanese organizational hierarchy in this and the next few paragraphs are based on a number of authors (Helper 1990; Aoki 1986; Smitka 1990). Specifically, the concept of "voice" was advanced by Helper and "trust" by Smitka, as they are noted here.

3. "Conflict resolution" is differentiated from "conflict regulation" and "conflict avoidance" in the Japanese society. While conflict regulation means suppression instead of removing the conflict, conflict avoidance refers to a refusal to address it. These compare to conflict resolution whereby the parties involved in a conflict tackle the problems directly (Ishida 1984).

4. Unless otherwise noted, the following discussion of the creation of modern investors in place of traditional traders for Japan's industrial development, transformation of the role of samurai and development of a new business ideology relies on Hirschmeier (1965), Horie (1965), Marshall (1967, Chap. 1) and Takahashi (1969, Chap. 6 of Book 2, Chap. 4 of Book 3). For the definition of the role of the Japanese government, refer to Johnson (1982).

5. Younger sons who could not get any inheritance as well as apprentices who had proven loyal to the house after long years of service could set up branch houses for Mitsui. They brought with them to the new branches not only the specialized knowledge which they had accumulated in the main branch, but also trust, which they had learned as the code of business conduct. Unless otherwise noted, the story on Mitsui in this and later paragraphs is based on Roberts (1973, Chap. 9). Refer particularly to pp.98-106.

6. In 1872, for example, one of the leading political oligarchs. Inoue and Shibusawa Eiichi, a top policy maker in the Ministry of Finance, "persuaded" Mitsui, by then the largest money exchange house, into setting up the first of Japan's four national banks. They indicated to Mitsui that it could continue to serve as a government mint and hold deposits for the army and government bureaucracy, both lucrative businesses, only if it did what the government had asked it to do. To enforce its policy, the government also chose the house of Ono, another money exchange house of the equal size, to be Mitsui's partner in establishing the First National Bank. Besides reducing entry risk, the policy must have also generated competitive pressure for Mitsui to follow the directive of its political patron in the government (Roberts 1973; Allen 1940, 680, 682; Wray 1989b).

7. This was because "the purpose of the modern bank" was "not just sound finance" but also promotion of "industrial stability and growth," claimed Shibusawa, the chairman (Hirschmeier 1965).

8. Unless otherwise noted, both this and the next paragraphs refer to Takahashi (1969) and Clark (1979).

9. Ibid. Also note that Mitsubishi had incorporated internal operating divisions in 1917, which created the institutional basis for voice to be adopted in intragroup relations (Wray 1989a).

10. The story is based on Wray (1989a, 186, 188, 195-197, 209-210) and for the quotation, see Wray (1989b, 321). For the classical method of dealing with in-group versus out-group conflict and mediation of a deadlock by a superior institution, see Ishida (1984).

11. For instance, he Law for Supporting the Production of Military Vehicles, introduced in 1918, provided subsidies in price, maintenance, production, and in the use of these vehicles by the defense contractors themselves as an alternative to cheaper transport tools such as railways (Adachi, Ono, and Odaka 1983, 335-344; Yakushiji 1984)

12. Unless otherwise noted, the analysis of the history of Japan's auto industry made in this chapter relies on Cusumano (1985). The discussion Toyota refers also to Toyota Jidosha Kabushiki Kaisha (1988).

13. This was the strategy which the founder of Toyoda Automatic Loom used consistently to establish market leadership for his innovative textile machineries, beginning with the first wooden hand loom whose design he had improved to raise the productivity of cottage weavers in the Nagoya area (Sawai 1988).

14. Toyota's concern was validated by the fact that the majority of the incoming parts were defective in spite of 100 percent inspection and they were causing breakdowns of Toyota's trucks. But defects were understandable, given the primitive technological conditions in which most of the cottage suppliers were operating. Most of the suppliers were supposedly like Kojima Press, which started with seven employees making washers for Toyota in 1937 using simple hand- and foot-powered tools (Smitka, 1991; 54-56, 60, 64-65; Allen 1940; Adachi, Ono, and Odaka 1983, 378-379, 381; Toyota Jidosha Kabushiki Kaisha 1988, 39, 64, 72, 99).

15. For the purchasing rule, see Toyota Jidosha Kabushiki Kaisha (1988, 27-28, 76; also Adachi, Ono and Odaka 1983, 347, 369, 373-373, 381; Smitka 1991, 55-56). For shifting the boundary of the concentric circle of in-group solidarity, see Ishida (1984).

16. The story on Nissan refers primarily to Cusumano (1985), unless otherwise noted.

17. Nissan reportedly faced a more severe labor problem than Toyota when recession hit both under the contraction policy of the Dodge regime in 1949-1950. One indication was that Nissan was much more ready to resort to dismissal whereas Toyota tried first to keep its employees with wage cuts before it shifted to dismissal (Cusumano 1985, 80, 94-95, 192-193, 239-242). However, the head of Toyota, Kiichiro fired 2,000 workers in 1950 after he reportedly tried to keep them for a couple of years when Toyota was struggling

at the brink of bankruptcy (Toyota Jidosha Kabushiki Kaisha 1988, 104-110, 145).

18. Unless otherwise noted, information on Ono and his contribution to the Toyota system is based primarily on these two authors, with occasional reference to Toyota Jidosha Kabushiki Kaisha (1988).

19. For the process of improvement which Kiichiro began during the 1930s, including using JIT concept to reduce in-process inventory and level production, see Toyota Jidosha Kabushiki Kaisha (1988, 69-72, 141-145, 408). For Kiichiro's instruction to Eiji Toyoda, see Ono (1988, 75), and Deming (1986, 24-25, 54, 65-69, 89, App.).

20. Shortages in materials reportedly forced the parts makers to deliver supplies only during the second half of the month. This in turn forced Toyota to cramp the production of the monthly output in the last two weeks of the month (Cusumano 1985, 265-319; Smitka 1991, 153).

21. Both were reportedly common practices among the auto makers (Broadbridge 1966, 75).

22. Toyota had stopped allowing Nissan and other auto makers to visit its facilities by this time (Cusumano 1985, 14).

23. This paragraph is inferred from the purchasing practices followed by Toyota as well as its competitors today, as compared to the problems that Toyota had to resolve in the 1950s. For detailed discussion and analysis of the former, see Asanuma (1989). For more detail see also B. Asanuma, "The Contractual Framework for Parts Supply in the Japanese Automotive Industry," *Japanese Economic Studies (JES)* (Summer 1984): 32-53 and "The Contractual Framework for Parts Supply in the Japanese Automotive Industry," *JES* (Summer 1985): 52-78.

24. The U-line process, of course, was pioneered by Ono (1988). For an analysis of the process, see an unpublished report by M. Ikeda, S. Sei, and T. Nishiguchi, *U-Line Auto Parts Production* (Cambridge, MA: MIT IMVP Research Affiliates Meeting, Oct. 1988).

25. Refer to Nishiguchi (1989b). The processes on which the direct suppliers of all the auto makers became more heavily dependent for external sourcing included casting, pressing machining, and, in late 1970s, die casting. The highest dependence as of 1978 occurred in casting, which amounted to roughly 37 percent of the orders the direct suppliers received from the assemblers (Ikeda 1987, 11). For a detailed discussion of the division of labor between the first- and lower-tiers of suppliers, see Asanuma (1989). Also B. Asanuma, "The Organization of Parts Supply in the Japanese Automotive Industry," *Japanese Economic Studies* (Summer 1985): 32-53.

26. Suppliers can engage in two types of product development activity in auto manufacturing. They can develop their own proprietary design or engineer black-box parts or "do the detailed engineering for parts based on functional specifications provided by auto makers" (Cusumano and Takeishi 1991, 565). Most of the direct suppliers of the Japanese auto assemblers had obviously developed the second type of technological capability by the 1980s. One study, for example, estimated that Toyota was providing Nippon Denso with seventy percent of the design specs by the early 1980s, leaving the remaining thrity percent to Nippon Denso (Hervey 1982). The assemblers are moving

towards developing proprietary technology following globalization, as will be discussed later in this chapter.

27. This and the next paragraph are based on Nishiguchi (1987; 1989b) an d Asanuma (1989).

28. For an insider's account of the loyalty which a subcontractor must give to an assembler in the electronics industry as a member of the assembler's "family" group, see Kuniyasu Sakai, "The Feudal World of Japanese Manufacturing," *Harvard Business Review* (November-December 1990): 38-49. For the "Alps" structure, see Nishiguchi (1987).

29. Unless otherwise noted, the story on Nissan, again, is an interpretation of Cusumano (1985).

30. One explanation why Nissan chose first to add high-speed, dedicated, automatic machinery and then introduce computerization and robotics in competition with Toyota (which reciprocated the game by relying on internal process redesign) was that Nissan did not start with a focused production site. This led to a preference for a greater degree of reliance on technological solutions to productivity and product quality while seeking to compete with teamwork. Geographical proximity, on the other hand, favored teamwork as a starting point for Toyota build its competitiveness (Cusumano 1985, 94-95, 217-220, 225-226, 241, 273-274, 308-309).

31. For the timing of Takara Kai's establishment, see Adachi, Ono, and Odaka (1983, 369). Note however that Cusumano records that Nissan first tried to establish such an association in 1949. The organization was said to have collapsed during the 1953 strike and became reestablished in 1958 under the title of Nissan Treasure Association. In 1963, according to Cusumano, the association was rationalized into branches of 109 suppliers according to product specialization. This is the number of suppliers which Adachi, Ono and Odaka cite as the total membership of Takara Kai in 1979. For this reason, 1954 is treated here as the formal year in which Nissan tried to establish its first supplier cooperation association in this thesis (Cusumano 1985, 243-247, 252-261).

32. The discussion of Nissan's supplier management strategy in the next few paragraphs is based on Wada (1976). For quotation, see pp.96-97.

33. Nissan established special offices in the late 1960s and early 1970s to perform the task (Cusumano 1985, 252-261; Wada 1976, 109).

34. The discussion of Japanese business culture in the next few paragraphs builds on the concept of conflict management as advanced in Ishida (1984).

35. Asanuma (1989, 5), and "Nissan Offers to Increase Purchases of U. S. Auto Parts if They Meet Criteria," *BNA International Trade Daily* (11 February 1992).

36. The discussion on Honda in the next few paragraphs relies on Sakiya (1982), unless otherwise noted.

37. See Sakiya (1982, chap. 7 and chap. 8) for this and the next few paragraphs. Note that the promotion system mentioned here applied also to the workers on the shop floor. They could move up to specialist status as the engineers (Shimokawa 1978).

38. By 1986, seventy-six percent of Honda's production was sold in the United States. This and the next few paragraphs draw on Nobeoka (1988).

39. This may be one reason that most of Honda's suppliers have remained medium-sized. Sumihiko Nonoichi, "Honda Motors Parts Affiliates Merge to create Showa Corp.," *Nikkei Weekly* (26 October 1992), 9.

40. The investment decisions of Japanese suppliers stemmed from their competitive strategy as much as from the investment incentives from the state government designed to create jobs locally. R. G. Newman and R. Rhee, "Midwest Auto Transplants: Japanese Investment Strategies and Policies," *Business Horizons* 33, no. 2 (March-April, 1990): 63-69.

41. Honda Research of America had a staff of 500 by the end of 1987, according to *Ward's Automotive International* 3, no. 1 (January 1988), 16.

42. D. Gelsanliter, "Japan's Auto makers in America's Heartland," *The JAMA Forum* 9, no. 3 (March 1991): 9-12.

43. For export to Europe, see ibid. All three vehicles were designed at Honda Research of America in California and built at Marysville, Ohio. For Honda's joint venture in Great Britain, see Nobeoka (1988). Reportedly, only 12,000 units of the Accord Coupe were sold in 1991, far short of the target of 50,000. This was despite the extra effort which Honda made for those who follow the fad of import by differentiating the sedan in a "unique" way--it left the steering wheels on the left side, the wrong side for Japan's driving system. The poor sales were reportedly due to the Japanese consumers' disappointment that the vehicle was incompatible with their expectation of a sporty car model from the company. Honda, on the other hand, blamed it on the barrier of the distribution system as much as on its failure to anticipate the market for a sportier car. Separately, the Accords made in Ohio were found in a 1987 sampling to have more defects than other imports. K. L. Miller and J. B. Treece, "Honda's Nightmare: Maybe You Can't Go Home Again," *Business Week* (25 April 1988), 36; S. Toy, N. Gross and J.B. Treece, "The Americanization of Honda," *Business Week* (April 25, 1988), 90; "Lean, Mean and through Your Windscreen," *Economist* (23 February, 1991), 68.

44. L. Armstrong and K. L. Miller, "So Far, Nissan's Catch-up Plan Hasn't Caught On", *Business Week* (17 September 1990), 59; S. Isaka, "Nissan Paves a New Road for Foreign Parts Suppliers," *The Japan Economic Journal* (18 May 1991), 1; "Local Input is Key Link in Building New Nissan," *The Toronto Star* (24 October 1992), Sec. 6, 15. For design-in development implemented for Altima, see "State-of-the-Art Plant Gives Altima an Edge," *The Toronto Star* (31 October 1992), Sec. 11, 10; S. Asami, "Companies Set up Overseas R&D Bases," *Nikkei Weekly* (9 November 1992), 13.

45. J. Dubrowski, "U. S. and Japanese Auto Chiefs Agree to More Talks on Cooperation," *The Reuters Business Report* (18 May 1992); "Japanese, U. S. Firms to Jointly Develop Chips for Toyota," *Japan Economic Newswire* (30 October 1992).

46. A. Pollack, "A Lower Gear for Japan's Auto Makers," *New York Times* (30 August 1992), Sec. 3, 1; L. Rosario, "Bumpy Road Ahead," *Far Eastern Economic Review* (17 September 1992), 70; and L. Helm, "Nissan Posts Its First-ever Loss," *Los Angeles Times* (3 November 1992), Sec. 4, 1.

47. Nissan was the most aggressive in pushing application of the computer-aided design and flexible manufacturing systems with robotics during the 1980s to increase the flexibility of both design and production. But to

resolve the dilemma of introducing as many vehicle models and varieties of product models as possible without sacrificing productivity and compromising on unit costs, they still have to return to the basics, namely, improving the coordination of design and production by bringing the design and production engineers together through more frequent rotation of jobs at the product design stage. Nissan calls this "simultaneous engineering." This strategy Honda began to follow in 1992 under a different name, "concurrent engineering." Honda also introduced its 300 some subcontractors to the program.   See Ward's *Automotive International* 1, no. 5 (December 1986), 5; K. Rafferty, "Japan: Nissan Cuts Costs to Tackle First Ever Loss," *Guardian* (3 November 1992); "Concurrent Engineering," *Nikkei Weekly* (2 November 1992), 11; Toshio Shinmura and Hidenaka Kato, "After Boom, Auto Bust Stalls Recovery," *Nikkei Weekly* (16 November 1992), 1, 9. In the competition to introduce as many models and model varieties to the market, Toyota was the first to install two super computers. *Ward's Automotive International* 3, no. 8 (April 1988), 4. Honda had stayed as No. 4 since 1987 and had sold only a few thousands fewer units of cars than Chrysler in 1990. S. Toy, N. Gross and J. B.. Treece, "The Americanization of Honda," *Business Week* (April 25, 1988), 90;   D. Gelsanliter, "Japan's Auto makers in America's Heartland," *The JAMA Forum* 9, no. 3 (March 1991): 9-12. Some in the American automobile industry have actually urged Japanese auto makers to restrain from taking up too much market share to avoid provoking even greater protectionist sentiment in the U. S. See D. Luria, "U. S.-Japan Trade and Investment Relations: Lessons from the Auto Industry," *The JAMA Forum* 10, no. 1 (March 1992), 17.

48.   T. Hanna, "Out of the '80s, Into the '90s," *The JAMA Forum* 9, no. 4 (May 1991), 8-21.   Traditionally, the Japanese assemblers would switch suppliers when a model year changed (Hervey 1982).

49.   For Toyota's shift to using merit as the sole criterion for granting supplies contracts, see Toyota Jidosha Kabushiki Kaisha (1988, 410).   TRW also had to find American parts makers who were willing and able to meet the faster delivery schedule it needed to compete with its rival, Nippon Denso. For the story on TRW in this and the next paragraph, see V. Torres, "TRW Division Finds Secret to Success in Dealing with Japanese," *Los Angeles Times*   (25 February 1992), sec. 4, 8.

50.   "Toyota to Develop Chips with U. S. Makers," *Agence France Presse* (30 October 1992); "Toyota Accelerates Design-in Business with Foreign Semiconductor Makers," *PR Newswire* (30 October 1992).

51. S. Isaka, "Nissan Paves a New Road for Foreign Parts Suppliers," *The Japan Economic Journal* (18 May 1991), 1.

52. "Bosch Seeking Niche in Car-Supply Network," *The Nikkei Weekly* (19 October 1992), 9; C. Leadbeater and E. Terazono, "Nissan Strengthens Bosch Alliance," *Financial Times* (14 October 1992), 30.

53.   *Ward's Automotive International* (February 1987), 13; ibid., (March 1987), 2; ibid., (April 1987), 3; *Automotive News* (10 September 1990), 8; A. Pollack, "A Lower Gear for Japan's Auto Makers," *New York Times* (30 August 1992), Sec. 3, 1.

54. *Ward's Automotive International* (September 1987), 7; E. Klamann, "Lowly Subcontractors Begin to Assert Technological Might," *Japan Economic Journal* (30 March 1991), 1.

55. Atsuhi Nakayama, "Car Parts Makers Declare Keiretsu Liberation," *Nikkei Weekly* (16 May 1992), 8.

56. See Cusumano (1985, 15, 17, 19-20, 23-25, 244). Japan Development Bank lent 14 percent of the fixed investment of the auto parts makers during these years. Special depreciation allowances for new machinery that came with low-interest loans were first applied to auto assemblers in 1951 before being extended to parts suppliers in 1956. 351 plants were qualified from 1948 to 1953 as licensed parts makers (Adachi, Ono, and Odaka 1983, 349, 352-353, 363, 382).

57. H. Nakamae, "Auto Rivals Unite under Green Banner," *Nikkei Weekly* (9 November 1992), 9.

Chapter Four

Globalization, Firm Organization, and Interfirm Market Relations in the Automobile Industry in the People's Republic of China

China's linkages with the global economy are different from those of the United States and Japan. In order to understand the difference, we must look at a complex set of circumstances surrounding their emergence and maintenance. First, the country has been trying to manage a limited yet significant transition from a command economy to at least a partial market orientation since 1978. Second, it is trying at the same time to develop global linkages for investment, technology acquisition and improvement in international trade. Third, while the Japanese and American economies have actual strength, the Chinese economy is based only on its potential. As such, the only contribution it can make to its global partners is a potential market instead of actual trade off in technology, R&D capacity and/or existing markets. This leads to a significantly different and possibly weaker position for China in terms of its ability to dictate and shape global linkages. While it is susceptible to some extent to the demands from managed trade as well as to threats as a means of conducting international economic relations, the socio-political reality at home does not allow global linkages to influence or dictate its internal politics. Nor is it necessary for China to be influenced by such means of conducting international investment and trade. Global linkages, after all, permit even weaker societies a great deal of flexibility in shifting partners and sources of capital and technology.

After WWII, Chinese studies in the West were no longer the object of exotic curiosity and museum-like interest treated as the examination of a dying civilization. But the exotic effect continues to influence many analysts who depend on the interpretive approach to inquiry. These analysts investigate the operation of the Chinese system and understand its reforms as they are determined by its culture and derivative institutions. In most cases, however, postwar analysts have moved away from the interpretive to rational-choice analysis, which examines and explains the Chinese system and its reforms in terms of system-wide goals and orientations. Rational choice analysts treat culture-specific variables as given. Therefore, they focus on identifying the constraints that frustrate the realization of the system's objectives and suggest ways in which improvement can be made rather than describing and making sense of China's social and culture particularities (Little 1991).

The rational choice approach is useful inasmuch as critical constraints must be located and investigated and reforms, if undertaken, must be evaluated. In comparison, the interpretive approach helps to explore why such constraints exist, and what use may be made of them before decision on whether such constraints should be reformed and removed, as well as how these tasks may be accomplished. These are questions which can be properly understood only if the constraints are traced to their origin, so a residual explanation[1] which rational-choice theory is inadequately equipped for considering, can be obtained.

Whether with the interpretive or rational-choice approach, center-periphery relations, thanks to Schurmann (1968a), has become the dominant schema of how China has been studied for over three decades. This schema has shaped both the intellectual questions selected for investigation and research design. In this schema, power lies in the political system rather than in the market (Schurmann 1968a). The Party is identified as responsible for organizing and maintaining the core of the administrative bureaucracies (Harding 1980) and supervising the organizational control of the masses for implementing policies (Schurmann 1960). It is at the bidding of the Party that the industrial bureaucracy works to realize China's technological and developmental objectives, which the bureaucracy ideally seeks to attain through specialization of production, economies of scale, and improvement and maintenance of the quality of products in line with the comparative advantages of each region, so that backward and advanced regions can develop in a more or less balanced way (Donnithorne 1964; 1967; 1972). The constraint on the economy is thus seen as determined by how power is divided between the political center and the periphery (Schurmann 1964).

Reforms of the Chinese economy are consequently investigated in terms of shifts in power relations between the two poles of the political system as well as in terms of control over the nation's resources. Since concentration of power and control in the center is often taken to be what frustrates policy implementation and what causes inefficiency in resource allocation, decentralization is called for. Other times, developments which go beyond the intention of such liberalization trigger re-centralization. This schema permeates discussion of the numerous reforms that have been introduced in the post-1978 period, whether they cover the areas of ideology (Goodman

1984; Schram 1988; Sullivan 1988; Gold 1991) and politics (Dittmer 1983; Kallgren 1985; Goodman 1985; Manion 1985; Chamberlain 1986; Schram 1988; Sullivan 1988) or concern China's economic (Griffin 1982; Vermeer 1982; Kueh 1983; 1989; Field 1984; Lardy 1984; Wang 1984; Howe and Walker 1984) and management systems (Korzec and Whyte 1981; Shirk 1981; Wang 1984; Lee 1986; Jackson 1986; White 1987; Chamberlain 1986; Davis 1988; Walder 1989; Wong 1989).

The result is a vertical model of reform which hardly investigates any horizontal problems in the Chinese system. When they are discussed, the horizontal problems are termed "bottlenecks" or treated as derivatives of the vertical constraints. They are assumed to disappear once the vertical constraints are removed (Cheng 1985; Lardy 1991). Most of the studies, further, stay at the macroeconomic level. Whereas a micro level of study is recently emerging, it is intrafirm in orientation (Jackson 1986; Koziara and Yan 1983; Walter 1985; Wong 1989; Walder 1989; Lee 1986; Manion 1985). The question of how the structural relations between firms may influence their performance remains undealt with in either research or analysis.

It must be pointed out that reform in China has come in cycles for more than three decades. Dittmer (1977) characterizes the reform of the pre-1978 period as commencing with intra-party rectification. It prepared the cadres for policy change, followed by mobilization in various segments of the society of constituencies whose function it was to produce a winner that had failed to emerge from the intra-party debate. This was, in turn, followed by the introduction of new policies which were sure to be implemented by all, including those who opposed the new policies yet had to keep the opposition to themselves, thanks to "criticism, self-criticism and unity", an instrument of the mass line that was employed for resolving "non-antagonistic" contradictions among the masses. An exception to this sequence of change came during the Cultural Revolution, when mass mobilization and intra-party campaigns traded places. Dittmer's analysis is valuable in that he succeeds in providing Chinese studies with a tool for predicting the cyclical visitation of reform. The exclusive claim which any reform makes to legitimacy as well as to the nation's scarce resources, indeed, dictates that when negative byproducts turn up, the reform's opponents hurry to set its reversal in motion.

In the post-1978 period, class struggle, which bridges the intra-party campaigns on the one hand and mass mobilization on the other has been abandoned as a legacy of the Cultural Revolution. The cycle of reform begins consequently to move from intra-party campaigns directly to policy change, with the mass line replaced by bureaucratization for implementation of policy (Manion 1991).

Whereas those who study Chinese policy have recorded radical changes like this, they continue to confine their analysis to the road maps drawn by the center-periphery relations. This applies not only to substantive investigations of specific policies and case studies of reforms (Hsiao 1982; Wang 1984; Kambara 1984; Yue 1984; Oi 1986; Lee 1986; Baark 1987; Wong 1989; Tam 1988; Watson 1988; Ash 1988; Kojima 1988; Sicular 1988; Dicks 1989; Simon 1989), but also to the discussion of the function of policy models. One author starts with the hypothesis that the models of technology acquisition alternate, as power and control shift vertically in the system. On this basis, he speculates, centralization will endure, as China takes off industrially with a renewed drive for foreign acquisition of process technology (Reynolds 1978). The prediction of stability is taken up by another writer when he concludes that because of the fatigue at the periphery, the models of policy now selected for emulation have to be disconnected from the power struggle and competition in policy priorities at the center, in order for reform to be implemented and given a chance to succeed (Friedman 1978; Petrick 1981).

This last observation points to discontinuity in the policy studies in terms of the implementation of policy (Friedman 1978; Kallgren 1985; Manion 1991). Various case studies indicate that since 1978 Party bureaucrats and managers instead of the masses have been asked to act as the carriers of reforms (Koziara and Yan 1983; Jackson 1986; White 1987; Walder 1989). This discontinuity is attributable to enhanced commitment to economic growth, which has necessitated discarding the mass line employed during the reforms to serve non-economic objectives. As a result, the behavioral habits of bureaucrats and managers are now to blame when the reforms fail to deliver their economic promises (Blechmer and Meisner 1981; Petrick 1981).

It has come as no surprise that debates have evolved in Chinese studies about the post-1978 reforms. Many have described growing unease in the party about unintended effects like widening inequality between regions, sectors of the economy, and households, as well as demoralization within the party and economic organizations (Goodman 1984; Sullivan 1988; Kallgren 1985; Xu 1990). Although they have noted Chinese worries about negative consequences on national development (Vermeer 1982; Wang 1984; Field 1984; Lardy 1984; Lee 1986; Kueh 1989), academic scholars cannot reach a consensus on just how the Chinese should cope with the problems of reforms. Some suggest pushing the reforms further into politics, continuing the trend which the Chinese have already initiated in their effort to provide ideological legitimacy to economic and management reforms (Dittmer 1983; Chamberlain 1986; Schram 1988). Others single out limitation in scope as the key reason for the failure of reforms to deliver the objectives of productivity and efficiency. Consequently, they propose total devolution of government control, so that markets can allocate labor and other critical yet scarce inputs (Shirk 1981; Howe and Walker 1984; Shirk and Stepanek 1985; Ross

1986; Walder 1987; White 1987; Friedman 1990; Cheung 1990; Roth 1990; Zhou 1990).

Some leading Chinese economists, however, do not believe that government direction of resource flow necessarily conflicts with the objectives or processes of an expansion in reform. They cite as an example the absorption of surplus rural labor by emerging township enterprises, a solution to the problem of structural shift in employment which differs from the experience of the developed economies in their early stages of industrialization (Pu 1990). In agriculture, certain specialization of production has also been achieved, thanks in great part to the assistance of the regional governments (Stone 1985).

While vertical studies of reform are becoming exhausted, a shift has occurred within the model from the interpretive to the rational-choice approach of analysis. With the interpretive approach, the inquiry focuses on understanding the Chinese political and economic systems for what they are, describing how the systemic processes work and interpreting why they differ from those in the West. Indeed, many of the writings in various social sciences in the past three decades fall in these categories (Little 1991; Wilson 1991; Tsou 1969; Harding 1982; 1984). Criticisms of intellectual parochialism have inspired some to experiment with rational-choice-based analysis, as they try to move out of the theoretical borrowing mode to construct generalizations which may be applied to studying the systems of other societies (Johnson 1974; 1982, Wilson 1971; Perry 1989).

By virtue of its means-ends analysis, rational-choice theory provides a useful tool for studying reform. If, for instance, constraints are located in the government-business relations, then their solution lies in reduction of government control over the economy. Assuming that the objective of the reform is maximizing growth and productivity, then the success or failure of the reform can be evaluated by whether it has fulfilled its economic promises and to what extent these goals are met. More often than not, the failure is traced to non-economic goals that interfere with the processes of reform.

The disadvantages of sole reliance on rational choice analysis are many. They begin with the assumption that economic benefits constitute the only objective of reform. But what if they are merely one of the objectives? Moreover, what if they are secondary to other goals of the Chinese political-economic system? Considerations like these raise the question of just precisely what needs to be reformed, a question which, given adherence to the vertical model, rational choice analysis is able to avoid answering. The philosophical belief that non-economic objectives are responsible for the problems of reform leads to the suggestion that ideology and party control be taken out of the management of the economy. If they are eliminated, it is assumed, then everything else will work.

As a result of its preoccupation with removing macro-vertical constraints, the rational choice approach has neglected investigating the micro-horizontal constraints in the Chinese political-economic system. This points to a fundamental question which the approach has failed to address. Insofar as reform means removal of the constraints, just what can be removed? Further, should the micro-horizontal constraints be handled in the same way as macro-vertical ones? What if the cost of removing the micro-horizontal constraints in terms of the social backlash is too high? Suppose these structural constraints cannot be removed. Would it be better, then, to accept the legacy, coping with them and making necessary trade-off to make them work, instead of eliminating them?

Vertical reform means change that is introduced on the basis of conceptualizing the constraints in terms of the hierarchical authority and power relations in the Chinese system. If the objective of the system is maximizing growth, then reform entails removing the sources of the rigidity in this hierarchy, so that the lower level of administrative agencies and production units have a certain autonomy in decision-making for attaining allocative efficiency and productivity. The success or failure of the reform is therefore a function of how much control the party or political center is willing to devolve. Non-economic objectives are extraneous in the vertical reform.

In comparison, a horizontal model conceives of systemic constraints in terms of the input-output relations between parallel organizations. It seeks the solution to the problems of the firms' performance in the nature of their institutional linkages rather than in the political system. This is despite the fact that politics and non-economic variables continue to bear on structural relations and an examination of these variables still provides an answer to how the constraints may have emerged. Market mechanisms such as pricing are, then, examined as a function of the structural linkages between the economic organizations. This method promises to deal more adequately with the question of how constraints on the economy may be handled, given the complexity of the environment in which the problem must be resolved.

It has been pointed out that vertical reform, coupled with sole application of the rational choice approach, focuses on diagnosing systemic constraints, prescribing the policies to deal with them, and devising the measures for evaluating the reforms. It seeks to find out whether reforms can enhance productivity and efficiency insofar as they must be implemented in the context of the structural relations that are inherited from China's culture, history, and past government policies. These are the questions which any serious study of reform must address. Yet because it can not be micro-horizontal in inquiry, the vertical model has left them uninvestigated.

In other words, the problems here are horizontal in nature. If this hypothesis is true, then such horizontal constraints as the control of supplies, in addition to those of finance, pricing, and distribution and storage, should receive more attention in reform. This shows that the Chinese reforms have not been conducted in a proper manner.[2]

Inasmuch as the structural aspect of the Chinese politico-economic system is germane to reform, the horizontal model is better equipped for its inquiry. The reasons are two. First, it deals with structural constraints directly rather than treating them as byproducts of the centralized control of supply and demand. Because it incorporates the interpretive approach in the analysis, the horizontal model can also trace constraints to their roots. Second, the horizontal model relies on cross-disciplinary rather than single disciplinary techniques in investigation. Consequently, micro-horizontal analysis that cannot be conducted under the vertical model becomes feasible. The horizontal model of analysis, of course, yields a different understanding from that already provided by the vertical model, partly by helping one to zero in on the crucial constraints in the system. Finally, the horizontal model is able to take into account the non-economic objectives as a part of the systemic problems that must be resolved, whether with or without reform.

Certainly, government policies influence the nature of the structural relations between firms. They also determine whether the reform can succeed or not. The intellectual question which awaits investigation, then, is why Japan and some other countries have used government policies to achieve their economic and technological objectives whereas China has failed to do the same? How have the government policies[3] influenced the structural relations between the Chinese enterprises?

Several propositions are made here to facilitate the analysis of reform. First, if the government control over the economy is where reform is needed, then reform means changing the way with which such control is exercised. Ownership is merely one of many ways for the government to control the resource flow. Government control may be altered, so that resources can be mobilized while the objective of efficiency in its use achieved. Second, if the method of control that restricts the government to making regulations while giving business the responsibility for running the economy is changed, then the objective of the system may also have to change. Indeed, certain non-economic goals may have to be surrendered. Such undesirable consequences as widening of income inequality may also have to be tolerated for some time to come.

In any event, the students of Chinese studies have identified three components of the Chinese politico-economic system for reform. The first is China's political system, with an analytical focus on power relations in the system. This is the perspective of the political scientists. China's economic system is the second component. The analytical focus here is on the relationship between central planning and other forms of controlling and allocating the nation's scarce resources. Adherents to this perspective, many of whom are economists, are particularly keen on comparing the allocative impact of the alternative means of balancing the economy's demand and supply. China's management system is the third component. The analysis in this respect concentrates on alternative methods of management of production as a function of the power relations and patterns of control and resource allocation in China's politico-economic system. Inevitably, most of the scholars examining this aspect of systemic reform have received disciplinary training in either political science or developmental economics.

In his seminal writings, Schurmann (1960; 1964; 1968) established himself as the authority on the reform of China's political system. After identifying the key function of the Chinese organization as controlling people for policy implementation, he argues that the constraints on the economy come from rigid control, as a result of too much concentration of power at the political center. Reform therefore requires decentralizing decision-making authority vertically downward, so that central policies may be more flexibly implemented to suit the local conditions. Power may be further decentralized to either the regional administrative authorities ("decentralization II") or the production units ("decentralization I"), depending on at which level it is perceived as necessary to remove administrative constraints while maintaining coordination of inter- and intra-sectorial growth to attain multiple developmental goals.[4]

Schurmann's hypotheses have been widely applied and supported. They have also received some revisions from the authors of the Chinese reforms during the 1980s. All, like the Chinese themselves, identify politics as the primary constraint on China's growth. All argue for its removal from the management of the economy (Dittmer 1983; Petrick 1981; Schram 1988). Ideological reforms, for example, are suggested as necessary for legitimizing economic reforms (White 1987; Schram 1988). Political reforms are also proposed to ensure that decentralization I proceed meaningfully. In this respect, some call for removing the political control of the Party in the production units so that managers can act according to the signals of the market or the "law of value" (Chamberlain 1987). This contrasts with concentration of power in the hands of the Party when highly centralized "vertical rule" shifted to "dual rule" during the first two waves of decentralization in the late 1950s and early 1970s (Schurmann 1964). Others argue for taking away such concerns as morality, the loyalty of the communist party members and equity in the processes of reform to prevent policy reversals like rectification campaigns from interfering with growth (Goodman 1984; Kallgren 1985; Sullivan 1988). Still others urge institutionalization of leadership changes so that the managers can have a stable environment in which they perform in response to the market incentives (Goodman 1986; Pu 1990).

Regarding China's economic reform, a debate has developed between competing hypotheses advanced by Donnithorne (1964; 1972; 1976) on the one hand and Snead (1975) and Lardy (1976) on the other. In the light of the experiments made between the late 1950s and early 1970s, Donnithorne hypothesizes that decentralization, introduced with "self-reliance," reduces trade between regions. She supports her argument with the observation that China has had to develop the backward interior regions and induce mass technical socialization, both accomplished with local initiatives, in the spirit of self-reliance, by sacrificing specialization of production, economy of scale, and comparative advantages which must be fostered and coordinated by central planning and centralized balancing of material transfers. Snead counters Donnithorne with respect to the impact of decentralization and self-reliance on internal trade. Self-reliance, in fact, promotes trade. For it promotes attainment of self-sufficiency in limited areas of production in a locality, thereby providing a basis on which it could exchange supplies with other localities. Donnithorne is wrong, criticizes Snead, to have equated self-sufficiency with total self-reliance and, hence, autarky. Her mistake may be attributed to identifying the system of supplies and marketing that remain in the hands of the central agencies with regional administrative control defined by geographically determined boundaries.

As for Donnithorne's other hypothesis that decentralization diminishes the center's control, leaving the interests of the backward provinces less attended to in the processes of growth, Lardy nullifies it on the basis of his investigation of China's fiscal system. The center must have retained its power, or it would not have had the capital to pursue the objectives of economic integration and equitable pattern of development, resulting in the build-up of a resource base in the interior that is large enough to market to the entire nation. Lardy shows that the central government continues to collect the size of tax revenue it wishes, despite decentralization and self-reliance. What has changed, then, involves merely the avenue of tax collection. It has shifted from the central ministries to provincial authorities. Indeed, what evidence can be more persuasive than the fact that the interior provinces have grown at a faster pace than more advanced industrial centers during the period of decentralization and self-reliance?

Some writers have produced evidence to show that decentralization has adversely affected inter-regional specialization of production and trade.   This supports one of Donnithorne's hypotheses.   The authors of the 1980s, however, go further to pinpoint the cause of the allocative dislocation as structural shortages of supplies highlighted under decentralization, a policy whose effectiveness is undermined by continued central and provincial control of supplies, related to control over the affiliated large- and medium-sized enterprises in the supply sector of the economy. Vertical integration and intra-regional trade at the *xian* (county) level have emerged as the solution to the shortages.   But they have also ended up digressing the materials destined for more efficient enterprises (Kueh 1983; 1989; Field 1984).   Observations like these led Lardy, who earlier tried to revise Donnithorne's hypothesis in the area of fiscal control, to revise her hypothesis in the area of internal trade.   Where the control of the supplies is not devolved from the center, Lardy insists, decentralization II that is carried out together with decentralization I drives autarkic tendencies at the regional level at the expense of inter-regional specialization of production, economy of scale, and trade.

Other authors have noticed a decline of the center's ability to collect revenue when the responsibility for revenue generation has been shifted to the enterprises following the introduction of the system of enterprise responsibility (Wang 1984; Field 1984; Lee 1986). But there is insufficient evidence to negate *in toto* the earlier findings of Lardy, namely, that the central authorities have been able to reverse the situation by substituting profit remission by enterprises with the requirement that they submit a fixed proportion of such profit as tax to guarantee the revenue collected.   Otherwise, why were the dependent interior provinces able to keep up with the growth rate while major industrial centers located in Shanghai, Beijing, and Liaoning province had to struggle to survive during the reforms of the 1980s, as some statistical results revealed?   The performance of the interior has been propped up by the funds which the center has transferred from the prosperous coastal areas, argues one author (Kueh 1989).   This supports Lardy's hypothesis that fiscal processes continue to be in the center's hands in spite of decentralization. Lardy himself supports his earlier hypothesis by tracing the sources of growth during the period of readjustment to increased consumer income, which is in turn derived from an increased number and variety of the state subsidies.[5]

The downside of the regional economy's dependence on central intervention for expansion, as in the case of the interior provinces, is that it slows down the growth of the more advanced coastal areas. Similarly, the dependence of the consumer goods sector on the state subsidies for expansion has its potential danger.   It raises speculation that the momentum of growth will stagnate when the state shifts its focus from increasing production of consumer goods to revitalizing and upgrading the producer goods sector with a new round of import substitution production.   Additionally, there is growing concern that structural shortages inevitably create uncertainty in the supplies and costs for Sino-foreign joint venture investment, an alternative source of growth.   All these observations point to the reality that further growth depends on improvement of productivity.   But the question remains whether this may necessitate giving up equity as an objective of the national development strategy (Kueh 1989; Lardy 1984).

The reform of China's management system has always been treated as a derivative of those of the Chinese political and economic systems.   Schurmann (1968), for example, records the adjustment in the relationship between the party and engineer-managers in state-owned enterprises when power relations in the political system as a whole shift with decentralization and re-centralization.   Similarly, Donnithorne (1967) observes a "competitive" orientation among state-owned enterprises toward verticalization so as to control supplies, each time as they are forced to cut costs according to instructions in the production plan.   "Import-substitution" production within a given region that is permitted under decentralization II, together with the enterprises' autonomy in retaining part of the cost savings generated in production that is granted under decentralization I, combine to induce such "rational" behavior among the state enterprises.

More recently, Korzec and Whyte (1981) have posited that salary increases alone in China's industry can not improve productivity. Three institutional and policy constraints are blamed, based on the co-authors' survey of four wage adjustments[6] made during the 1960s and 1970s (1963, 1971-72, 1977-78, 1979). First, the seniority system, in which the length of service in an enterprise is the primary determinant of both the salaries and the size of fringe benefits renders it difficult to link rewards to labor productivity.   Further, in the process of implementation, the policy becomes reduced to a measure for narrowing income gaps, and ends up taking priority over the objective of rewarding productivity.   Politicization of the process of evaluating an employee's seniority status and related prospects for promotion, finally, helps to sever the link between remuneration and merit. Effort and skills simply do not count when one is dismissed as a political and ideological deviant.

In comparison, Shirk (1981) hypothesizes that China's attempt to introduce examination-based system of recruitment, promotion, and wage raises during the 1980s is transforming the country's organization-oriented enterprises into efficiency-oriented ones. Full implementation of the new recruitment policy, however, has been impossible, because of the resilience of China's seniority system.   A number of authors have compiled a list of the institutional constraints responsible for frustrating this aspect of the management reform. One draws attention to the dilemma between the long-term need to improve productivity for which the policy is designed and short-term exigencies of job creation that is faced by Chinese enterprises, particularly for the children of their own employees (White 1987; Walder 1987; Jackson 1986). A co-author argues, additionally, that, as an institution which the urban state enterprises have inherited from the 1970s when it was established for stabilizing supplies and augmenting the income of factory employees, the *dingti* or inter-generational job substitution system is difficult to discard (Tang and Ma 1985). A third author concludes that to the extent that China has succeeded in replacing the *dingti* system with unified examination and placement under the management of the state labor bureau, it has incurred other social costs, too. The new labor policy has worsened inter-generational and gender inequality (Davis 1988).

It is worth noting an argument against the reform. White (1987), for example, observes that many in China still cherish lifetime employment as a superior institution of socialism. This explains why it is so difficult to replace it with the new recruitment policy, unless the new system of labor contracts allows an emerging free labor market to deliver not only productivity but also security. On this score, one can not ignore a legitimate question raised by opponents of the reform. Why can productivity not be achieved with lifetime employment, as has been done in Japan? Furthermore, a free labor market seems unlikely to contribute fundamentally to productivity, even though it is desirable for stimulating competition. This is true as long as retaining a "core" of the skilled work force, including its loyalty, morale and solidarity, continues to be vital for keeping the large- and technology-intensive enterprises in operation. For this reason, White suggests reforming China's larger institutional environment and its infrastructure, such as its systems of education, social welfare, and housing, as well as Chinese laws, to enable the new recruitment system to take root.

Shirk (1981) qualifies her hypothesis, finally, with an observation similar to Donnithorne's (1972). She identifies shortages in supplies as a structural constraint on the manager's autonomy, preventing him from single-mindedly pursuing productivity and efficiency. This compares with Walder's analysis (1987) of intrafirm systemic constraint on one hand and its relationship with larger institutional constraints on the other. Given the two sets of constraints, he argues, the manager is induced to use the enterprise autonomy and monetary incentives to maximize profit retention instead of productivity and efficiency. Irrational price systems, as well as chronic shortages in the supplies, are responsible for such unintended policy consequences.

Insofar as supplies are concerned, the disappearance of the principle of self-reliance in the 1980s has brought about a different motivational incentive for an enterprise managers differing from those of the previous rounds of industrial reforms. To be sure, a manager under both regimes would seek to make extra-budgetary capital construction investment in supplies. Under the principle of self-reliance, he followed this policy to localize production of certain items that were in short supply. This promoted internal trade, as well as a certain degree of local economic equilibrium (Snead 1975). Managers have continued with this practice under the enterprise responsibility system since the early 1980s. But in so doing they are often driven by competition in manufacturing those products which promise high profit rates under the irrational structure of the state-fixed prices rather than the goods genuinely in short supply (Field 1984). The situation is undesirable, because the items which are essential for people's livelihood yet are the least profitable according to the state-fixed prices get dumped in production (Kueh 1983).

Consequently, inflation has appeared, particularly with pricing becoming partly decentralized. Two-tier pricing has inevitably emerged, making it easier for managers to maximize profits retained not only to deliver quotas, as stipulated by the superior administrative governments, but also to fulfill obligations in welfare provision, as expected by subordinate employees. To achieve these objectives, managers often have to resort to illicit practices. Hence, the common practice of bribing superior agencies into allocating more supplies at the planned prices and reselling them on the black market at a lucrative premium (Walder 1987).

Walder's observation is echoed by other writers when they identify such lawless behavior of the managers as rational under the constraints of the seniority system, structural shortages of supplies, and the irrational structure of costs and prices (Kueh, 1989). If a manager can cover losses and boost profits by manipulating product prices in the context of shortages, why indeed should he go through hell to improve productivity (Field 1984)? This risk-averse strategy finds support among Chinese workers who have themselves become bonus maximizers under the enterprise responsibility system, even if this means plowing in quick profits by sacrificing the interests of consumers (Walder 1989).

The price system, consequently, is suggested as the next in line for reform (Kueh 1983; Field 1984; Pu 1990; Xu 1990). Enterprise autonomy, observes one co-author, has had the effect of helping the Chinese enterprises to achieve some degree of productivity improvement by forming industrial partnerships across administrative and geographical boundaries. But price reform is still necessary to further rationalize the allocation of resources. It is, thus, in exploring how control of prices can be removed to further rationalize the allocation of resources that more administrative decentralization is urged (Howe and Walker 1984; Davis 1988; Walder 1987; 1989; Jackson 1986).

Similarly, the reform of the wage structure is important to improving intrafirm as well as intra- and interindustry productivity (Hu, Li, and Shi 1988). Wage reform is expected to complement reduction of absenteeism and an increased interest among workers in skill acquisition after regulations on monetary incentives came into effect under the new labor contract system (Walder 1987). But the problem remains how to use workers' skills to improve productivity in the enterprises.

The discussion of management system reform has therefore come full circle. Many are convinced that efficiency and productivity are unlikely to make real headway if China limits reform to its industrial organizations alone. Reforms of the Chinese price and wage systems, and other institutions has become crucial. Attention now zeroes in on Chinese policies. Policy shift, it is believed, reflects shifts in power relations and, thus, in systemic priorities as well as the strategy for running the economy. Generalizations can be made through analyzing this more dynamic aspect of power relations so that a measure of predictability is obtained. A debate has subsequently emerged (Petrick 1981). On one side is Winckler (1976), who champions the policy cycle hypothesis. On the other, Nathan (1976) argues that China follows a learning model in policy making and implementation.

In his criticism of Hart's book, Winckler advances the hypothesis that the incentives of Chinese organizations change cyclically, as goals and tasks take turns becoming the systemic priority. Hart tries to explain the shift in policy incentives as a function of the velocity of revolution raging in China's politico-economic system.[7] Winckler, in comparison, insists that the Chinese seek more than one goals, including equity, control (dictatorship), and growth. Each goal is promoted by transforming the Chinese organizations with a matching set of policy incentives.

But what causes the priority goals to rotate and policies to oscillate? In line with the tradition set by Schurmann (1968), Winckler argues that it has to do with the dialectic epistemology of the Chinese. This adherence to the dialectics results in diametrically opposed coalitions among power holders and the Chinese organizations that are designed to handle dialectically contradictory demands of national development. As power shifts between competing coalitions, systemic priorities and their supporting developmental programs change radically. Swings occur not only because of constraints on resources available for implementing competing priority goals, but also because of competing ideological predilections which dictate that certain policies be used together to advance the new priority more effectively. Covariation of policies is also suggested as necessary in order to undo the damage of the previous policy.

Nathan (1976) challenges Winckler with the argument that the differences between political coalitions lie merely in the means used to attain these objectives rather than in the objectives per se. What is more, the differences come primarily from learning to set the policy right through trial and error. Thus, it is misleading to explain them in terms of power struggles within the elite. Otherwise, why are both "leftist" and "rightist" policies found in any single package, irrespective of which way it oscillates? Similarly, why has any policy in any single area shifted both back and forth? For that matter, why has decentralization proceeded hand in glove with centralization, except for the period of the Great Leap Forward? Why, finally, have mass campaigns been used by both those on the left and those on the right, by both those advocating decentralization and those following a more centralized strategy? It is in this light that he suggests that mass campaigns, which policy cycle hypothesis takes as an indication of a new round of radical change, be treated instead as a normal "administrative" tool for implementing policy.

Petrick (1981) seeks to settle this disagreement with his "cyclical problem-solving model" of Chinese policy and reform. He acknowledges both Winckler's hypothesis on policy oscillation and Nathan's view on the continuity of the elite consensus on the ideology of development and its shared commitment to removing developmental bottlenecks. Petrick argues that policy learning occurs precisely while the emphasis of each policy package that is used experimentally to remove such bottlenecks oscillates. It oscillates in a direction that permits political learning to take place when the role of ideology is reduced and compromise in politics is stressed. Thus, Petrick contributes not so much to resolving the dispute but rather to offer a mechanism to predict the success or failure of reforms.[8]

Reynolds (1978), following Winckler, hypothesizes that Chinese policy fluctuates with the changes in the models of national development. The shift in models correlates, in turn, with shifts in the objectives of development, bringing with them vertical shifts of power. When the goal is acquiring new technology, for example, a technology-intensive model is followed. China begins to emphasize plant import. In this period, the central government tightens the control of inputs as well as of agricultural surplus needed for export so as to balance external payments. But this strategy frequently gives rise to bottlenecks in diffusion, another objective of technology acquisition. When the bottlenecks emerge, China makes a switch to a factor-intensive or "agriculture-first" model of development that stresses decentralized management with local initiatives so as to encourage diffusion of technology from the manufacturers of the industrial producer goods to the agricultural producer goods sector.

Decentralization II, however, provides regional governments and lower level authorities with an opportunity to pursue different ends from the central objectives.   When deviation occurs, the center initiates a return to the technology-intensive model of development, thereby completing the cyclical change. At this point, Reynolds (1978) mends Winckler's hypothesis with a proposition that a structural change in favor of industrial takeoff may break the cyclical return to a factor-intensive and decentralized model of development.   The evidence of the 1980s, however, provides conflicting proofs. Acquisition for foreign technology, for instance, became decentralized when China replaced plant imports with Sino-foreign joint ventures. This nullifies Reynolds' prediction of the trend toward permanent centralization.   On the other hand, small-scale agrobusiness is flourishing, lending support to his argument that structural change is occurring in China, which is seeing the demise of an "agriculture first" model of development.[9]

Friedman's study (1978), in comparison, casts doubts on the relationship between the shifts in policy models on the one hand and those in priority objectives and central political power on the other. In agriculture where a model is used by both camps to launch emulation campaigns, he finds that one model can serve to implement competing policy priorities, were its function redefined. Savings can certainly be made from using the same model for policy emulation, were the model flexible enough to switch political loyalty when power changes hands. It not only helps legitimize radical policy shifts, but also reduces the costs that must be incurred for searching and promoting a new policy model. Friedman supports his hypothesis with the observation that the Chinese debate on a policy model centers largely on what function it should serve and for what purpose.

But Friedman assigns more power to the local authorities than Reynolds. He argues that the local leaders may continue to emulate a model in a fashion they choose despite the new definition given by the center. Thus, the center is not able to force a new priority on a locality, even though it has the power to destroy the model and support its competitor with a new round of emulation campaigns. Indeed, it is this power in the local organizations which contributes to the continuity of the policy objectives that Nathan perceives. The resilience of power in the local organizations, Friedman concludes, derives from the fatigue growing among the masses about the ceaseless debate over national policy models as well as their redefinition and change. This is in addition to growing unease about abuses perpetrated by competing policy camps at the center of the emulation campaigns. For reforms to endure, therefore, stability of national models has become a necessity, regardless of which camp employs which model for implementing which policy objectives. Ultimately, Friedman's analysis serves more to criticize the negative impact of policy oscillation than to deny the oscillation per se. It finds support in Korzec and Whyte's conclusion (1981) that cyclical commitment to wage adjustment diminishes its incentive effect on enhancement of productivity.

When the emphasis on growth leads to an erosion in ideology, political rectification intervenes, bringing with it economic retrenchment and recentralization (Shambaugh 1989). One author finds competition between diametrically opposed camps of the central elite and their supporters at the periphery to be responsible for causing the cyclical shifts in reform. When the system of labor contracts runs into institutional resistance, for instance, the reformers at the center are forced to water down its content. But they await an opportunity to regroup support to introduce the reform again (White 1987). Another author detects a resemblance between the cyclical change in politics and macroeconomic management in China and that in Eastern Europe prior to the latest democratization. He draws attention to the simultaneous occurrence of political succession and an expansionary policy on consumption, which gives way to power consolidation that entails a policy adjustment, reducing the rate of increase in the production of the consumer goods (Lardy 1984).

The intellectual question haunting the economists, on the other hand, concerns how efficiency may be improved in a command economic system and with what mechanisms. Specifically, should central planning be perfected or should it be modified or even abandoned?

Donnithorne (1964; 1972; 1976) alone stands for perfection. This is because central planning is essential for achieving specialization of production and economy of scale in a command economy. Planning by centralized balancing of material transfers, of course, has its weaknesses. But to overcome allocative dislocation, argues Donnithorne, the policy should be to create more mechanisms for implementing the plans and supervising their implementation rather than to reduce the control of the central government. Decentralization, after all, merely results in patterns of allocation and production that run counter to the principles of economic rationality and technological imperatives, particularly when it is introduced with self-reliance. As soon as the euphoria of expansion and technical improvisation dies away, the system must turn to deal with its disastrous consequences·

There are others who argue for improving planning by decentralizing the control to the lower levels of the administrative authorities. Indeed, much literature on the Chinese economy until the latter 1970s upholds this proposition (Perkins 1966; Lardy 1976; Snead 1975). But this partial approach to systemic reform has been criticized as inadequate and outdated by a number of authors since the late 1980s. Cheng (1985), for example, argues that horizontal coordination is inherently lacking in the system of central planning.

He contends that planning by the lower level of the administrative authorities under the policy of decentralization will only cause verticalization within each region and give rise to greater inefficiency, just as Donnithorn predicted earlier. This means that the time for discarding planning and balancing of the physical inputs and outputs has come, even though they have proven useful for forming an initial capital base for China.

Milton Friedman, while consulting for the Chinese government, argued more concretely for total replacement of central planning by "free private markets" (Friedman 1990). Privatization can take politics out of the minds of the manager-bureaucrats, explains the supply-side theorist, so that they can concentrate on taking risks and competing in cutting costs and improving productivity. At the macroeconomic level, a new generation of privately-owned small urban enterprises promises automatic absorption of the surplus labor that is bound to emerge with structural shifts in the economy. Where private firms emerge, they render it unnecessary for the government to keep state enterprises afloat, which it has to accomplish by pumping credit and printing notes. Privatization, therefore, provides a way for China to eliminate a major source of inflation and corruption. It also takes the opportunities away from the opponents of reforms to reverse the processes of change.

Support for privatization abounds. Cheung (1990), like Milton Friedman, calls for coupling privatization with decontrolling the price system in order to achieve allocative efficiency. Breaking up the state monopoly and its resistance to total reform is Cheung's particular concern. He suggests that shares be sold and transfer of shares be permitted. Prices in the monopolized supply sector should also be decontrolled, so that entry, competition, and productivity instead of profiteering are stimulated.

In the area of policy studies, economists likewise argue for abandoning planning and replacing it with total privatization. Ross (1986), in his counter to Petrick (1981), argues that only a market system can provide the type of policy stability which China needs for switching from risk-averse to risk-taking entrepreneurship. If the government wants control at all, urges Ross, it should focus on creating institutions which facilitate the functioning of the market rather than continuing with central planning.

It is interesting to compare the positions which some Chinese authors have taken toward the debate on whether China should pursue partial or total reforms. Pu Shan, an establishment academician, disagrees with Milton Friedman, Cheung, and Dorn's proposition for linking price reform to privatization. He believes China's real problem lies in how to make partial reform work instead of seeking solution in privatization. In other words, how can China achieve efficiency and productivity with "the state regulat[ing] the market and the market guid[ing] the enterprises"? The trick, he argues, rests on finding the mechanisms that can link the collective- and individual-owned enterprises to the state sector in such a way that the subcontractors and state-owned manufacturers thrive together. Pu insists that contractual management and cooperative management, in which Cheung has lost faith, can serve the function. It is to insulate the managers in the state enterprises from interference from the owner-government and to motivate them to work for efficiency and profits that Pu supports the experiment with stock ownership (Pu 1990, 18-20).

Xu, on the other hand, sides with total reform. A technical consultant in Shanghai, Xu argues that the only way to improve productivity is to "completely decontrol market prices" and let the prices "fluctuate according to the law of supply and demand" (1990, 36). The change from centralization to a double-track system that combines a planned with a market economy with a dual price structure and two extremes of social psychology is simply not enough, he insists. Meanwhile, Xu urges that equity be kept as a developmental objective, along with growth. He also urges that such established political mechanisms as nationalist moral education be retained, in addition to punitive measures, for cracking down on corruption.

Privatization, however, has become trendy among those who study the reform of China's system of industrial management, corresponding to the proposition for changing from the partial to total approaches to reforming China's economic system. Increasingly, the Chinese see the "conservative"[10] or partial approach as promoting increased use in capacity without achieving greater efficiency within the planned economy. Under this "mixed" system, the annual state plan continues to be the primary instrument for coordinating enterprise activities, following the official principle of the leading role of the planned economy and the supplementary role of the market regulation. The only difference is that the enterprises get to keep a portion of the profit from their production and plan a part of their output according to the market demand after they have fulfilled the mandatory production quota provided under the state plan.

But how may this new managerial authority translate into necessary investment for productivity improvement when central planning and administrative control remain the chief mechanisms for coordinating economic activities? For instance, an enterprise that experiences troubles in the supplies may try to eliminate the bottleneck by petitioning superior agencies for investable funds and critical equipment. Or it may form joint ventures with local machinery producers or even production units in distant provinces. Indeed, when its petition for obtaining new machinery is denied because of the shortages in the system, the said enterprise is left with no other choice than using retained production funds to transform its outdated equipment. But this has often ended up incurring serious financial costs as well as waste in technical manpower (Jackson 1986).

In investigating the reform of China's political, economic and managerial systems, the students of the Chinese studies share a descriptive emphasis. Although it has provided much insight, such an analytical orientation has also obstructed efforts to generate independent theories contributing to social science disciplines.

This methodological weakness may partly be attributed to the dominance of the field by sinologists, historians, and other scholars of the humanities (Wilson 1971). As pioneers, they started with the interpretive analysis. This predilection is followed by the social scientists, based on the premise that history and culture define the characteristics of contemporary China. Subsequently, they confine their inquiry to documenting and elaborating the country's uniqueness (Harding 1984; Gaenslen 1986). This characterizes a number of major volumes on the Chinese political (Schurmann 1968; Townsend 1974; Harding 1981; Lieberthal and Oksenberg 1988; Goodman 1989), economic (Donnithorne 1967; Eckstein 1975; Perkins 1966, 1975; Prybyla 1978) and management systems (Andors 1977; Laaksonen 1988). Numerous articles that have appeared over the past three decades reviewing the Chinese systems and explaining their reforms carry the same bias, whether they concern politics (Doolin 1961; Townsend 1963; Schurmann 1964; Goodman 1984; 1986; Manion 1985); economics (Hoffman 1964; Cheng 1970; Wallace 1970; Donnithorne 1972; 1976; Snead 1975; Lardy 1975; 1976; Kueh 1983; 1989; Wang 1984; Howe and Walker 1984; Walter 1984; 1985; Yue 1984; Tang and Ma 1985; Oi 1986; Tam 1988; Watson 1988; Davis 1988; Kojima 1988; Sicular 1988); or management topics (Pfeffer 1963, 1966; Andors 1974; Korzec and Whyte 1981; Shirk 1981; Wong 1989; Hu, Li, and Shi 1988; Dicks 1989; Simon 1989).

The tendency toward adopting this so-called data-centered (Wilson 1971) or highly empirical methodology of study is reinforced by the academic foci and analytical tools of comparative politics (Schurmann 1968; Pye 1971; Solomon 1971; Eisenstadt 1973) and comparative economic and management studies (Richman 1969; Prybyla 1969; Hare 1988; Nee and Stark 1989). When the concepts, models and generalizations that are developed for explaining the processes of industrialization and development in the West and the Soviet Union are applied to China, the inclination is toward validating them. An essential task, then, becomes finding out to what extent they work for China and in what ways revisions have to be made to verify China as an exceptional case. Its deviation is explained in terms of cultural and historical continuity, thanks to the longitudinal typology of tradition and modernity.

Nonetheless, the development in the other economies of Confucian culture and China's latest drive to modernization have brought about a self-examination in the field of Chinese studies. The result is a reorientation in both the methodology and foci of analytical inquiry. Previously, reliance on the interpretive approach led China scholars to leave it up to the Chinese themselves to identify and define their systemic problems. The advantage of this strategy lies in acquiring an initial comprehension of the system before alternative methodologies are developed for a more sophisticated inquiry. Additionally, it helps to avoid outright imposition of western conceptual thinking on the field of study. But the approach also has an obvious disadvantage. It induces students to focus on the gymnastics of statistical and model testing. Although one may perfect validation of China as a unique case by increasing systematization in the testing of alternative models, one cannot make any theoretical generalization from the exercise (Harding 1984).

Rational choice theory is not without influence in the field, of course. To begin with, it provides the underpinning for the western concepts, generalizations, and models which social scientists have borrowed to aid Chinese studies.[11] The need for adopting it as a formal methodology of inquiry emerges when they attempt to move beyond describing what China is to probe the question "So what?" By treating culture and tradition as given, they hope to build with some generalization with the means-ends analysis (Little 1991).

As it turns out, the effort has run into difficulties. When rational-choice analysis is applied to the Chinese policy studies, for example, hypotheses are generated that argue for both China's uniqueness (Winckler 1973; 1976) and its convergence with other societies (Nathan 1976; Petrick 1981). The argument for China's idiosyncrasy holds, too, when attempts are made to examine the country's development and growth as a model for other developing economies (Oksenberg 1973; Eckstein 1977).

It has been proposed that without changing the horizontal structural relations between firms, vertical reform in China will not succeed. The proposition is raised in the light of recent studies on the relationship between the nature of supplier-manufacturer linkages on one hand and the firms' competitive performance on the other in two established systems of market economy, those of the United States and Japan. All in all, the inquiry here centers on what difference the horizontal relationship makes for the development of technology and improvement of productivity. An essential question therefore concerns to whom the nature of such institutional linkages makes a difference. What does it mean for China, as it moves toward a market economy, aiming ultimately to manufacture products of competitive quality and costs for overseas markets?

As China turns to the principles of the market system for managing the economy, it faces the critical question of how to carry out the reform of the supplier-manufacturer linkages.   Indeed, without changing government control over the inputs and other critical linkages, changing ownership and pricing seems useless. This is because comparative allocative efficiency and productivity of industries will remain a function of how government exercises its control (Shirk 1985).

In their effort to satisfy both the tax revenue demands of higher supervisory authorities and the welfare demands of the workers, tasks which they sought to accomplish by expanding above-plan production, enterprise managers met with grave difficulties in securing critical input supplies.   Partly, this was because local governments did not simultaneously devolve the control of production planning and material supplies while the central government was granting the enterprise managers greater autonomy in production planning, procurement, and marketing, first with the factory director responsibility system in 1984, and then with a more comprehensive system of contractual management responsibility in 1986.   Given their proximity to the enterprises under their geographical jurisdiction and their higher degree of reliance on profit tax for revenue income, the local authorities, in fact, had tighter control on enterprises than the central ministries. The power of the managers was further reduced by the emergence of industrial corporations under the local functional departments charged with the responsibility for managing supplies and prices.   As they were impelled to deliver immediate profit, managers tried to bargain down production quotas with the local authorities. They also began to seek supplies through such unconventional means as barter. After all, barter gave a better reflection of the value of their products in an emerging multi-tier price system. More aggressive and risk-oriented managers even began to initiate collaborative relations with enterprises engaged in the production of supplies (Fischer 1986; Fujimoto 1987; 1990; Naughton 1983; Takai 1990; Zhai 1992).

Inevitably, decentralization swept through the automobile industry during the Sixth and Seventh five-year plan (FYP) periods in the 1980s.   As elsewhere, the system of self-management, profit retention, and profit-tax kicked off in some one hundred and thirty automobile manufacturing plants. Some of them experimented with direct sales in response both to rapidly expanding markets in the rural areas and rising demand for special-purpose vehicles. For large enterprises like the Second Auto Works (SAW), direct sales also appeared to be a solution to the problem of the State Bureau of Material Supply's abstention from continuing to distribute their output to institutional users when the latter had to cut back on procurement with the budgetary contraction of fiscal 1981-1982. As they began to build their marketing channels, the auto makers started simultaneously to produce some vehicles outside the state plan (Byrd 1992b).

Vertical conflicts in the automobile industry were exacerbated with the decentralization of decision-making authority. This happened not only to the relationship between an auto maker and its direct supervisory agency, but also that between the local governments and the central bureaucracy. A classic example was the fight between SAW at Shiyan, Hubei province, and the Ministry (previously Bureau) of Material Supply (MMS). The issue concerned who should market its vehicles through the ups and downs of the business cycles that resulted from radical shifts in the budgetary expenditure of institutional users. Since SAW was forced to take on market risks in the downside of the production cycle, it did not want MMS to take back distribution power when the economy picked up. This was despite the fact that MMS had been supplying SAW with the materials needed to make its products. SAW also found itself locked in perennial bickering with the China Automobile Industry General Corp. (CAIGC)[12] that was a formerly competent bureau in the First Ministry of Machine-Building responsible for supervising the operation of the motor vehicle industry. With the enterprise responsibility system, SAW wanted to focus on maximizing its production capacity and technological competitiveness, particularly versus the First Auto Work's (FAW) located in Changchun, Jilin province, which produced the same range of four- to five-ton trucks. But CAIGC seemed to be more interested in balancing the forces between the two largest Chinese auto makers over whom it retained some supervisory authority. CAIGC was trying to increase the effectiveness of its oversight by improving its revenue income. This included an attempt to take away such profitable and strategic segments of business as the marketing of the spare parts from SAW, the business that proved critical for promoting SAW's sales and reputation. In both cases, SAW had to compromise with some concessions.[13]

Historically, the central industrial ministries were responsible for coordinating the interfirm as well as inter provincial relationships in specific industries. In automobile manufacturing, the First Ministry of Machine-Building had coordinated development among automotive enterprises. During the Sixth FYP period, CAIGC had taken over this function.

But one result of micro-vertical reform was a significant reduction of the fiscal power of CAIGC. Short of funds, it had no capacity to use its oversight positively to push its pet projects and direct the industry towards long-term development of specialization, standardization, and a larger scale of production. So it used power negatively. In technology imports, for example, CAIGC sought indirectly to orient enterprise investment by exercising its approval authority over foreign exchange spending.[14] It was by and large successful in advising defense enterprises on what products and production lines to license and from which foreign producers to license them so as to convert to automotive production. But CAIGC could not control the number of licensing projects.

For example, CAIGC had to let four plants divide up the action when it introduced assembly of the Austrian Styre-91 series of sixteen- to thirty-two-ton heavy trucks, a high priority project since 1983, with two plants located in Jinan and Qingdao in Shandong province on the eastern coast, a third in Xi'an in central northwest Shaanxi, and the last one in Dazu, probably in southwest Sichuan. When it came to importing auto transmission production technology to support assembly of these heavy trucks, two members of the Heavy Duty Group that was formed surrounding the project decided independently to import two separate lines. One of them received funding from CAIGC in conjunction with the Xi'an municipal government and Shaanxi province, whereas the other, the Qijiang Gear Plant in Sichuan probably acted with the help of the central defense apparatus and the Sichuan government. In fact, CAIGC was so strapped financially that it had to fight with SAW for the right to market SAW's lucrative spare parts. Inevitably, such conflict was resolved with some concession from SAW. Instances like this could only weaken CAIGC's bargaining position with SAW. They bred dissatisfaction in SAW and motivated it to maximize its autonomy from the state bureaucracy. In this context, the "combined management company" evolved to become a coordinating institution, an alternative to both central governmental coordination and local administrative control.

In managing the combined management company, however, the core assemblers found themselves under severe constraints. The problem was that relationships between enterprises were subject to interference from the superior government authorities. In the case of the Dongfeng Group,[15] membership had arisen to two hundred and two of some four-thousand Chinese automotive enterprises in twenty-four provinces by 1987. Yet the degree of SAW's management authority must have depended on how much the local governments of these provinces were willing to relinquish their control. Besides the integrated management over the six in-house workshops or "close associates," SAW was able to take charge of management in a number of "semi-close associates" as an equity holder, after it had won "independence" from CAIGC in 1986 and come under direct supervision of the State Planning Commission (SPC). Of course, SAW also shared profits with them. But SAW had to operate under the financial and administrative oversight of the local governments. As for the "loosely associated" enterprises with whom it had concluded contractual cooperative production arrangements, SAW only offered certain technical assistance, including a degree of quality supervision and marketing help. Finally, SAW affirmed long-term matching relations with seventy-eight factories in production and supply.

Thus, some degree of division of labor had begun to evolve in the Dongfeng Group. In addition to six in-house workshops and one R&D unit among the two hundred and two members, sixty-four fitted special-purpose vehicles, sixty-two supplied spare parts and components, thirty-four made vehicles under the Dongfeng brand, twenty supplied parts to SAW, and fourteen specialized in the production of chassis and engine kits for fitting by other members. This was a remarkable achievement, despite the fact that SAW was probably helped by a certain degree of good luck in trying to hold the group together, particularly toward the end of the Sixth FYP period. In 1985, for example, the price of automobiles inflated drastically. With permission to set prices flexibly, one hundred and twenty-six of some two hundred members of the group were able to post profits.[16]

The key area of business tension with superior government authorities, however, remained structural, namely, shortages of quality inputs over which the government retained control. To resolve such constraints on the above-plan production, its main profit earner, SAW came up with some innovative answers.

SAW's managers used counter trade both to overcome shortages in supplies and control the quality of incoming inputs. It assembled trucks for steel mills in exchange for critical materials like rolled steel. From 1983 onwards, such exchange had become sufficiently regularized to warrant the description of "processing of materials on behalf of customers." The terms of the transactions in fact reflected more truly the market values which each trading party assigned to the other's products. This was shown in SAW's decision to set its vehicle prices higher than the state-fixed prices. But to maintain long-term cooperative relations with suppliers SAW priced them at a lower premium than the going rate for its above-plan output. In return, SAW got more steel per truck from the steel suppliers, better than the one-to-one ratio it would have received from the state supply system. SAW also bartered scrap steel, one of its surplus by-products, for pig iron with the Linxian Steel Plant. This allowed SAW to obtain more pig iron of sufficient quality for building vehicles that maintained the image of its Dongfeng brand while making up for some of the materials deficits occasioned by its refusal to accept substandard inputs from the Wuhan and Chongqing Iron and Steel Mills, its matching suppliers.

The competitiveness of SAW brought about a diffusion effect. It had obviously drawn attention from CAIGC, which wanted to rationalize the structure of China's auto industry around a few manufacturing centers, with each focusing on production of one or a limited number of motor vehicle models. In any event, five other combined management companies--Jiefang, Nanjing, Heavy Duty, Beijing-Tianjin, and Shenxi--had emerged by 1983 with CAIGC's approval, followed by the Shanghai Auto-Tractor Industry Co., as well as an Auto Parts Industry Co. It was claimed that these companies had first grouped together two hundred and ninety enterprises from ten industrial branches and twenty-seven provinces and cities. The total membership increased to four hundred and sixty by 1986, while the number of the combined management companies reduced with consolidation. Most of the members seemed to follow the path blazed by Dongfeng--they fitted parts to the main assemblies supplied by the respective core assemblers (Ding 1984; Kagawa 1983; Iwagaki 1986; Fujimoto 1987).

In some instances, collaboration produced surprising spin-off results. After it had established a stable relationship with Dongfeng, for example, Yunnan Auto Works was able to develop outsourcing with some thirty suppliers in its home province (Byrd 1992b). Nationwide, however, the factories that operated under the protection of the local governments continued their external development, adding facilities to expand production and integrate the manufacture of certain inputs so as to guarantee the production under their own plans whose profits they could fully retain, known as above-plan production. Such behavior, of course, caused severe shortages. It also diverted supplies from centrally targeted "key enterprises."

With the enterprises' habitual approach to production expansion giving rise to such disturbances in supplies and with the obviously diminishing effect of various incentive schemes and responsibilities on productivity improvement, one wonders what measures China took to improve product designs and modernize factories. In this respect, the central problem is that China has overlooked design and development in most of its state enterprises. Historically, the main function of the enterprises was simple reproduction for meeting the basic needs of the society. Product design fell in the realm of the functional responsibilities of the specialized research and design institutes affiliated with the industrial ministries or universities. Only defense enterprises operating under the pressure of the arms race fostered internal design capacity. Key civilian enterprises may have had design offices, too, but their main task remained fulfillment of production quotas according to the annual state plans.

In auto manufacturing, FAW--China's first auto builder--had a product design division that was separate from the industry-wide Automotive Research Institute (ARI) and Motor Vehicle College (MVC), both located in Changchun, formerly China's auto "capital." Under the direct supervision of the First Ministry of Machine

Building, FAW, ARI, and MVC had gathered together most of China's talents in automotive engineering (Xue 1988). But from the late 1950s onwards, they did not generate any new products. Besides reverse engineering a few vehicle models, China's biggest success came by way of constructing SAW by duplicating FAW, with the help of organizations in other industries under the jurisdiction of other central ministries. Moreover, both this plant engineering project (1971) and establishment of Sichuan Auto Works with the imported products and process technologies (1965) were initiated under the Third Front strategy.[17]

Given the circumstances, a sure and quick way to modernize China's industrial products and factories would have been to call in foreign technology. By discarding self-reliance, the legitimacy for transferring foreign technology had at least been established. This paved the way for decentralization in foreign economic dealings, which proceeded in tandem with the main momentum of internal reform. New legislation was introduced from 1979 onwards for handling contractual relations with foreign businesses. These laws were followed by amendments written to improve China's business climate further. Although they targeted mainly joint ventures in the officially sanctioned policy enclaves or special economic zones, these provisions were equally applicable to technology import projects in general, because they allowed local governments and enterprises to interpret broadly their decision-making authority in foreign dealings.[18]

But an important issue remained in regard to the approach China was taking in transferring foreign technology. As it found out, the special economic zones experimenting with the strategy of export-led growth could not attract the type of technology that China needed to transform the large and medium-sized state enterprises--its main industrial assets. Thus, it launched an internal development or renovation campaign to revamp the products and facilities there. This, of course, called for self-help from the Chinese enterprises. Foreign technology, on the other hand, was to be imported for resolving technological bottlenecks.

In auto manufacturing, the two largest assemblers acted swiftly. As early as 1982, FAW took advantage of its geographical proximity to the Automotive Research Institute, China's only auto research facility, to merge with it. FAW then assumed joint administrative authority. SAW responded with unparalleled aggressiveness. Since its Dongfeng trucks were selling well, SAW was able to accumulate earnings. This at least provided part of the funding needed for building a research center at Shiyan, Hubei province, SAW's operational base. To break FAW's monopoly on the existing pool of engineering talents in China's auto industry, SAW also pursued a progressive human resource development strategy. It augmented its research center with graduates recruited from Qinghua University and Jilin University of Technology, formerly Changchun Motor Vehicle College--the two universities that offered the best programs with automotive engineering degrees (Xue 1988). Both, however, had to import critical parts and production lines and/or introduce tie-ups with foreign businesses to make up for their weakness in experience and internal capability.

The question is what happened to the other auto assemblers when FAW and SAW were scrambling for China's limited engineering resources. According to one source, FAW's integration of the Automotive Research Institute had dealt them an especially hard blow, because it practically deprived them of the most important source of technical help previously available.[19] This surely gave local assemblers added incentives to launch technology transfer projects, whether they made economic sense or not. Of course, these imports and various types of tie-ups received backing from local governments, as did projects designed for external development.

Emergence of technology transfer projects in automotive enterprises reflected improvement in the regulatory environment in China's foreign economic relations. By 1983, China had evidently learned a major lesson from implementing the first joint venture laws,[20] namely, that the linkages it needed with the world economy in industries of higher risks differed from those in small processing businesses, such as those concentrated in the special economic zones. To attract the right type of technology, China had not only to reduce investment risks by lengthening the tie-up period so that foreign investors could recover their initial investment and to work out more reasonable requirements on domestic sourcing, so that foreign partners could maintain product quality in conformity with the competitive image of their brand names, but also to open up its domestic market, so that they could broaden product sale.

These considerations found expression in the 1983 provision that allowed joint ventures to sell more output in China, provided that they met the requirements on product and process technologies transferred and on the rate of product content localized (Cohen and Horseley 1983). The concession on marketing provided opportunities to those businesses that were searching for not only new sites to extend product life cycles, but also markets to expand sales, a strategy that was compatible with the linkage structural changes at home. In retrospect, however, one of the most important contributions of the 1983 provisions was in laying out a foundation for resolving the problem of shortages in foreign exchange that had been plaguing the joint ventures as a result of their reliance on imported knock-down parts and materials for maintaining the quality of their products while keeping production in operation.

The 1983 provisions, for example, gave joint ventures the right to choose whether to source inputs in China or to import them, provided that they gave China the priority consideration if the performance specs of both were equal. This constituted a concession on domestic sourcing for the initial stage of import substitution production. Additionally, the provisions moderated import duties on intermediate inputs and equipment so as to facilitate progress in the transfer of full assembly operations to China. Most importantly, they stipulated that the competent superior agencies shoulder the responsibility for finding extra foreign exchange currencies needed by the joint ventures for continuing their production. In the event they were unable to resolve the problem of foreign exchange shortages, the relevant joint ventures could submit their output plans to the Ministry of Foreign Economic Relations and Trade (MOFERT), and ultimately to the State Planning Commission, for approval to obtain foreign exchange at the official currency conversion rate.

One suspects that the clause was at least partly designed to make local governments accountable for the joint ventures they had either initiated on their own or lent critical support. As it turned out, the clause not only anticipated conflicts between ACM-Beijing Jeep and the Beijing Municipal government in 1985-1986, but also provided the ground for the State Planning Commission's decision to help the joint venture to solve its foreign exchange crisis.

Finally, the power of the managers in foreign dealings increased further, as the emphasis on the content of the technology imports shifted from hardware such as equipment, facilities, and turnkey plants toward software, including technical expertise and managerial know-how, in support of factory modernization in China's main industrial enterprises (Sakurai 1984; Yabuchi 1986; Yuann 1987). The managers became directly involved in the processes of technology import when they received permission to work together with foreign corporations to prepare for the launching of import projects. A limited number of Chinese enterprises obtained authorization as "legal persons" under the General Principles of Civil Law of 1986 to sign contracts directly with foreign technology suppliers, even though they had to petition for approval first from the superior industrial ministry, and then from MOFERT, before sealing the contract (Cohen, 1986). Probably in response to the cry of the joint ventures surrounding the foreign exchange conflicts between Beijing Jeep and the Beijing municipal government, the "Provision of the State Council for the Encouragement of Foreign Investment" was promulgated in October 1986 to reaffirm the joint ventures' autonomy in management, which ranged from formulation of production and operating plans, financing and marketing to procurement, in addition to determination of wage levels and incentive schemes (Xue 1988). Now the question is how technology transfer was organized in the auto industry during the first wave of the post-Mao reform.

In assembly operation, the first technology transfer deals materialized in 1982. A defense enterprise in Beijing under the jurisdiction of the Ministry of Aviation Industry obtained technology and sample parts from Japan's Fuji Heavy Industries for manufacturing a thirty-five-seat bus. Additionally, a provincial auto builder, Guangzhou Auto Works (Guangdong province), licensed production of truck trailers and container chassis from an American company, Fryegayf Corp. These were followed by Nanjing Auto Works' (Jiangsu province) decision to import designs, molds, and technical assistance from Japan's Isuzu to introduce the manufacture of small diesel trucks in 1983. As one of the major assemblers formerly under the joint jurisdiction of local and central governments, Nanjing Auto Works' deal was on a bigger scale than that of the provincial Guangzhou Auto Works, necessitating involvement of MACHIMPEX, a centrally controlled trading corporation that specialized in imports and exports of capital goods and related know-how for large- and medium-sized Chinese enterprises in the transaction. In the same year, a construction machinery plant under the jurisdiction of Hubei province also reached a deal with a Japanese corporation, Ishikawajima-Harima Heavy Industries, for assembling concrete-pumping vehicles in Wuhan, using components from Japan.[21]

The most eye-catching development in 1983, however, was the Heavy Duty Group project. It was the only key undertaking sponsored by CAIGC during the first wave of the post-Mao reform. The central bureaucracy of the automotive industry imported both product and manufacturing technologies from Styre-Daimler-Push, a European conglomerate, to initiate the production of a range of heavy trucks in China. It let four plants participate in the turnkey assembly. Besides Jinan Auto Works of Shandong province, the maker of China's reverse engineered eight-ton Huanghe truck, and an enterprise located in Qingdao, the same province, two factories related to China's defense establishment that were situated at Xi'an, Shaanxi province, and Dazu, probably also in an interior province, also joined in (Ding 1984).[22]

In 1984, three more technology transfer projects developed. A local assembler, Dandong Auto Works of Jilin province, situated on the Sino-Korean border, obtained parts from Nissan Diesel to assemble the chassis of fifty-ton cranes. Shanghai Tractor and Auto Corp., in comparison, transferred both product and process technology from Wabco Construction and Mining Equipment Co., of the United States, for assembling thirty-two-ton mining trucks. Lastly, another enterprise in Jilin concluded a deal with Japan's Suzuki on coproduction of mini-trucks and mini-buses. As indicated by the presence of the China National Aero-Technology Import-Export Corp. at the conclusion of the Sino-Japanese contract, the anonymous Jilin enterprise must have been affiliated with the Ministry of Aviation Industry in the former's previous engagement in aircraft production.[23]

1985 witnessed a boom in Sino-foreign technology-sharing deals, as the Sixth FYP (1981-1985) headed for its completion. No less than ten transactions were realized. Notably, both volume producers, SAW and FAW, initiated tie-ups with foreign assemblers. FAW, which had craft-manufactured Hongqi limo until the early 1980s, began trial assembly of the 200 series of Mercedes cars. According to the terms of the arrangement, FAW was to modify one of the German models, probably both to render it more suitable to Chinese driving conditions and to gain badly needed experience in design and engineering. SAW, in comparison, tied up with Nissan Diesel to enter the production of eight-ton diesel trucks, using engines whose production SAW had licensed from Cummins of America two years earlier. SAW probably was also the party working out a technology sharing scheme with France's Citroen for manufacturing car horns, head lamps, instrument boards, and mirrors, with Citroen considering buying back sixty-five percent of the parts for use in its own cars.[24]

Additionally, a central agency backed up a project on licensed assembly of Komatsu's large dump trucks. This was in addition to the technology-sharing arrangements which two local producers concluded with two Italian companies in 1985. First, a plant in Hubei, SAW's home province, licensed production of heavy trucks from Goldani Spa. Next, Nanjing Auto Works, which had elicited the technology for small diesel trucks from Isuzu, approached Iveco for the design, machinery, equipment, and so on to broaden its range of production to include three- to five-ton trucks. The remaining four technology transfer deals taking shape in the year all involved defense enterprises. Chongqing Auto Industry Corp. in Sichuan province, where auto assembly first began in the 1960s, established the Qingling Motor Corp. to manufacture small trucks, using Isuzu's technology. In comparison, Yuxing Industries Corp., a second automotive business located in Chongqing, entered the assembly of light trucks and vans with knockdown components from Isuzu's competitor, Suzuki. Finally, Songling Machinery Corp. in Shenyang, Liaoning province, in northeastern China, approached a third Japanese producer, Fuji Heavy Industries Corp., for the technology needed for knockdown bus assembly. Like the factory in the Suzuki deal in neighboring Jilin province, Songling was also affiliated with the aviation industry.[25]

In automobile assembly, as in the rest of the Chinese industry, more significant was the entry of equity investment during the first wave of the post-Mao reform, setting a precedent in the history of the People's Republic. Two municipal builders under the jurisdiction of the Shanghai and Beijing governments spearheaded the experiment in 1983. Shanghai Tractor and Auto Corp. established Shanghai-Volkswagen to assemble Santanas with knockdown units from the German producer. Beijing Auto Works, on the other hand, formed Beijing Jeep with American Motors, now Chrysler Corp., to launch knockdown assembly of four-wheel-drive Cherokees. Compared to Beijing Jeep in which the American assembler booked a minority stake, Shanghai-VW was fifty percent owned by the German producer, reflecting the longer term of commitment it had made to the venture.[26] Figure 4.1 presents a graphic summary of the location of Sino-foreign joint ventures in automobile assembly established from the first half of 1980s to mid-1993.

A flurry of imports and various other types of technical and managerial tie-ups on automotive parts and components proceeded simultaneously during the first wave of post-Mao reform, beginning from 1981, a year earlier than those on auto assembly. As shown in Table 4.1, one plant in Hubei, SAW's home province, signed an agreement with Parker-Hannifin of the United States to introduce the production technology for automotive O-ring seals, whereas another factory in Hubei's capital, Wuhan, lined up with a counterpart in Shanghai to approach Japan's Koto Manufacturing Co. for know-how on fabricating auto lamps.[27]

In the next year, SAW acquired what might have been the third technology transfer deals for Dongfeng Group when it licensed production of engine thermostats and other temperature control products from Thomson International Corp. of the United States. In both 1982 and 1983, the production of automotive tires and diesel engines received attention for technology transfer. Two factories in Shanghai and Guangzhou respectively implemented three deals with Germany's Michelin and Britain's Dunlop International and Farrel Bridge on tire manufacturing technology. Compared to these local initiatives, licensing of diesel engine production from Cummins Engine of the United States enjoyed central backing. Both CAIGC and China National Technical Import and Export Corp. were present to broker the deal, whose recipients included SAW, a defense enterprise in Chongqing, and the latter's supplier in Wuxi.[28]

In 1984, both Dongfeng and Shanghai auto groups continued the lead in technology import. The Wuhan Auto Parts Plant, for one, signed a memorandum with Japan's Riken for the production know-how on piston rings. Three other plants in Shanghai contracted separately with Johnson Controls of the United States for equipment and related know-how on auto batteries, with Armstrong Equipment, Britain, for licensed production of shock absorbers, and with BASF on fabrication of polyurethane auto parts. In this last deal, FAW was a

Figure 4.1
Geographical Distribution of Selected Joint Ventures and Technology Sharing Arrangements in Auto Assembly in the People's Republic of China, May 1993

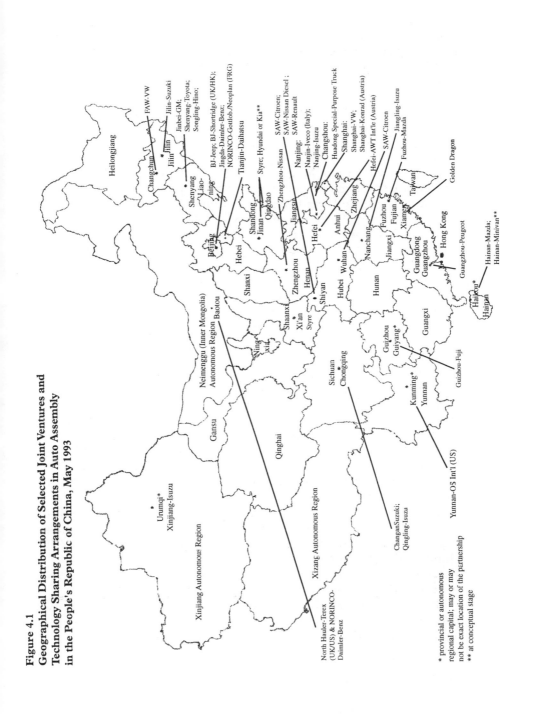

* provincial or autonomous regional capital; may or may not be exact location of the partnership
** at conceptual stage

Table 4.1
**Growth of Market for Automobiles
in the People's Republic of China,
Comparison of Total Annual Output and Imports, 1959-2000[1]**

Year	Total Annual Output (TQ)[2]	TQ w/o Truck Chassis	TQ of Trucks	TQ of Cars & Jeeps[15]	Total Vehicles in Use[3]
1959	19,601	5,325	18,938	382	
1960	22,574	4,146	21,294	667	
1961	3,589	423	3,169	295	
1962	9,740	1,363	9,160	322	
1963	20,579	3,762	20,500	78	
1964	28,062	6,787	27,542	202	
1965	40,542	11,516	38,054	511	
1966	55,861	14,279	48,478	1,072	289,873
1967	20,381	6,300	16,996	743	322,904
1968	25,000	7,100	19,076	1,878	374,446
1969	53,100	10,200	40,616	5,008	384,939
1970	87,166	18,585	65,686	9,094	436,413
1971	111,022	25,548	83,616	13,312	487,557
1972	108,227	21,609	82,102	13,919	542,896
1973	116,192	23,687	88,070	16,216	642,792
1974	104,771	19,111	76,054	18,823	717,583
1975	139,800	27,497	105,103	21,310	825,226
1976	135,200	28,310	102,849	21,791	946,833
1977	125,400	23,540	99,460	17,313	1,100,463
1978	149,062	28,970	125,073	15,578	1,250,827
1979	185,700	34,585	154,086	21,333	1,429,229
1980	222,288	48,321	163,853	25,800	1,565,678
1981	175,645	39,986	148,247	18,880	1,680,960
1982	196,304	42,541	164,330	19,356	1,873,049
1983	239,886	62,263	199,363	24,293	2,053,174
1984	316,367	85,348	265,194	22,563	2,227,130
1985	443,377	114,069	351,003	26,454	2,433,713
1986	372,753	71,821	228,304	36,036	1,887,126
1987	472,538	92,065	288,066	31,369	3,574,463
1988	644,951	136,234	364,000	72,776	4,122,939
1989	586,936	103,896	342,835	77,111	4,776,352
1991	645,000[4]			63,000[12]	5,274,663
1992	1,080,000[23]			180,000[21]	

Table 4.1 (cont.)

Year	Total Annual Imports (TM)	Annual Imports of Trucks	Annual Imports of Cars & Jeeps[15]	Annual TM/TQ[16]
1983	25,156[11]	10,776[14]	5,086*[11]	10.50%
1984	148,743[11]	32,813[14]	21,651*[11]	47.00%
1985	353,979[11]	138,018[14]	119,501[13]	80.00%
1986	150,051[11]	77,397[14]	55,302[13]	40.00%
1987	90,399[11]	28,413[14]	33,629[13]	19.00%
1988	93,211[5]	17,557[5]	55,737[5]	14.50%
1989	67,283[5]	12,587[5]	44,984[20]	11.50%
1990	65,000[6]	15,392[20]	34,064[20]	
1991	84,000[6]		54,409[8]	
1992	225,000[7]			

Projection of Michigan-China Study[9]				
Year	Total Output	Cars, Jeeps & Minivans	Other Projection: Total	Other Projection: Cars
1990				42,000[17]
1991				66,000[17]
1994				240,000[18]
1995	1,150,000	470,000[10]		600,000[17]
2000	1,740,000	830,000[10]	3,000,000[19]	1,950,000[19]

Notes
* Excluding jeeps.
    1. The annual output until 1989 draws from *World Motor Vehicle Data* (Michigan Motor Vehicle Manufacturers Association, 1991, 44. These are in turn based on the data of the China Automotive Technology and Research Center in Beijing.
    2. Includes all vehicle types, such as buses and others. Ibid.
    3. The data until 1989 is based on the same source as 1. The total also includes all vehicles, such as buses and other vehicles.
    4. R. Johnson, "GMC May Build AVP in China," *Automotive News* (18 January 1993): 1.
    5. Page 46 of the same source as 1. Note that of the cars and trucks imported in 1988, 20,447 were knockdown units for cars and 1,694 were for trucks. In 1989, the knockdown car units were 20,560, whereas the knockdown truck units were 1,598. If chassis were included, the total imports in 1989 would have been 85,742. *Zhongguo Haiguan (China Customs)* (Beijing, Customs Office: February 1990): 22.

6. S. Vine, et al, "China Puts Out Welcome Mat for Imports," *Automotive News* (19 April 1993):22. Excluding chassis, which would have totaled the imports for 1991 as 98,000 units; *Zhongguo Haiguan (China Customs)* (Beijing, Customs Office: February 1990): 38. The February 1991 issue of *Zhongguo Haiguan (China Customs)*, however, puts the total imports of automobiles and chassis as 63,000, which it reported was a 26.1% decline from the previous year (p.20).

7. The latter number includes 50,000 units of illegal imports. Ibid.

8. S. Vine, "Car Imports Business Slips into Top Gear," *South China Morning Post* (28 march 1993): 3. The huge imports in 1985 and reportedly for 1986 resulted from Hainan government's using its special status to import cars either at low tariffs or without them.

9. *US-China automotive Industry Cooperation Project, Final Report, vol. 1* (Ann Arbor, MI: University of Michigan, 1989), Task 1.1., Table 1.1.11.

10. These are listed in a separate category because they represent a Sino-Western consensus on future growth area in the Chinese auto industry. They have also been where foreign investment is penetrating. The projected figures for cars, minivans, and jeeps are 320k, 90k and 60k for 1995, 60k for 2000. In the truck category, the projection for light trucks was 350k and 530k for 1995 and 2000; medium trucks 260k and 270k; heavy trucks 50k and 90k; and buses 20k and 20k. Ibid.

11. Complete vehicles only. The same as footnote 9, Table 1.1.6, which bases data on sources in the *China Automotive Industry Year, 1986; China Statistical Yearbook,* and *General Administration for Customs,* PRC of the relevant years.

12. Karp, "Back on the Road: China Auto Ventures Rebound from 1989 Squeeze," *Far Eastern Economic Review,* vol. 155, no. 12 (26 March 1992): 49-50.

13. Note the total number of cars imported were 105,775; 48275; and 30,536 from 1983 through 1987.

14. The vans here most likely refer to minivans. Ibid.

15. They are grouped together because the Chinese consider both as luxury consumer goods compared to trucks that are used for production, and vans and buses for public transportation.

16. Rounded to two decimal points.

17. "China to Build Largest Automobile Bearing Factory," *Xinhua General Overseas News Service* (17 Sept. 1991).

18. "China's Auto Industry Focuses on Sedans," *Xinhua General Overseas News Service* (13 December 1991).

19. For the projection of CNAIC, see *Xinhua General Overseas News Service* (19 February 1993).

20. Excluding jeeps. *Zhongguo Jingji Nianjian, 1991 (China Economic Annals, 1991),* VIII-101. In 1989, almost half of the car imports, however, are those of the knockdown units. See 5.

21. G. Murray, "China Seeks Foreign Investment to Update Car Industry," *Japan Economic Newswire* (12 April 1993).

22. Ibid.

23. "Plans to Upgrade Motor Industry," *BBC Summary of World Broadcast,* NCNA in English 1542 GMT (19 February 1993).

----

co-recipient of the German technology. FAW, late in seeking foreign tieups for upgrading its automotive supplies, also contracted automotive radiator technology from the American Prefex Co.[29]

Among newcomers to import automotive parts technology in 1985 were factories from Liaoning province. Two in Shenyang, its capital, sought partners in Japan. One licensed auto paint technology from Kansai Paint; the other imported machinery for making truck transmissions from Mitsubishi Heavy Industries. A plant in Chaoyang received a turnkey facility for manufacturing truck tires from Britain's Dunlop International in a counter trade arrangement. This was accompanied by China's fourth deal on tire manufacturing, broached between a plant in Heilongjiang province and Italy's Pirelli, that had the blessing of the Ministry of Chemical Industry, represented by China's National Chemical Construction Corp.[30]

In the last year of the Sixth FYP (1981-1985), three components licensing deals also came in place to support the Styre heavy project that CAIGC had launched in 1983. Besides the transaction on the production of gears with Germany's Zahnradfabrik Friedrichshaften, two separate production lines for transmissions were imported from North America's Eaton Corp. and GM's Allison Division. China's defense enterprises seemed to be involved in all these deals. NORINCO, for instance, was a party in the licensing of the gear technology. By virtue of their location in the interior provinces hosting China's Third Front industries, the plants in Shaanxi and Sichuan that were responsible for implementing the transmission projects may also have had connections with the military industrial bureaucracy.[31]

Finally, 1985 witnessed the evolution of several other imports or licensing contracts on auto supplies technology, such as two licensing deals with British firms, York International for parts manufacturing and Automotive Products for technology for making automotive clutches for commercial vehicles, and a transaction involving procurement of crankshaft pin-turning machines from Saginaw Machinery Systems Inc. of the United States. Additionally, CAIGC brokered a parts manufacturing deal with France's Citroen. One suspects that either the central auto agency or its counterpart in other branches of the central industrial bureaucracy also had a hand in the negotiations between seven Chinese radiator makers and the American Livermois Engineering Co. on the design, production and servicing of the machinery used in manufacturing automotive radiators and components.[32]

Thus, China introduced at least twenty-six technology-sharing projects for auto parts and components manufacturing in the first half of the 1980s. These compared with only two equity partnerships formed during the same period. Of these two equity linkages, the localized production of thermostats which SAW sought with Thomson International Corp. in 1984 represented an upgrading of their relationship since 1982. The production of automotive batteries, in comparison, was a joint venture, with ownership split equally between a Shenyang company and a Portuguese firm.[33]

With reform, therefore, not only various branches of the central bureaucracy, but also local governments and individual enterprises were starting technology transfer projects. The initiative came first from local authorities who had obtained special trading status as well as discretion in disposing a limited amount of the foreign exchange needed in international dealings. This included three municipalities, Beijing, Shanghai, and Guangzhou. Major local assemblers like Nanjing Auto Works also actively pursued technology transfer, with the support of superior governments. Some local authorities established an umbrella organization, a provincial auto company, to help the subordinate auto builders to launch modernization projects. This at least was the experience in Hubei and Liaoning provinces.[34] Defense bureaucracy provided the third entrepreneurial source in technology imports and partnerships. Besides projects they initiated on their own, the Styre heavy trucks targeted by CAIGC provided an excellent opportunity for it to assist the factories under its jurisdiction in entering automotive assembly and components manufacturing. Finally, SAW and FAW sought technology from both foreign assemblers and parts and equipment suppliers. But SAW went after it more aggressively than its competitor.

Acquisition of foreign technology in China's auto industry began as early as 1979 when Wuhan Auto Works placed an equipment order with Mitsubishi Heavy Industries.[35] But the momentum for imports and cross-border partnerships did not pick up until after 1982. Auto enterprises had to wait for the slump of 1981 and 1982 that was induced by budget cutbacks and a subsequent contraction in foreign exchange allocations to ease off. They had also to wait for government policy to switch from relying on special economic zones towards using China's large- and medium-sized state enterprises to transfer the type of foreign technology that the country needed for upgrading its technological capabilities.

The automotive enterprises had to go beyond external expansion and simple improvement in labor productivity to increase profits after delivering income and profit tax to the government. For local assemblers that sought transition from assembling a few hundreds or thousands of vehicles a year to making more than 10,000 annually, the technological leap was too big to accomplish through revamping outdated equipment and facilities. Acquisition of foreign technology was especially critical when it became linked to adding new products for the Chinese economy. On the supply side, decades of emphasis on simple reproduction to the neglect of R&D and improvement in product design meant that the Chinese had no experience in coming up with new products of their own. Yet demands were growing rapidly not only for light and heavy trucks, with a thriving rural economy and anticipated expansion in the mining and manufacturing industries, but also for luxury coaches, taxis and vans, with China's door opened to foreign tourists and businessmen. Demand for specialty vehicles also rose, as the consumption of the urban population became more sophisticated.

But the rush for launching technology transfer projects stemmed also from other environmental stimuli. Indeed, a sense of exigency must have prevailed among the automotive enterprises, as it did for their counterparts in other industries. First, the vertical control of superior administrative authorities in the past had left them perennially short of investment capital. Second, the cyclical pattern of reform must have created much uncertainty about their new autonomy. These combined to generate hunger and anxiety for action. They had to use whatever money was available to get their share of modernization before policy reversed again. Although it may not have been rational for scale-related technological reasons, their investment decision made sense economically, given that vehicle assembly continued to be lucrative under tariff protection and administrative barriers of the local governments. Price inflation and speculation by entrepreneurial elements among the local authorities themselves toward the mid-1980s added further impetus to modernization through technology transfer.

Imported technology allowed established assemblers to make products of superior designs, such as the diesel engines used in the light and heavy trucks which the Chinese found more fuel-efficient than the gas-driven midsized ones they had been producing in volume. Likewise, it provided a golden opportunity for the defense enterprises, now under "self-management," to convert to civilian production by taking advantage of their experience in reverse engineering and precision processing.

With so many parties launching projects simultaneously, duplication became inevitable. It has already been mentioned that two transmission lines were imported in 1985 for centrally targeted Styre trucks, whose outputs reached 8,600 the next year.[36] Between 1982 and 1985, four tire production projects were introduced. By all accounts, they probably occurred exclusive of one another, because the local authorities in Shanghai and in Guangdong, Liaoning and Heilongjiang provinces obviously initiated these projects without talking with one another or with the central bureaucracy. The transaction between Heilongjiang province and Italy's Pirelli was the only project supported by the center, with the China National Chemical Construction Corp., an import-export arm of the chemical industry that had supervisory authority over the production, involved in the technological acquisition for the plant. While this deal-making was going on, its neighbor, Liaoning province, installed a tire plant of its own through counter trade.[37]

The danger of duplication is not only waste, but, more seriously, its constraints on the scale and depth of the technology transferred.

When resources are scattered, both the scale of the projects and subsequent volume of production may be limited. Minimally, low volume hinders the recipients' ability to bring imported production lines to full capacity to climb up a scale-related learning curve. The problem in China for these years was that many technology transfer projects began precisely with a low threshold. This both reflected and reinforced local protection in production and procurement. As a result, Beijing, Tianjin, Liaoning, Shanghai, Jiangsu, Shandong, and Sichuan, where foreign assembly technology had made inroads, achieved an annual outputs of 50,064; 20,787; 32,730; 12,165; 24,474; 15,517; and 16,901 units respectively in 1985, while fourteen other provinces made one to several thousand vehicles each. In 1986, three assemblers in Beijing, including Beijing Jeep,[38] Nanjing Auto Works, and Tianjin Auto Works, produced 58,392; 20,403; and 21,542 units respectively. Shanghai-Volkswagen made about 5,000 sedans, whereas Guangzhou Peugeot only 790 cars and 592 pickup trucks. In fact, most of the 130 auto assemblers in China built only hundreds of vehicles each this year.[39]

More fundamentally, constraints on scale-related learning arose from the bottlenecks in supplies. Shortages and poor quality forced the assemblers with various forms of partnerships to rely on imported knockdown kits. When this arrangement was prolonged, it worsened their foreign exchange imbalance, which in turn hurt their expansion plans. Beijing Jeep, for one, had to halt production while fighting with the Beijing government for an additional foreign exchange allocation. Meanwhile, it continued to produce the outdated BJ212 as a main bread earner instead of phasing it out as planned (Xue 1988).

The question is what happened to coordination in technology transfer on the one hand and how technology transfer fit into the overall development of China's auto industry during the first wave of post-Mao reform on the other. A few ways of imposing partially systemic coordination were emerging during this period of time. Shanghai occupies a unique position. The five parts projects for auto lamps, car tires, car batteries, shock absorbers, and polyurethane products between 1981 and 1984 were obviously introduced around Shanghai's car venture with Volkswagen.[40] The other projects seemed to be less coherently orchestrated by other provincial authorities, the defense industrial system, and the central bureaucracies of the automotive-related industries respectively.

The explanation of Shanghai's uniqueness is simple. Along with Sichuan, it had pioneered one of two approaches to industrial reform since 1979. Unlike Sichuan, where individual factories made investment and other decisions, the municipal bureaus in Shanghai coordinated investment by assuming the responsibility for aggregating tax revenue as well as planning and supervising how their subordinate enterprises might use the retained funds (Fujimoto 1981). This pro-business method of economic management proved extremely helpful in later years for Shanghai-VW when it began to introduce domestic production of parts and components.

It is difficult to tell which provincial authorities extended which approach to investment, Shanghai or Sichuan, when they transferred technology. But at least Hubei and Liaoning appreciated the need for local coordination and perhaps that for aggregation insofar as it affected the bargaining position of the local enterprises versus foreign businesses. They used provincial auto industry corporations to influence and support locally started imports and cross-border partnerships. The effort of Hubei authorities overlapped, additionally, with the interests of the Dongfeng Group. Three Hubei plants' deals on O-ring seals, auto lamps and piston rings made between 1981 and 1984, complemented SAW's projects on thermostats and diesel engines. While introducing knockdown assembly of concrete-pumping trucks with kits from Ishikawajima-Harima Heavy Industries and licensing production of Goldani's heavy trucks, two Hubei machine builders may also have referred to the overall strategy of product specialization[41] in the group, so that they focused on acquiring the technology of specialty vehicles while SAW licensed production of eight-ton diesel trucks.[42]

Dongfeng's competitive strategy obviously had an emulation effect on other combined management companies. Shanghai Auto and Tractor Corp., for instance, entered the heavy truck business with Wabco's technology while setting up car production with Volkswagen. Although FAW did not begin to transfer parts technology until 1984, it is likely that the projects in Liaoning and Heilongjiang next door were established with some reference to the strategy of the Jiefang group that was headed by its core manufacturer, FAW.

It is fair to say that CAIGC had worked hard on sorting out the chaos in technological acquisition to make some sense of its role in the broad development of China's auto industry. In this effort, it took over part of the MACHIMPEX as a specialized arm in imports and exports. The objective was evidently to influence the direction and scale of technology transfer and coordinate various projects so that they supported or at least would not conflict with CAIGC's pet targets. This strategy revealed its deep suspicion about the ability of locally initiated projects to move beyond production for local consumption so as to climb the learning curve. Surely, this suspicion was grounded in an understanding of the paucity of resources, engineering manpower, in particular, among local assemblers. It explained partly the local governments' intransigence in maintaining their administrative barriers.

Despite its official capacity, CAIGC ran into much difficulty in performing its functions in control and coordination. Not only did its policy preference differ from the rational interests of most of the local governments and their subordinate assemblers, but also its financial weakness rendered it unable to enforce its authority effectively. Consequently, CAIGC left those local governments capable of devising their own financing to pull their own acts. Guangzhou-Peugeot was a case in point. Its Chinese partner, Guangzhou Auto Works, had been a stranger in car production. Before the post-Mao reforms began in the late 1980s, FAW and Shanghai Auto Works had been China's car assemblers. By 1980, FAW had terminated its production of the Hongqi or Red Flag limos. If it planned to build sedans again, CAIGC would have done so at either of these enterprises. Indeed, CAIGC supported Shanghai Auto Works by lending its presence in the conclusion of its partnership with Volkswagen.[43]

But Guangzhou had the special autonomy as well as the capital mobilization capability to cut its own deal. One year after Shanghai formed its joint venture with Volkswagen, Guangzhou tied up with the French producer Peugeot. Compared to Shanghai-VW which received official backing from the cautious Bank of China (BOC), CAIGC, and the German producer itself, Guangzhou-Peugeot got financial support from China International Trust and Investment Corp. (CITIC), a newly established state investment firm that tended to be more risk-taking than BOC in decisions, the French assembler and its French bank, and World Bank's International Finance Corp. (IFC). IFC reportedly loaned Guangzhou-Peugeot $15 million for a ten percent stake on the condition that it would pursue autonomy by issuing stocks to the public.[44]

Where possible, CAIGC refrains from confrontation with defiant local authorities, particularly when the latter's decision does not threaten to divert the resources it can otherwise access itself. When Jinggangshan Auto Works, Jiangxi province, decided to import production lines for engines and driver's cabs from Isuzu to upgrade its production of small trucks, for example, CAIGC put in a favorable word for it before the superior authorities, even though the central agency generally did not like the local authorities to take their own initiatives on transferring assembly technology without first consulting the CAIGC's opinion. It granted the symbolic sanction, not only because small trucks remained in short supply, so that one more project would not conflict with CAIGC's priority target, the Styre trucks, but also because Jiangxi planned to finance the deal with its own money without asking for foreign exchange from Beijing.[45]

Finally, the constraint on CAIGC's coordinating function came from a lack of cooperation from other branches of the central industrial bureaucracies. CAIGC had to give a green light to the technology transfer projects of the defense enterprises. After all, they fell under the control of the military industrial apparatus, an independent system with independent resources. But CAIGC was also aware of the technological contributions these enterprises could make to China's auto industry upon conversion. More problematic was the slow response which the materials industries[46] were making to the demands of the auto assemblers and parts makers that had modernized their products and facilities with foreign technology. The boom in auto imports in the mid-1980s (Table 4.1) and subsequent hype in auto production must have further compounded the problems in supplies. As a result, forty percent of the steel products, twenty-three percent of the pig iron and from thirty percent to sixty percent of the non-ferrous metals needs of the automotive industry went unmet.[47]

Partly, the shortages resulted from the poor quality of the inputs supplied, as the experience of both SAW, a wholly domestic enterprise, and Beijing Jeep, a joint venture, suggested. It has already been mentioned that SAW refused to accept some of the steel products from its matching supplier, Wuhan Steel Mill. Similarly, dissatisfaction with the quality of locally made parts forced Beijing Jeep to prolong its dependence on the imported knockdown kits. But the chaos in the auto industry reflected also the disruptive forces of the pent-up demand triggered by the speculative behavior of certain local authorities. Hainan government, for instance, gained notoriety for abusing its duty-free status to import most of the complete cars in 1984 and 1985 and profit from sales to the interior provinces at inflated prices. This surely undermined further the central bureaucracy's ability in concentrating resources to develop a few major bases of production, which entailed suppressing duplicate assembly and technology acquisition projects.

Likewise, the situation reflected the absence of a concerted national transportation strategy that targeted transformation of China's auto industry. In fact, the major modes of transportation continued to be rail and water in these years. The role of the auto industry in the overall development of China's economy and that of the technology in this process were also unclear. For example, the Chinese seemed to be using auto manufacturing to join the world economy at a higher value-adding level than light processing enterprises in special economic zones. This outward orientation explained why Shanghai reportedly chose Volkswagen over its Japanese competitors in forming the joint venture.[48] It also explained why future exports were part of the deal for Shanghai-VW and Beijing Jeep, based on the Chinese delivery of quality and performance specs.[49] But the question is how China could move from assembly of the imported knockdown units to exports of some automotive parts and components and even complete cars. The prolonged dependence of Beijing Jeep on the imported knockdown kits and the subsequent foreign exchange crisis, followed by a dramatic conflict with the Beijing government, reflected a confusion about how export orientation, that was so easily put in place in the special economic zones, could be built into a technologically sophisticated infant industry.

At one level, the confusion concerned what role import substitution could play in transforming China's auto industry and how it should be linked to export promotion to develop its technological capabilities. This was reinforced by a lack of vision of precisely which product category, trucks or sedans, should be the engine of growth in the long run. At another level, it concerned what function technology transfer should assume in this process of change. It seemed that the Chinese continued to use it solely for overcoming bottlenecks in technology, perhaps as a result of the legacy of the planned system that assigned foreign trade an incidental instead of a strategic role in national economic development so that imports served to bridge the gap in domestic demand and production. This explained why turnkey projects continued to dominate in the first half of the 1980s. Consequently, automotive enterprises held onto self-help in technological development while shifting to include technical expertise and managerial know-how--so-called software, as compared to hardware like equipment, facilities and turnkey plants, in technological acquisition.

In Table 4.2, one can see that SAW and FAW shouldered the main burden in developing automotive technology during the Sixth FYP period. Both faced the problem of improving the design of their five-ton gas guzzlers while diversifying production. FAW, the older of the two, had also a tougher time modernizing its workshops and facilities. This pressure found expression in the expert services they sought from foreign companies. Between them, SAW seemed to be the more aggressive in acquiring the technological software. Indeed, it displayed a commitment to the development of product technology by seeking advice from a British firm on how to construct China's first auto proving ground. Its aggressiveness probably reflected SAW's attempt to build up an internal technological base in competition with FAW. FAW, in comparison, seemed to have closer backing and probably also greater interference from the central authorities. It had to give CAIGC more prominence in foreign dealings. CAIGC, of course, was behind the licensing of blueprints and technical expertise in support of China's entry in the production of heavy trucks. Finally, the difficulties which Beijing Auto Works (BAW) experienced in implementing the order of the central authorities on redesigning its BJ212, a product which Changchun Automotive Research Institute had reverse engineered yet which probably would no longer render assistance freely after its merger with FAW (Xue 1988), must have influenced BAW's decision to call in help from Japan's Hitachi and Britain's Haden Drysys when it experienced difficulties in redesigning the carburetors and designing and managing the construction of the production lines for paint finishing.

This shows that longer-term liaisons than turnkey imports were beginning to develop while automotive enterprises switched towards licensing, coproduction and other technology-sharing schemes to acquire engineering knowhow and expertise. Nonetheless, the pattern of these activities still reflected an emphasis on seeking engineering solutions to problems that were fundamentally structural in nature. In other words, the fundamental constraints on the automotive enterprises' performance, including their ability to learn and improve after implementing factory and product modernization with foreign partnerships, were rooted in interfirm organizational linkages that remained subject to the intervention of the local administrative directives. The lack of measures addressing this problem showed that China had underestimated the structural changes required by technological upgrading through foreign linkages. It also points out the policy changes of the local authorities as one indication of a trend towards structural transformation in China's auto manufacturing.

During the Seventh FYP period (1986-1990), China began to ease into the second wave of post-Mao reform. This was indicated by a transition from technology imports to joint ventures, with equity investment in auto assembly spearheading the latter trend. Following Shanghai-VW and Beijing Jeep, a number of joint ventures was formed in this period, including Beijing Light Auto Co., a partnership among the former Beijing No. 2 Auto Works, CITIC, and the Hong Kong subsidiary of Britain's Shortridge, for assembling light trucks with product design from Isuzu; Huadong Special Purpose Truck Co. Ltd., a venture between an assembler in Jiangsu province and Japan's Onga Trade Corp. for building container and garbage trucks; Golden Dragon Auto Corp., a venture between SAW and Sofrasia, GM's sales representative in Hong Kong, for fabricating auto bodies for passenger vehicles; as well as North Hauler Ltd., a twenty-year equity venture between No. 2 Machinery Co. in Inner Mongolia, probably a defense enterprise, and Northwest Engineering of Terex, an Anglo-American corporation, for building off-highway dump trucks.[50]

The momentum in joint ventures picked up further from the late 1980s through the first few years of the Eighth FYP (1990-1995). First of all, some assemblers have shifted from knockdown assembly of foreign makes to joint ventures with their partners. They include Tianjin-Daihatsu, a venture between Tianjin Minibus Works, Ohana Industrial Corp., and Daihatsu, a member of the Toyota group, that

Table 4.2
Technology Transfer in the Automobile Industry
and Development of Domestic R&D in China, 1983-1993

Project	Location	$ Transact'n	Term/Status	Parties
1983:				
design of 5-ton truck driver's cabin[1]	Shiyan, Hubei Province	NA	memorandum signed on provision of expertise[1]	• SAW • Motor Panels Ltd. (UK)[1]
designing 3 plants for painting truck cabs[2]	Changchun, Jilin Prov.; Jinan, Shandong Prov.; Shiyan, Hubei Prov.[2]	NA	licensing contract signed on transfer of expertise[2]	• FAW • Jinan AW • SAW • Hayden Drysys (UK)[2]
1985:				
redesigning carburetor of Beijing Jeep[3]	Beijing	NA	commission made[3]	• BJ Auto Accessories Lab • Hitachi[3]
design consultancy for building auto proving ground[3]	Xiangfan, Hubei Province	NA	contract signed[3]	• SAW • Motor Industry Research Assn. (UK)[3]
consultancy on factory modernization[4]	Changchun, Jilin province	189,000[4]	agreement reached on draft proposal[4]	• FAW • GNK Forgings (UK)[4]
design&mgt of construction of paint finishing lines[5]	Beijing	NA	order won & granted[5]	• BJ JEEP • Haden Drysys (UK)[5]
technology for cabin design & mgt. of metallic molds & dies[6]	Changchun, Jilin Province	121 million[6]	NA	• FAW • CNAI Import-Export Corp. • Mitsubishi Motor Corp.[6]

Table 4.2 (cont.)

engineering documentation, technical assistance&training for 3 9-speed road ranger trans mission[16]	NA	NA	Licensing[16]	• CAIGCIEC • Heavy Duty Group • Eaton Corp. (Canada)[16]
1987:				
drafting & video-digitizing system for designing auto parts & bodies[7]	Changchun, Jilin Province	450,000[7]	NA	• FAW • Changchun Auto Research Institute •Garber Scientific Instrument Co. (US)[7]
building vehicle testing ground for cars,[8] heavy duty & cross country vehicles[17]	Shiyan or Xiangfan, Hubei Province	64 million yuan[17]	NA	• SAW • British Motor Industry Research Association[8]
expertise in manufactur ing & QC for truck production[9]	Shiyan, Hubei Province	NA	NA	• SAW • Nissan Diesel[9]
design,devt. of compressed natural gas tech. for large truck & bus engines; training in mktg & technical expertise[10]	NA	459,940[10]	deal concluded[10]	•NORINCO • Wekgas Holdings Ltd. (New Zealand)[10]

Table 4.2 (cont.)

1992:				
devt. of new generation of 4WD Cherokee[11]	Beijing	N A	N A	• BJ JEEP • Chrysler • Visioneer-ing (US)[11]
1993:				
establishing an R&D center in China[12]	Shanghai	N A	letter of intent sighed to conduct feasibility study of R&D joint venture[12]	• CNAIC • 1st Auto Group Co. • Dongfeng Motor Co. • Shanghai Auto Ind. Corp. • Nanjing Auto Corp. • Ford (US)[13]
technology & devt. for bus chassis & truck axle prod.[15]	Shiyan, Hubei Province	N A	agreement signed, continuing technical assistance since 1985 on design & prod of cabs, transmis-sions & axles[15]	• Dongfeng Motor Corp. • Nissan Diesel[15]

Sources
1. *China Business Review (CBR)*, vol. 10, no. 5 (1983): 64.
2. Idem., 66; vol. 11, no. 4 (1984): 50.
3. *CBR*, 12, no. 1 (1985): 66.
4. Ibid.
5. Ibid.
6. *CBR*, 13, no. 3 (1985): 54.
7. *CBR*, 14, no. 1 (1987): 58.
8. Ibid.
9. Ibid.
10. *CBR*, 14, no. 2 (1987): 59.
11. *CBR*, 19, no. 1 (1992): 49; *China Trade Report* (April 1992): 2.
12. "Big 3, Chinese Officials Sweeten Partnership," *Reuters* (19 April 1993): 3.

13. "U.S. to Cooperate in Auto Research, Development," *Xinhua General News Service* (24 March 1993).
14. "Ford to Set up Parts Plant in Shanghai," *Reuters* (25 April 1993); "Ford in China," *The Daily Telegraph* (26 April 1993): 23.
15. "Nissan Diesel to Supply Chinese Firm with Bus Chassis and Truck Axle Production Technology," COMLINE Daily News Transportation (25 February 1993) from *Nikkan Kogyo Shimbun* (24 February 1993): 15.
16. *CBR*, 12, no. 5 (1985): 65.
17. "Motor Vehicle Testing Ground Operational," *Xinhua News Agency*, Peking, in English 1060 GMT (16 October 1989); *BBC Summary of World Broadcasts* (24 October 1990).

----

assembles Daihatsu's mini-car, Charade; Jiangling-Isuzu Motor Co., a partnership between Jinggangshan Auto Co., Jiangxi province, Isuzu, and C. Itoh Co., that assembles pickup trucks; and Nanjing-Iveco, a tie-up between Nanjing Auto Works and Italy's Iveco, that builds light trucks and diesel engines.[51] Two defense enterprises in Sichuan have also switched to joint ventures after converting to knockdown assembly of motor vehicles during the 1980s . One, Qingling-Isuzu, is an assembler of light trucks and vans with equity participation from Chongqing Auto Industry Corp., Isuzu, and Da Chong Hong, CITIC Hong Kong's automobile sales arm. The other, Changan-Suzuki Auto Co., is a builder of Suzuki's Alto, a minicar model that is sold under the name of "Changan." Its stake holders include Changan Auto Corp., a superior organization of Changan Machine Building Plant, Suzuki, and Nissho Iwai.[52]

Second, new equity ventures have taken shape. Besides Hainan-Mazda Motor and Stamping, which assembles Mazda's Luce Van; Jinbei or Golden Cup Vehicle Manufacturing Co., which assembles GM's S-10 series of pickup trucks and Jingda-Daimler-Benz which plans to manufacture luxury buses at Beijing Bus, with equity participation from Singapore's TIBS as well as the German producer, China's two largest auto builders have also shifted to joint ventures in production and technological upgrading. FAW, for example, has formed partnership with Volkswagen for manufacturing Golf and Jetta. This compares to SAW's partnership with Citroen for building VX cars and engines. SAW, additionally, has participated in the joint venture at Zhengzhou, the capital of Henan province, between Zhengzhou Light Truck Plant and Nissan, through the Dongfeng Group, along with other equity holders, the Industrial and Commercial Bank of China, and Thailand's Sammitra Motor Group.[53]

During both five-year plan periods, Sino-foreign partnerships that involve no equity investment have continued to evolve, especially for heavy and specialty vehicles. These include SAW's deal with Renault to produce diesel trucks jointly at Shiyan, Hubei province, and a few partnerships which the local producers have formed with foreign assemblers, such as Hainan's decision on co-production of the forklift truck with Britain's Lancer Boss Co.; Shanghai Fire-Fighting Equipment Plant's partnership with Konrad Ropsenbauer for the manufacture of heavy-duty fire engines; as well as Hefei Auto Works and Anhui General Bus Plant's tie-up with Austria's AWT Internationale Handels Und Finanzierungs for assembly of large buses at Hefei, capital of Anhui province.[54]

The enterprises that have ties with the Third Front industry have engaged actively in the production of heavy and specialty vehicles. NORINCO or North Industrial Corp., one of the most powerful business organizations for the defense industrial establishment, sponsored at least two partnerships with foreign auto producers, such as its contract with Daimler-Benz on knockdown assembly of fourteen types of heavy trucks by Nos. 1 and 2 Machinery Plants at Baotou, Inner Mongolia, and its agreement with a German firm on knockdown assembly of transit and city buses by No. 1 Bus Plant in Beijing. These compare with Xinjiang Auto Works' deal with Isuzu on the assembly of eight-ton trucks in Xinjiang Autonomous Region and Yunnan province's decision to co-produce fire engines, engineering trucks, and military vehicles with OS International of the United States.[55]

Finally, a number of new car projects based on some type of technological sharing arrangement have emerged during the same period. They include licensed assembly of Mazda's Proceed pickups at Fuzhou, Fujian province; Jinbei Vehicle Manufacturing Co.'s deal with Toyota on licensed production of Hi Ace Vans; and Guizhou Aviation Industry Corp.'s preliminary agreement with Subaru Inc. of Fuji Heavy Industries on the assembly of minicars.[56]

In the auto parts and components business, equity joint ventures have also increasingly become an important means for transferring technology while partnerships without equity investment rise in scale and number. During the first two years of the Seventh FYP, five joint ventures evolved, compared to two in 1984 and 1985. In 1986 Tianjin Rubber Industry Corp. entered into a joint venture with Canada's United Tire and Rubber Co. and Hong Kong's Sam Yed Co. Ltd. for manufacturing engineering tires in the northern coastal city. Ma'anshan Steel and Iron Corp., in comparison, formed an eighteen-year venture with Britain's Shaw Tegee to produce axles at its mills at Ma'anshan, Anhui province. This was followed by Nantong Bearing Factory's decision to establish a facility with another British firm at the former's existing plant site at Nantong, Jiangsu province, to make plane bearing components and materials in 1987. In the same year, a newly formed Rich Island Enterprise Ltd. signed an agreement with a Hong Kong concern to manufacture ignition coils in Hainan province. Similarly, a factory in Shanghai established Xiangdao

Machinery Manufacturing Co. Ltd. with Hong Kong Shanghai Investment Co. to produce auto parts in Shanghai.[57]

In 1988, seven more joint ventures in automotive supplies materialized. Besides Zhejiang Electric, which the Zhejiang branch of CITIC established with Ezaki Electric Co. Ltd. for processing auto parts and electric wire, three auto parts ventures were set up in Shanghai and one in Suzhou. First, Shanghai Auto and Tractor Industry Corp. established Shanghai GKN Drive Shaft Co. with Uni-Cargen of GKN to make drive shafts for the Santana cars, VW's nameplate assembled at Shanghai-VW. The second venture in Shanghai involved Purolator Products for making auto filters in the port city. Third, Shanghai Piston Factory signed an agreement with Germany's Kolbenschmidt AG on the production of aluminum pistons. The venture, introduced in Suzhou, Jiangsu province, by an auto electric factory in Suzhou, also had the participation of an automotive concern in Shanghai. Interestingly, Changsha Electric of Hunan province was a party to the venture, too. In other words, two Chinese auto suppliers formed the same partnership with SAF Auto-electric of ITT Automotive Industries to obtain an initial capacity of one to two million units of automotive parts annually. Finally, SAW which had entered into technical partnership with Thomson International, the United States, in the early 1980s to upgrade SAW's production of automotive thermostats and related temperature control components set up a joint venture, Dongfeng Thomson, to further improve the production of thermostats.[58]

In the last two years of the Seventh FYP, joint ventures in auto parts and components manufacturing began to diffuse to other cities in China. Baoxing Plastics Plant, for one, entered into a fifteen-year joint venture with Japan's Precision Instrument Manufacturing in 1989 to make auto brakes at Baoding, the capital of Hebei province. Chongqing Tire Plant in Sichuan province, similarly, decided to form a joint venture to build steel-belted radial truck tires with Dunlop International, China's fourth deal with the British supplier of the technology for tire production. Back in the coastal province of Zhejiang, Hangzhou General Glass Plant formed Hangzhou Safety Glass Co. Ltd. with Singapore's Safety Glass Manufacturing to produce windscreen glass for Shanghai-VW. These partnerships were followed by the 1990 decision of a concern at Qingdao to establish a venture with South Korea's Tong Il Co. to build auto components at the port city in Shandong province, and a venture established in the same year between the Joints Plant at Suzhou University, Jiangsu province, and an American company, for making universal joints and cross axles for motor vehicles. Significantly, FAW reportedly decided to modernize its metal casting foundry with Chrysler's technology through a joint venture instead of imports.[59]

Five more joint ventures emerged in 1991, the first year of the Eighth FYP (1991-1995).   Among them were one involving an Australian firm constructing a plant to make tubes and other components for automobiles and another venture between Hainan province and a Hong Kong concern for manufacturing tire cord. Shanghai Storage Battery Plant, in comparison, formed a joint venture with Thailand's Chia Tai Group to make automotive batteries, whereas Yangzhou Bearing Plant established equity partnership with a Hong Kong firm to supply automotive bearings at Yangzhou, Jiangsu.   Hubei Asbestos Product Mill rounded up the year's equity investment deals for automotive supplies with a venture with Italy's ALA to produce car disc-brake pads at Xiangfan, Hubei, the same location as SAW.[60]

In the next year and a half, eight more ventures mushroomed. Two of them were established in Beijing in 1992, with one between the Auto Furnishing Plant and a Hong Kong company for producing bolstered automotive armchairs, and the other between the Red Lion Coatings Corp. and Akzo Coatings International for fabricating auto finishes and related products.   Additionally, two companies at Zhongshan, Guangdong province, established an auto paints business with a Japanese company, Ohashi Chemical Industry, and a Taiwanese firm named Hong Kong Central Paint Shop.   In comparison, Chengdu Engine Co., a venture between a Chengdu plant at the capital of Sichuan province and Isuzu, went into operation.[61]

New developments evolved in the first half of 1993 when Shanghai Auto Industry Corp., together with Shanghai Yafeng Accessories Factory, sealed a letter of intent with Ford on investing $90 million to produce plastic and trim parts in the Pudong Development Zone, which may evolve to include fabrication of glass and climate control components through a number of related joint ventures.   This compares with a venture on processing labor-intensive parts with three affiliates of Nissan, and SAW's intent to build auto components with Nissan Diesel to substitute for the knockdown kits.[62]

In addition to about thirty joint ventures, more than forty other Sino-foreign linkages on automotive supplies have been reached through first years of the Seventh and Eighth FYPs.   At least seven projects were established in 1986 alone, including a licensing deal between Beijing and Italy's Piaggio and C. Spa. on automotive supplies for small trucks; Cangzhou Platinum Factory's contract with Toho Metal Co. on the equipment and knowhow for fabricating tungsten contracting points used in auto ignition systems at Cangzhou, Hebei province, licensed design and production technology which FAW sought with Britain's Automotive Products PEC; a production line which an enterprise acquired from Japan for producing auto sealing materials; a Guangzhou tire plant's contract for a factory for making steel radial truck tires; and the deal which CNAIC made with Isuzu, probably in behalf of Nanjing Auto Works, for producing components for Isuzu's light trucks. Finally, a plant that was affiliated with China's aviation industry decided to sign a five-year contract with Japan's Mikuni Corp. for annual production of 100,000 carburetors in Changchun city, Jilin province, the same locale as that of FAW.[63]

In 1987, no less than nine projects were introduced, mostly by the Three Bigs (FAW, SAW and Shanghai-VW). SAW, backed by CNAIC, signed a ten-year licensing contract with Cummins Engines, the second between the two in decade, on knockdown assembly of 60,000 diesel engines annually for use in heavy trucks, relying on technology, knowhow, and training provided by the American company. FAW, in comparison, concluded two engine deals. One concerned acquisition of the facilities and technology from Chrysler for eventually making 300,000 engines a year for use in light trucks and cars. The other involved purchasing five-liter diesel engines for use in the Jiefang trucks. Shanghai Auto and Tractor Corp., on the other hand, participated in the signing of an agreement between Shanghai Clutch Plant and a German supplier to transfer the technology for producing diaphragm string clutches for automobiles. This was accompanied by another deal in Shanghai with Britain's Versons International Ltd. and Verson Wilkins on acquiring the presses, engine design, and critical components for car production. Shanghai Heavy Machinery Works was the third enterprise in the city to transfer technology for automotive business. Along with its counterparts in Beijing, Taiyuan, Shenxi province, and Qiqihar, Heilongjiang province, it reached an agreement with Japan's Komatsu on the technology for making large presses used in auto manufacturing. Another multi-party deal involved joint acquisition of four continuous profile scanning systems by four tire manufacturing plants in Anhui, Guangxi, Shandong and Sichuan provinces from Selective Electronic, Inc., of the United States. Two other transactions were concluded in Shenyang and Nantong cities respectively. While a Shenyang enterprise sought assistance in the production of car batteries from Japan's Yuasa Battery, Nantong Bearing Factory in Jiangsu province licensed production technology for auto bearings and bearing materials from the British AE Group.[64]

Six more technology sharing deals were arranged in the next year. These included three transactions related to tire-making technology, one between China Chemical Construction Corp. and Pirelli of Italy for radial tire production facilities; the second between Dazhonghua Rubber Factory, Shanghai, and Firestone Tire of the United States for the technology for fabricating steel cord radial tire; and the third between Guizhou Tire Factory, Guizhou province, and Daimler-Benz for technology and equipment for tire production. In 1988, Liuzhou Minicar Factory, Guangxi province, also concluded a deal with Grotnes Metalforming Systems, the United States, on an automotive rim manufacturing line. One of two most prominent transactions during the year, however, was struck by the Beijing General Internal Combustion Engine Plant, a national key supplier, when it purchased a secondhand two-liter gas engine assembly line from GM with the support of CNAIC. The other deal concerned China's import of an engine plant from Chrysler, which was most likely completed by FAW.[65]

The momentum slowed down during the last two years of the Seventh FYP, with four deals taking shape in each year. Two more tire projects were introduced in 1989. Guangzhou Tire Factory signed a contract with Firestone Co. on a production line, whereas Qingdao No. 2 Rubber Co. transferred production technology from Pirelli with a loan from the Asian Development Bank. In addition, there were two auto battery projects in the two years, with one involving plant import by Shenyang Battery Plant from Britain's Chloride Technical and Trading, and the other involving acquisition of a production line by Beihai Storage Battery Plant, Guangxi province, from Austria's Akkummulatorenfabrik Junger. In 1989, an enterprise affiliated with the aviation industry also imported parts from Japan's Mikini Corp. to manufacture carburetors. This was followed by three major transactional events in 1990. Besides the second plant import which Beijing General Internal Combustion Engine Plant made from GM, this time entailing moving the latter's iron casting plant at Saginaw, MI, to Beijing; and FAW's imports of stamping dies for stamping metal parts for the Audi 100 from Fujima International Inc., a Japan-Canada joint venture, Siping Instrument and Meter Plant at Siping, Jilin province, witnessed the auto meter production line which it had acquired from Japan going into operation.[66]

In the next two years, the number of automotive parts transactions was sharply reduced. One project, introduced to acquire the technology for establishing China's largest auto bearing plant, Zhenhua Auto Bearing Factory, with a designed capacity of 100 million units annually, required merger of two plants, Shanghai Xinhua Bearing Plant and Shanghai Zhenxin Chemical Factory. The second project involved import of ten 600-metric ton heavy auto body presses by Shanghai-VW from the British subsidiary of Germany's Emst Komroski and Co. Significantly, a GM office was also opened in Shanghai through its sole agency in Hong Kong, Sofrasia Ltd., with the objective of not only producing but also purchasing automotive parts from China.[67]

But the pace picked up in 1993 when at least ten technological sharing arrangements were made. Both Beijing and Shanghai hosted two projects. In the Chinese capital, the General Internal Combustion

Engine Plant, along with Jiangxi Motors Co. and a defense enterprise, Changsha Auto Engine Works, jointly ordered three crankshaft balance machines from Balance Engineering Corp. Another Beijing parts maker reached an agreement with Budd Co. to provide technical assistance for the production of sheet molding compound materials as well as components. The foreign parties to both deals were American. The transactions in Shanghai were made by Shanghai-VW with Litton for import of a grinding system and by Shanghai Machine Tool Works with the same American company for licensed production and sale of grinding machines. Two other Chinese plants also chose Litton as a partner in technology transfer, including Jiangxi Motors at Nanchang, which placed an order for two engine-production systems, and a rotary compressor manufacturer in Nanjing, Jiangxu, which purchased disc grinders. Tianjin Sanfeng Minibus Co. Ltd., on the other hand, placed an order with Volvo for engines and gear boxes for the assembly of minibuses. Finally, SAW imported axles from Nissan Diesel for knockdown assembly of trucks and buses, along with production technology for both the truck axles and chassis.[68]

A striking feature of the foreign linkages established during the second wave of the post-Mao reform is an escalation of their scale. Leading the drive are what is known as China's "Three Bigs", SAW-Citroen, FAW-Volkswagen and Shanghai-Volkswagen, all three producers of small cars. The first two ventures have, in particular, overshadowed other projects, whether joint ventures or partnerships on the basis of other technology-sharing arrangements.

China's dash to small car production seems fueled by a match between FAW and SAW. Both are switching from relying on equipment imports and various types of technology-sharing schemes to upgrade their capabilities in truck production and design toward utilizing equity investment to initiate knockdown car assembly. Both are racing for the scale of the assembly venture, with each determined to produce 150,000 cars annually upon completing the first phase of the construction projects in the mid-1990s. Shanghai-VW, in comparison, intends to match up by raising the knockdown assembly to an annual capacity of 150,000 by mid-decade.[69] The aggressive move of the three largest joint venture producers compares with mere thousands or tens of thousands of outputs typically obtainable each year by the local auto works through foreign tie-ups in the first half of the 1980s.

Of course, local governments and the defense establishment have given continued support to their pet assembly projects. But, except for the "Three Smalls" (Beijing Jeep, Tianjin-Daihatsu and Guangzhou-Peugeot), which have earned recognition of their de facto status from the center, and Changan-Suzuki, which the military industrial authorities have pushed through of their own will, they are playing a lesser role in China's overall development of car assembly. To better position themselves, some of these assembly plants have sought alliances with the Three Bigs. This seems to benefit SAW well, since it pioneered the conglomeration strategy in the early 1980s. Through the Dongfeng group, for example, SAW has obtained thirty-five percent of the stake in Zhengzhou-Nissan, a new light truck venture in which the number two Japanese producer has taken a five percent interest. SAW has also been able to launch the Golden Dragon auto body shop at Xiamen, together with GM's Hong Kong sales representative, while considering whether to escalate the licensed truck production with Nissan Diesel to a joint venture. On its part, FAW maintains an interest in Changan Auto Corp., which will convert its knockdown assembly of minicars to a joint venture with Suzuki.[70]

An interesting question is why the two volume truck producers in China have switched strategies in foreign technology acquisition. After all, are they not more used to reverse engineering products and processes handled behind closed doors? One explanation is that a joint venture provides a quick way for entering car manufacturing. It allows producers to begin mass production almost immediately by relying on the designs and processes of foreign partners instead of struggling to develop anything of their own. Indeed, the Chinese have had much difficulty in redesigning fuel inefficient engines in mid-sized trucks. Furthermore, the experience they have gained in volume production derives from trucks rather than cars.

With a joint venture, FAW and SAW can also easily mobilize capital for diversifying production. Because there are many idle plants available in the world since the auto assemblers in the Triad have had a decade of slumping sales, the Chinese have found it easy to persuade them and their banks to leverage some of these facilities as a part of the stake in Chinese ventures. A joint venture may prove cheaper, too. It saves the Chinese builders development costs. Shipping secondhand equipment and facilities and producing cars whose product life cycles have already ended in the advanced economies comes at a bargain price. Finally, a joint venture, through its domestic content clause, obligates foreign investors to teach the Chinese how to improve product quality and maintain the image of the brand names in a manner that helps to maintain the position of these nameplates in the Chinese market in the future. This may bring spillover effects to the transfer of technological know-how. But the decision of SAW and FAW to switch to joint venture car assembly has also come in response to the investment opportunities revealed by car imports of 1984-1985 (Table 4.1).

In parts and components production, as in auto assembly, change is also on the way. First, the sources of capital for joint ventures have diversified. While investment from the Triad continues to flow in, newly industrialized countries (NICs) have also joined the game. As shown previously in the discussion of the origin of investors for these ventures, Hong Kong has been particularly active in China's automotive supplies business since 1986. The prospects of market expansion are so great that Taiwan and South Korea have also come in. Some of them seem to aim beyond local consumption for sale in the regional or even national market, evidenced by the scale of their investment. A few examples include a $29 million venture on the production of storage batteries in Shanghai, in which Thailand's Chia Thai group made an investment in 1991, and a $48 million tire cord business in Hainan in which Hong Kong took a stake in the same year. One expects the ventures involving the participation of the Triad to be of larger scale. This is true to some extent, as in the case of the $90 million venture between Shanghai and Ford.[71]

What is more, clusters of joint ventures in automotive supplies seem to be emerging in support of the joint venture assemblers' effort to switch from knockdown assembly to sourcing parts and components in China. As of mid-1993, nine parts makers in Shanghai and neighboring Jiangsu and Zhejiang provinces have formed linkages with foreign investors, the most concentrated of the supply clusters. Surely, some of these ventures may be established to serve the demands of Nanjing-Iveco, in addition to Shanghai-Volkswagen. But Shanghai has the advantage of its new Pudong Development Zone as the location for a comprehensive parts supplies site through its deal with Ford as well as a base for a large research facility for which CNAIC, Shanghai Auto Industry Corp. and four other Chinese auto makers have approached Ford for help in establishing.[72]

Beijing and Guangzhou, which host two of China's Three Smalls, come next in line. Beijing is moving aggressively, because it has two joint venture assemblers, Beijing Jeep and Beijing Light, to support. Guangzhou, in comparison, may benefit from the parts projects established in both Hainan and Guangdong provinces. A supply base seems also to be emerging in Sichuan. The tire project initiated in Chongqing in 1989 aimed probably to supply not only the assembly operations in Chongqing but also the Styre project. Similarly, the venture on diesel engines set up in Chengdu in 1992 intended probably to introduce domestic sourcing of some of the parts for the same assemblers. Clusters of joint ventures, of course, have also been established surrounding SAW and FAW. Besides the projects on factory modernization and domestic sourcing they themselves have introduced, some locally initiated ventures such as the contract between the Changchun plant and Japan's Mikuni Corp. for improving the supply of the carburetors (1986) and Hubei Asbestos Product Mill's partnership with Italy's ALA for production of car disc-brake pads (1991) surely are intended for the benefit of the two respective producers.

Lastly, Ma'anshan Iron and Steel Corp. decided in 1986 to enter automotive parts production through a joint venture arrangement, following the strategy of vertical integration, and received partial funding from CITIC.[73] Once in operation, it could threaten some suppliers in the same business.

Unlike joint ventures for which the foreign partners of the Chinese automotive enterprises have diversified, our review of the other types of technology sharing deals that involve no equity involvement indicates that they continue to be dominated by the European, Japanese, and North American firms from 1986 onwards. One reason may be that many of the technology-sharing deals of the latter type are more sophisticated in technology. Additionally, one detects a rising scale for these deals compared to the first half of the 1980s, evidently to support expansion in assembly joint ventures. For instance, the counter trade deal for tire production equipment and facilities which Changzheng Tire Plant at Chaoyang, Liaoning, reached with Dunlop International in 1985, provided for an annual capacity 150,000 pairs of tires. The contract for a tire production line which Guangzhou Tire Factory signed with Firestone in 1989 aimed at twice the capacity of the Changzheng Plant.[74]

Moreover, the central bureaucracy has participated frequently in these deals. Both CNAIC, the successor of CAIGC, and the central apparatus of the related industries are involved. This is probably because the Chinese parties to these deals are enterprises still under the supervision of the central agencies. Administratively, a transaction above a certain cap may require involvement of the superior authorities. Alternatively, the latter may have joined in to strengthen the bargaining position of the Chinese enterprises versus the technologically and financially powerful firms from the advanced economies.

Corresponding to the trend for joint ventures in automotive parts and components, clustering is showing for tie-ups that involve no equity investment. Shanghai, again, has built up the largest number of linkages. Beijing has also been active in this category of Sino-foreign partnerships, matching its number in joint ventures. Besides the projects which SAW and FAW have supported one way or another to acquire the parts and components technology from their foreign partners, the Heavy Duty Group has also geared up its parts and components technology-sharing arrangements. A reasonable guess includes the projects installed in Cangzhou, Hebei province, and Guiyang, Guizhou province, in 1986; in Guilin, Guangxi province, Qingdao, Shandong province, and Chongqing, Sichuan province, as well as a place in southwest China in 1987; in Liuzhou, Guangxi province, and Guizhou again in 1988; in Qingdao again in

1989; Guangxi again in 1990; and, finally, in Changsha, Hunan province, in 1993.

This suggests that local parts makers are also under pressure to upgrade their parts processing capabilities in order to maintain their business by supplying the joint venture assemblers. Liaoning province, for instance, introduced two more parts projects, the car battery manufacturing project in Shenyang in 1987 and import of the facilities for tire production in Shenyang in 1989, in addition to the tire production project at Chaoyang in 1986. Interestingly, the car battery project introduced in 1989 coincided with Shenyang's initiation of knockdown assembly of Toyota's Hi Ace vans. Such local initiatives surely have put pressure on automotive enterprises elsewhere in China to continue upgrading their capabilities.

The years 1991-1992 were slow for technology-sharing deals not involving foreign equity investment. This was evidently because of a freeze on the institutional buyers' vehicle procurement programs following a "recession" that resulted from a second budgetary contraction in the 1980s. A reduction in foreign exchange allocations to the auto assemblers may have forced them to slow down technology imports temporarily. As a result, only three technology-sharing projects with foreign automotive suppliers on automotive parts and components were introduced. But the same recession seemed unable to affect the number of equity joint ventures being established. Nine of them emerged in these years.

On the other hand, a trend seems to be emerging towards supply beyond a local destination, with the scale of Sino-foreign technological sharing deals increasing. For instance, the tire plant which the factory at Chaoyang, Liaoning province, obtained from Dunlop International in 1986 was evidently intended to supply to other places in China besides Liaoning, because the annual capacity of 150,000 pairs of tires could satisfy well beyond the provincial needs. Additionally, the facility for automotive meters that went into operation in 1990 at Siping, Jilin province, clearly aimed at cross-regional supply. With a designed capacity of 400,000 sets of auto meters a year for fitting 200 different specifications, the Siping plant's clientele outside Jilin included not only auto assemblers in Beijing, Tianjin, Shenyang, and Harbin in north and northeast China, but also Jiangxi and Sichuan in the central and southwestern part of the country. Similarly, the Shenyang Battery Plant that purchased the plant for making 600,000 batteries annually by 1990 should be supplying cross-regionally. One expects it to reach at least FAW, with whom the Shenyang plant may have had either matching relations, thanks to geographical proximity, or a combined management relationship thanks to membership in the same Jiefang Group. It is certainly not inconceivable that the battery project was introduced as a divisionalized production programs under the Jiefang Group. In comparison, the technology jointly acquired by two plants in Shanghai under their merger plan may eventually sell to not only Shanghai-VW, but also to other assemblers, given its designed capacity of 100 million units a year.[75]

Finally, the modernization programs launched at Beijing General Internal Combustion Engine Plant in 1988 and 1990 came in time to maintain its matching relationship with assemblers in China's national market. This compares with the obvious intent of the $48 million joint venture investment in the production of tire cords in Hainan to supply products nationally. Projects like these, of course, are matched by the Three Bigs' efforts to upgrade their parts and components manufacturing. Through its $90 million parts production deal with Ford in 1993 in Pudong Development Zone, however, Shanghai appears to be pushing joint ventures more vigorously than SAW and FAW.

In both assembly and parts and components supplies, proliferation of technology-sharing deals after 1986 has received an impetus from a number of political and economic forces evolving with the deepening of post-Mao reforms. For instance, defense enterprises have had to maintain their commitment to auto assembly because pressure has been rising for them to find new businesses and new sources of income, now that government procurement contracts are being reduced and budgetary allocations from the military industrial authorities are shrinking.[76] The local suppliers have had to begin factory modernization, because reliance on the protection of the local authorities alone no longer suffices for keeping business orders. SAW and FAW, China's two largest producers, have had to form joint ventures in car assembly and various other deals for parts and components production, because they of all the automotive enterprises must rise in a great haste to defend the position of China's auto industry after imports flooded the domestic market in the mid-1980s.

This points to the fact that an increasing number of foreign corporate linkages has been made in response to pressures from superior political authorities as much as from the challenges of the world market forces. In this respect, no challenge is more serious than the issue of domestic sourcing. It has already been mentioned that the success of technology transfer in auto assembly depends on how stably production can run, to what extent the assembly operation can reach its designed capacity, and how fast an assembler can climb up the technological learning curve or reach its intended scale of production. Similarly, it is known that the foreign currency costs in knockdown assembly have been frustrating the joint venture assemblers' transition to full-scale production.

The problem is that the Chinese did not anticipate the extent of their future dependence on the imported knockdown kits when they installed joint ventures in auto assembly. Partly, this was because they did not give adequate consideration to the tough demands the new technology placed on the domestic supply capabilities before import replacement could be realized. But such inattention is not new. Besides being the side effect of a vertically integrated system of production, the backward state of China's automotive supplies sector is due to government neglect. For decades, both central planners and local decision makers made assembly an investment priority. Parts supply, in comparison, always played an adjunct instead of a strategic role in investment plans. Consequently, the intended investment for parts manufacturing always failed to keep up with assembly. This bias displayed itself again when the local authorities pumped in support for assemblers in their areas of jurisdiction to import technology and set up joint ventures while giving minimal financing to suppliers for modernization.[77]

But modernization of parts manufacturing became an urgent matter after China enlarged the scale of the import substitute assembly of automobiles and began to tackle the difficult issue of domestic sourcing. As with knockdown assembly, major responsibility has fallen on the Three Bigs. If our review of the Sino-foreign linkages in automotive parts and components production is any indication, then Shanghai-VW has been the most active of the three in using such linkages to replace imports with domestic procurement. It is associated with at least seven joint ventures and fourteen other technology sharing arrangements in automotive supplies. SAW, in comparison, has ties with a minimum of three joint ventures and eight projects without foreign equity participation on parts production, sometimes through its relationship with other members of the Dongfeng Group, such as Wuhan Auto Works. This compares to one joint venture and at least seven other technology sharing schemes in parts production which FAW has either introduced by itself or with which it has had a relationship since the early 1980s. The coordinated fashion with which the parts projects have come together for Shanghai-VW may have much to do with the experience of the Shanghai enterprises in working with one another. But it must have also benefited from the pro-business policy which the Shanghai government has adopted since the beginning of the post-Mao reforms.

By relying more on transferring technology in parts and components manufacturing without foreign investment, SAW and FAW have simultaneously sought to use domestic sourcing to complement their strategies in market positioning in the whole country. Both have diversified production. Both have also encouraged the member firms in their combined management companies to enter assembly operations through joint ventures while introducing three-party investment themselves. FAW, one step behind SAW in strategic grouping, has also sought to strengthen its competitive position by merging and acquiring plants in Jilin as well as research facilities and plants in such distant provinces as Qinghai.[78]

Defense enterprises have likewise cashed in on the movement to raise the domestic content of motor vehicle assembly. Aside from meeting growing demands from within the military industrial system, they are taking advantage of their relatively advanced facilities and more experienced engineering manpower to internalize imported parts and components technology while solving certain problems of product quality. This explains why NORINCO, the umbrella corporation for the defense industry, has joined SAW and FAW in acquiring "soft" auto technology or design and engineering capabilities as well as managerial know-how and expertise (Table 4.2). In fact, both FAW and SAW have sought assistance from former aircraft manufacturers in developing devices for vehicle safety. Similarly, the strength of the defense contractors has lured Shanghai-Volkswagen and Beijing Jeep to seek them out in domestic sourcing.[79]

Thus, the defense enterprises have become a competitive force in China's automotive supplies business. With their ability to quickly reverse engineer products of superior quality and swiftly enter a new business, the defense enterprises help to keep suppliers in the civilian sector on their toes. The following story is illustrative. In the late 1980s, Chinese drivers began to converge on their preference for trucks fitted with engines made by the Beijing General Internal Combustion Engine Plant (BICE). Nanjing-Iveco had thus shifted procurement from a local supplier to BICE. This forced a competitor in Shenyang to adopt the same purchasing strategy. When demand surged, however, BICE failed to expand supply accordingly, partly because it had to guarantee priority supply to its main users in Beijing, as Beijing authorities, who had superior administrative authorities over BICE had stipulated. But an engine plant affiliated with the military industry in Changsha, Hunan province immediately filled the gap. Since the reverse engineered engines supplied by the Changsha plant proved better in quality, BICE was left to maintain its market share by relying on the cost advantage in production.[80] One suspects that the competitive challenge of the Changsha plant must have something to do with BICE's decision to import facilities from GM again in 1990, after having done so in 1988. But the counter-offensive of BICE also revealed a weakness of the Changsha plant, namely, its small volume of production and high unit costs. This points to scale expansion as the direction toward which the defense enterprises must go, particularly if the Chinese auto assemblers have to become price elastic, as China's institutional buyers probably will, when the country joins GATT.

The above discussion suggests that a detectable change in the nature of the pressure for localization has had a serious structural impact on China's auto industry. While both local governments and joint venture assemblers have felt pressure for localization, the nature of the pressure for them differs. Many local governments' initiatives in localization continue to derive from the need to improve their tax revenues. This contrasts with the need of the joint venture assemblers to ensure the quality of the locally procured incoming inputs to maintain the quality of their nameplates. Consequently, the joint ventures and local governments have often differed on where to engage in domestic sourcing and how to raise the domestic content. Local governments may prefer sourcing in the areas under their own geographical jurisdiction. But the joint venture assemblers are more likely to follow a national instead of a local perspective to procurement and source supplies where an enterprise's competitive advantage lies. Beijing Jeep, for instance, decided to buy tires from a factory in Qingdao after a thorough search in China instead of from a local supplier as the Beijing government would have preferred (Mann 1989).

Through bidding, therefore, the joint venture assemblers have provided an even stronger competitive challenge to the parts and components makers than entry of the defense enterprises. This is reinforced by the assemblers' bias in procurement towards those enterprises which have implemented product and factory modernization. Indeed, it was not a coincidence that the tire factory in Qingdao won the deal from Beijing Jeep, overcoming the barrier of matching relations the tire factory in Beijing had had with Beijing Auto Works, the Chinese partner of the joint venture assembler. The Qingdao factory had committed a $30 million loan to acquiring Pirelli's equipment and technology in 1989. The disruptive impact of both the purchasing strategy of the joint venture assemblers and the competitive drive of factories that have implemented technology transfer projects combine to force automotive suppliers to consider how to measure up in performance rather than continue to wait for the directives of superior agencies to ensure the sale of their outputs.

Suppliers have begun to join the race in factory and product modernization to defend business turf formerly secured by matching relations. The manager of Shenyang's Fuyang Parts Plant, for instance, imported a new generation of heat furnaces and bundled assistance to modernize its cast metal process in the late 1980s when he realized that it might lose its matching assembler, FAW, to two plants in Guangzhou, Guangdong province, and Dalian, Liaoning province. Both of these plants had acquired foreign technology to improve supplies (Grow 1987). But most parts makers continue to feel the pinch in financing while trying to upgrade product designs, product quality and processing capabilities to meet the demands of joint venture assemblers. Some of them team up with the assemblers to solve this problem. For instance, some parts makers in Beijing accepted compensation arrangements with the matching assembler, Beijing Light Auto Ltd., to improve product quality. They took dies and imported equipment from Beijing Light. In return, they sourced orders and subtracted service charges from the fees on the more advanced hardware.[81]

Other parts suppliers are finding relief in more diversified sources of financing from neighboring Hong Kong, South Korea, Taiwan, Thailand, and Singapore. Since China has installed a combined tax and tariff barrier of up to 250 percent of the wholesale price of an imported vehicle following the import frenzy of the mid-1980s and put up a tariff of 120 percent on imported knockdown inputs,[82] both car assembly and parts processing have become hugely profitable. This is especially true as joint ventures begin to intensify localization to reduce costs and scale up production. Furthermore, acute shortages in quality parts and in the parts makers that can deliver sufficient quality have allowed suppliers to fatten up with high charges (Mann 1989). Such profit-making opportunities, together with new rules permitting three-party joint ventures that serves to reduce the risks of investment, have subsequently lured capital from the East Asian NICs, including risk-averse capital from Hong Kong.

By the early 1990s, CNAIC was finally able to convince the State Planning Commission (SPC) that limits have to be placed on the number of automobile plants for mass manufacturing and that some control has to be imposed on the haphazard expansion of assembly plants and their suppliers. At present, there are eight officially endorsed major ventures among one hundred and thirty assembly plants who have fixed matching relations with over two thousand direct suppliers.[83] The situation is so chaotic that it is becoming increasingly difficult for the Chinese regulatory authorities to keep track of the small scale assemblers and suppliers. In addition, provincial competition sometimes bypasses central authority and enters into joint venture agreements or direct import of technology without authorization. This happened in the Jiangxi Auto Works, which modernized truck production by importing critical components technology. The central government controls product cataloguing, the only channel by which national marketing is possible, and refuses to mention Jiangxi Auto Works so that other provinces will not copy its strategy of bypassing the central government in importation of technology.[84]

CNAIC is also trying hard to guarantee delivery of scarce quality inputs to the few big auto assembly centers, the Three Bigs in particular. One of its objectives is to protect these centers from supply disruptions resulting from the policies of local governments, who have gained most of the allocative control over the industrial outputs and who remain interested in fostering local auto assembly capabilities.[85] By 1995, CNAIC hopes to consolidate suppliers by establishing fifty auto parts manufacturing groups, which CNAIC's chairman hopes to accomplish through "cooperation, regrouping, and merging." Such consolidation will reduce the number of parts makers and hopefully upgrade their quality by the end of the century.[86]

The turnabout in CNAIC's management of the industry has been impressive. The explanation points to the possibility of rethinking on the part of CNAIC and the highest economic decision-making apparatus, the SPC and the State Economic Commission, on how to help Chinese assemblers to position themselves in the domestic market, now a matter of exigency for China's auto industry. The pressure of raising the domestic content of the automobile assembly has also forced them to tailor policies to the interests of the targeted joint ventures.[87] Thus, the SPC had to allocate special funds twice to help the Three Bigs and Three Smalls out of policy-induced recessions in 1988 and 1989. This contrasts with the hands-off policy which the central authorities adopted through the previous budgetary recession in 1980 and 1981. CNAIC also tried to stimulate demand by forcing the retirement of the gas guzzlers still on the road.[88] Both measures were taken to stabilize production in the joint ventures, thereby ensuring the progress in localization.

But CNAIC has not been the only one to change. While trying to maintain the fixed matching relations with administrative directives, some of the local authorities are also beginning to support subordinate suppliers in modernization. For instance, the Beijing government reportedly allocated much of its own funds to help some 100 parts makers under its jurisdiction to implement the domestic sourcing for the Cherokees of Beijing Jeep.[89] Yet most local governments have to find ways to overcome shortages of capital financing. Hubei government tried a strategy of concentration. In one instance, it focused investment on setting up a competitive base for manufacturing automotive clutches at Huangshi.[90] Other local authorities seek to upgrade the products and production processes of local parts makers through alliances with the Three Bigs. Qinghai government, for one, let FAW merge an axle factory and a vehicle refitting plant, in addition to an auto research institute, in support of FAW's development of eight-ton trucks in competition with licensed production at SAW. In exchange, Qinghai received a multi-year profit-sharing contract.[91]

Some local authorities have become even bolder in policy innovation. The government of Wuhan, for example, introduced its own targeting after SAW selected the provincial capital as its operational center in order to break out of its isolation in Shiyan. Wuhan established a bonded warehouse to facilitate trans-shipment of automotive products. It is also planning to link manufacturing, trade, and storage facilities with "a state level of auto market" that is large enough to allow business transactions for the entire nation. One suspects that the Wuhan government is emulating its Shanghai counterpart in providing an infrastructure supporting the development programs of its member of the Three Bigs, especially after Shanghai established Pudong Development Zone to attract foreign investment for upgrading the city's industries. Certainly, Wuhan hopes to bring in more capital from the NICs by creating a friendly investment climate with a series of liberal policies, including privatizing some state enterprises for majority foreign ownership. Wuhan and Shanghai were followed by Guangdong province, which announced its plan to establish a free trade zone to handle transshipment of complete vehicles and parts and components for Guangzhou Peugeot and other automotive joint ventures in spring 1993.[92]

This means that the local authorities are breaking their own administrative barriers after raising them in the first half of the 1980s. They are converging with Shanghai on a pro-business approach to intervention. But what has caused this enlightenment? One possibility is that the joint venture assemblers have demonstrated their bargaining power to the superior governments. As the latter have found out, the joint venture assemblers do not have to make concessions on matching supplies like other Chinese enterprises. They can always overcome shortages of quality inputs with imports. Additionally, they would rather halt production to protect the product image of the foreign partners than keep the operation going by accepting inferior parts. Of course, such strategy incurs high costs to the joint venture assemblers. But in the end, local protection that hinders their development always hurts back. On the other hand, the new approach to intervention promises to broaden the sources of investment capital and stabilize tax income for the local governments. This must explain why the local Qinghai government approved FAW's offer to take over a few of its subordinate enterprises. It must have also driven the competition among the local authorities in policy liberalization.

Inspite of CNAIC's effort to impose some control for achieving coordination and quality improvement, the pressure of decentralization which the reforms have put in place will make it extremely difficult to develop a total rationalization of the automobile industry in China. Rationalization through market forces is not possible at the moment. Competition is not based on market but on the needs and ambitions of regions. The provincial governments now have the authority to bypass central regulations. For the sake of prestige or economic necessity, they strive to develop their own auto industry.

Thus, regional boundaries are getting stronger through decentralization while national boundaries are becoming porous. One of the problems which all planned economies are now facing, and China is not an exception, is that liberalization by the central government to forge linkages with the global economy is often frustrated by local autonomy and competition fostered by the local governments instead of the market. In the long run, this will create problems of standardization, and it will certainly affect China's plan to become a world-class producer of automobiles.[93] Neither the Chinese market nor the global market can sustain so many small auto producers and parts suppliers who do not possess the economy of scale and thus do not have the capacity to compete successfully in the global economy.

I am grateful to Professor Michael A. Cusumano for introducing me to the International Motor Vehicle Program (IMVP) at Massachusetts Institute of Technology, where I wrote a paper on the evolution of the Chinese automobile industry based on an earlier version of this chapter. Professor Cusumano proffered valuable comment on the content and organization of the paper. I would also like to thank Dr. Frank Schuller for securing limited funding in support of my paper. The work at IMVP enabled me to revise portions of the first and fourth chapters of this book.

NOTES

1. For culture treated as a residual rather than critical causal factor that explains the characteristics of a system as well as its performance, see Johnson (1982).

2. For how important it is first to correctly identify the nature of the systemic problems before proper policy solutions can be designed and reforms targeted, consult Drucker's comparison of the methods of policy-making and structures of operation and decision in an American versus Japanese corporation in P. Drucker, "What We Can Learn from Japanese Management," *Harvard Business Review* (March-April 1971): 110-122.

3. As an example of how the government has intervened in the Chinese economy historically, see R. Thaxton, "Peasants, Capitalism, and Revolution: On Capitalism as a Force for Liberation in Revolutionary China," *Comparative Political Studies* 12, no. 3 (October 1979): 289-334.

4. For two types of decentralization, see (Schurmann 1968, 175, 196). Indeed, decentralization during the Great Leap Forward, through the first half of the 1960s, was designed to link agriculture with industry so as to attain a more balanced development. Decentralization I and II were both experienced, sometimes jointly (Schurmann 1964).

5. For the difference between "readjustment" and "reform", see S. Ishikawa, "China's Economic Growth since 1949--An Assessment," *China Quarterly* 86: 242.

6. The coauthor distinguishes wage reform from wage adjustment. The former refers to a change in the wage structure, the latter to an increase in salary in conjunction with an adjustment in the employee's occupational rank that involves no alteration in the structure. Until 1979, China had introduced wage reform only once in 1956 (Korzec and Whyte 1981).

7. Hart's hypothesis, summarizes Winckler, goes as follows: When revolution accelerates, ideological control tightens up. This is followed by a period of relaxation when development receives more emphasis. As bureaucratization creeps in, however, revolution re-intensifies, bringing with it reorganization and ideological purge. The reorganization and purge are carried out through struggle-criticism-transformation, involving broad-based social participation (Winckler 1976).

8. "Political learning" is defined as reduction of politics in policy decision and implementation as well as institutionalization of the mechanisms for compromise and conflict resolution. This is compared to policy learning or "zero(ing) in" of a policy package that is designed to remove the developmental bottlenecks. Petrick argues that if political and policy learning occur simultaneously, then reform will succeed. The example of success is China's reform in science and technology. An example of failure is what Johnson has observed happened to previous reforms in China when non-economic objectives got the upper hand. As for the outcome of Chinese reforms in the 1980s Petrick is by no means optimistic, since politics come in and out at liberty (Petrick 1981, 108-109, 111-112, 114-118). Petrick has invited refutation of his own analysis from some economists like Ross (Ross 1986).

9. The prosperity of village and township businesses is reported by some as responsible for absorbing the labor released from agriculture, a task that otherwise has to be undertaken by urban enterprises (Pu 1990, 18-19).

10. Note that the term is defined in reference to the degree of the range and depth of reform. In his study, Jackson compares management reform in China with two levels of reform which the Eastern European countries introduced during the late 1960s and 1970s. The "conservative" model was followed by the Eastern European economies other than Hungary and Yugoslavia. This is comparable to decentralization II in Schurmann's schema of reform in China, involving "administrative decentralization" that transfers some authority for making detailed decisions to the lower level of the administrative authorities. Hungary and Yugoslavia, on the other hand, sought to reform theirs into a "socialist market" model of economy, a model which Jackson believes the Chinese copied in the early 1980s (Jackson 1986, 406-407).

11. For example, Schurmann defines the communist institutions in China in means-ends terms. He terms the party organization as "the ordered mobilization, control, and manipulation of people for certain ends" (Schurmann 1960, 47).

12. The central body was first established in 1964, but it ceased to function shortly. It was reestablished in 1982, when the central government sought to impose some control on the auto industry after introducing the

enterprise responsibility system. CAIGC took charge of the total supervisory authority over functional activities in the auto industry, ranging from research, production, sale of complete vehicles, engines, special-purpose vehicles, parts and accessories to provision of technical services and, finally, to exports and imports (Xue 1988, 45, 49).

13. Unless otherwise noted, the story on SAW in the next few paragraphs is based on Byrd (1992b, 371-426). The market risk here refers partly to SAW's decision in 1981 and 1982 to produce dump trucks outside the mandatory plan without the MMS's commitment to procurement. In its 1983 dispute with CAIGC, SAW got to retain the marketing right to one-third of the spare parts it produced while CAIGC two-thirds.

14. This paragraphs also refers to M. Weil, "Overhauling the Automotive Industry," *China Business Review (CBR)* 13, no. 4 (1986): 28-33.

15. Unless otherwise noted, the information on Dongfeng, as for SAW, the core company of the group, is based on Byrd's account (1992b).

16. For a discussion of how the Chinese industrial enterprises sought easy expansion through inflationary growth, an analysis that surely applies to the auto industry, see Iwagaki (1986).

17. The history of China's auto industry refers to Xue (Xue 1988, 33, 47, 64, 66). The "Third Front" industries were established in the 1960s and 1970s following a "defense in-depth" strategy. Enterprises were set up in the interior provinces of China away from the country's original centers of industry, the coastal provinces, and away from the Sino-Soviet border so that China would have an alternative industrial base in the event that the original centers of industry were destroyed in an armed conflict with either the United States or the Soviet Union. Because of the strategic nature of their origin, many of these factories fell under the control and administration of the central military industrial bureaucracy. See B. Naughton, "The Third Front: Defence Industrialization in the Chinese Interior," *China Quarterly* (September 1988): 351-386.

18. The first wave of decentralization in foreign economic dealings came on two levels. It included local governments as the providers of Chinese land and labor in Sino-foreign contractual negotiations. It also included the Chinese enterprises as signatories to Sino-foreign contracts. See "China's New Joint Venture Law, Xinhua, Beijing, July 8 1979," *CBR* 6, no. 4 (1979): 46-47.

19. The Automotive Research Institute was previously charged with providing technical support to the whole of China's auto industry (Xue 1988, 64. 67).

20. For examples of problems of technology transfer in the initial period of post-Mao reform, see M. Tomozo, "Sino-Japanese Joint Ventures: Taking It Slow," *CN 30* (February 1981): 14-19, and S. Sato, "Joint Ventures in China and Related Problems," *CN* (July-August 1984): 15-22.

21. *CBR* 9, no. 4 (1982): 52; *CBR* 9, no. 6 (1982): 49; *CN* 42 (1983): 22-24; *CBR 10*, no. 5 (1983): 64.

22. Also Weil, "Overhauling the Automotive Industry," *CBR* 10, no. 5 (1983): 66; CBR 11, no. 4 (1984): 57.

23. *CBR* 11, no. 4 (1984): 50; *CBR* 11, no. 5 (1984): 69; *CBR* 11, no. 6 (1984): 63; *China Trade Report (CTR)* (January 1985): 3.

24. *CBR* 12, no. 6 (1985): 60; *CBR* 13, no. 2 (1986): 54; *CTR* (November 1983): 4; Ding (1984).

25. *CBR* 12, no. 3 (1985), 55, 58; *CBR* 12, no. 6 (1985): 60; *CBR* 13, no. 2 (1986): 54; *CBR* 13, no. 4 (1986): 65; *CN* 56 (1985): 21-23.

26. *CTR* (January 1983): 3; *CBR* 10, no. 4 (1983): 51; *CBR* 12, no. 1 (1985): 68; K. Johnson, "Big Three, Chinese Officials Sweeten Partnership," *Automotive News (AN)* (19 April 1993): 3.

27. *CBR* 6, no. 5 (1979): 70; *CBR* 9, no. 1 (1982): 58, 63.

28. *CBR* 9, no. 3 (1982): 55; *CBR* 9, no. 5 (1982): 58; *CBR* 10, no. 1 (1983): 51; *CBR* 10, no. 2 (1983): 49; *CBR* 10, no. 6 (1983): 62; *CTR* (February 1983): 3.

29. *CBR* 11, no. 3 (1984): 66, 69.

30. *CBR* 12, no. 1 (1985): 68; *CBR* 12, no. 2 (1985): 59; *CBR* 12, no. 3 (1985): 54-55.

31. *CBR* 12, no. 3 (1985): 55.

32. *CBR* 12, no. 2 (1985): 59, 62; ; *CBR* 12, no. 6 (1985): 60.

33. *CBR* 11, no. 6 (1984): 64; *CBR* 12, no. 5 (1985): 66.

34. For instance, the deal on the production of O-ring seals for automobiles in Hubei in 1981 and import of the gear-making machinery for manufacturing truck transmissions at Shenyang, provincial capital of Liaoning, in 1985. See *CBR* 9, no. 1 (1982): 63; *CBR* 12, no. 3 (1985): 54.

35. *CBR* 9, no. 1 (1982): 63.

36. The output figure should be correct if it includes the output of the defense enterprises. The figure comes from that for "heavy" trucks in University of Michigan report (1989, Tab. 1.1.9).

37. *CBR* 9, no. 5 (1982): 58; *CBR* 10, no. 2 (1983): 49; *CTR* (February 1983): 3; *CBR* 12, no. 2 (1985): 59.

38. Beijing Jeep produced 24,087 jeeps; Beijing Auto Works, the Chinese partner of Beijing Jeep, made 11,805 light trucks; and Beijing Second Auto Works made 22,500 light trucks. For the output figures quoted in this paragraph, see the University of Michigan report cited previously (1989, Tab. 1.1.2, Tab. 1.1.9).

39. In 1986, the assemblers in Shenyang, Qinghai, Chongqing, and Xi'an were reportedly producing one thousand vehicles per year (Iwagaki 1986).

40. The car venture was formed in 1983-1984, but its negotiation began in 1980-1981.

41. The term is borrowed from Adachi, Ono, and Odaka (1983, 384-389). In this report, it refers merely to concentration of resources on making one or a limited number of products on the basis of some agreement among Chinese enterprises, with some of them having matching relations. This differs from the sophisticated engineering approach to production design and organization to which the same term referred when Toyota first used it in the 1930s. Product specialization in Toyota began with a decentralized structural relations. It contrasted with the Ford system that was "process specialized" and centralized in technology and production. For more discussion on this point, see the last section of this report on the transferability of "lean production."

42. *CBR* 9, no. 1 (1982): 58; *CBR* 9, no. 3 (1982): 55; *CBR* 10, no. 5 (1983): 64; *CTR* (November 1983): 4; *CBR* 11, no. 3 (1984): 66; *CBR* 12, no. 6 (1985): 60; Ding 1984.

43. *CBR* 12, no. 1 (1985): 68.

44. "Public Listing Considered for Guangzhou Peugeot," *Agence France Presse*, (1 April 1993).

45. *Interview with Hua Qi*, Beijing, January 1992. Note Hua Qi is a fictitious name adopted to maintain the anonymity of the interviewee.

46. The production of steel and pig iron, for example, fell under the jurisdiction of the Ministry of Metallurgical Industry.

47. M. Lee, "More Desired than Driven in China," *Far Eastern Economic Review (FEER)* (3 October 1985): 72-74.

48. L. Do Rosario, "Who Will Pick the Plum of a 1 Billion Market?" *FEER* (22 August 1985): 79-84.

49. *CTR* (January 1983): 3.

50. *CBR*, 15, no. 2 (1988): 62; *CBR* 15, no. 3 (1988): 64; *CBR* 15, no. 5 (1988): 61; *CBR* 15, no. 6 (1988): 52; *CBR* 16, no. 5 (1989): 69; "Hong Kong Company Sets up Office in Shanghai," *Xinhua General Overseas News Service* (3 July 1991).

51. "Daihatsu Motor to Set up Joint Venture in China," *Nikkan Kogyo Shimbun* (24 March 1993): 14; Hidenaka Kato, "Automakers Switch Focus to China," *Nikkei Weekly* (1 March 1993): 9; R. Johnson, "Isuzu Sets up China Venture to Build Trucks," *Automotive News (AN)* (15 February 1993); "Fiat's Iveco to Sign Truck Deal with China," *Reuters* (6 May 1993); K. Done, "Iveco in Talks on Joint Venture with Nanjing," *Financial Times* (5 May 1993): 6.

52. *CBR* 12, no. 3 (1985), 54; Hidenaka Kato, "Automakers Switch Focus to China," *Nikkei Weekly* (1 March 1993): 9; S. Holberton, "Rise of 21% in Per Share Earnings at CITIC Pacific," *Financial Times*, 23 April 1993, 4; "Suzuki Pact to Make Small Cars in China," *Financial Times* (6 November 1990): 8; "Suzuki to Launch Car, Motorcycle Ventures in China," *Japan Economic Newswire* (15 April 1993); R. Johnson, "Suzuki Plans China Venture," *AN* (19 April 1993): 2; "Suzuki Venture to Build Passenger Cars in China," *New York Times* (21 April 1993): Sec. A, 4.

53. R. Johnson, "Mazda to Help Increase Truck Production, Double Number of Service Outlets in China," *AN* (10 May 1993): 20; R. Johnson, "GM Maya Build APV in China," *AN* (18 January 1993): 1; A. Harmon and D. Holley, "GM Announces It Will Assemble Trucks in China," *Los Angeles Times* (16 January 1992): 5; *CBR* 19, no. 2 (1992): 44; *CBR* 17, no. 1 (1990): 59; "Mercedes Plans china Bus Production Deal," *Reuters* (7 May 1993); "Global Joint Ventures and Affiliations for 1993," *AN* (18 January 1993): 1; S. Vines and J. R. Crate, "Car-Making Again on Track, But Experts Scoff at Goals," *AN* (4 March 1993): 3; "Nissan to Set up Joint Venture to Produce Commercial Vehicles in China," *Nikkei Sangyo Shimbun* (12 March 1993): 8; *Japan Industrial Journal* (12 March 1993): 7.

54. *CBR* 13, no. 1 (1986): 61; *CBR* 13, no. 5 (1986): 58; *CBR* 15, no. 5 (1988): 61; *CBR* 15, no. 6 (1988): 52; *CBR* 16, no. 3 (1989): 52; *CBR* 17, no. 3 (1990): 58.

55. *CBR* 13, no. 2 (1986): 57; *CBR* 13, no. 6 (1986): 59; *CBR* 14, no. 5 (1987): 61;

56. R. Johnson, "Mazda to Help Increase Truck Production, Double Number of Service Outlets in China," *AN* (10 May 1993): 20; "Mazda to Assist Chinese

Firm in Truck Production," *Nikkan Kogyo Shimbun* (22 April 1993): 17; F. Gibney, "No Time to Waste on Theory," *Newsweek* (18 January 1993): 43; *CBR* 19, no. 2 (1992): 44.

57. *CBR* 13, no. 5 (1986): 60; *CBR* 13, no. 6 (1986): 61; *CBR* 14, no. 1 (1987): 58; *CBR* 14, no. 5 (1987): 61.

58. *CN* 71 (1987): 22; *CBR* 15, no. 2 (1988): 62; *CBR* 15, no. 5 (1988): 61-62; *CBR* 16, no. 1 (1989): 58.

59. *CBR* 16, no. 3 (1989): 52; *CBR* 16, no. 6 (1989): 62; *CBR* 17, no. 1 (1990): 59; *CBR* 17, no. 2 (1990): 60; *CBR* 17, no. 3 (1990): 58; D. R. Robin, "Foundry Show in China Attracts U.S. Exhibitors," *Foundry Management and Technology* 118, no. 9 (September 1990): 45.

60. *CBR* 18, no. 2 (1991): 65; *CBR* 18, no. 5 (1991): 55; *CTR* (April 1991): 13; *CTR* (September 1991): 11.

61. *CBR* 19, no. 1 (1992): 47; *CBR* 19, no. 2 (1992): 49.

62. R. Johnson, "Ford Calls China Report about Plant Premature," *AN* 3 May 1993, 22; Walker, "Ford Agrees to $90 Million Part Venture in China," *Financial Times* (23 May 1993): 30; "Nissan Diesel to Supply Chinese Firm with Bus Chassis and Truck Axle Production Technology," *COMLINE Daily News Transportation* (25 February, 1993).

63. *CBR* 13, no. 1 (1986): 61; *CBR* 13, no. 3 (1986): 72; *CBR* 13, no. 4 (1986): 65; *CBR* 13, no. 5 (1986): 58; *CBR* 16, no. 2 (1989): 58; *CTR* (April 1986): 4; *CN* 77 (1988): 64.

64. *CBR* 14, no. 2 (1987): 59; *CBR* 14, no. 4 (1987): 62; *CBR* 14, no. 6 (1987): 62; *CTR* 70 (1987): 22.

65. *CBR* 15, no. 3 (1988): 64; *CBR* 15, no. 5 (1988): 61; *CBR* 16, no. 1 (1989): 52; *CBR* 15, no. 6 (1989): 52; *CTR* (March 1988): 15.

66. *CBR* 16, no. 1 (1989): 52-53; *CBR* 16, no. 2 (1989): 58; *CBR* 16, no. 3 (1989): 52; *CTR* (April 1989): 14; *CTR* (November 1989): 14; *CBR* 17, no. 2 (1990): 60; "Magna Unit Wins Job from Chinese Auto Firm," *Toronto Star* (4 October 1990): Sec. H, 11; "China's Largest Auto Meter Production Line Operational in Jilin," *Xinhua General Overseas News Service* (15 November 1990).

67. *CBR* 19, no. 1 (1992): 49; "Hong Kong Company Sets up Office in Shanghai," *Xinhua General Overseas News Service* (3 July 1991); "China to Build Largest Automobile Bearing Factory," *Xinhua General Overseas News Service* (17 September 1991).

68. "Nissan Diesel to Supply Chinese Firm with Bus Chassis and Truck Axle Production Technology," *Nikkan Kogyo Shimbun* (24 February 1993): 15; "A Growing Asian Market," *Business Times* (24 May 1993).

69. *CTR* (January 1991): 11-12; "Global Joint Ventures and Affiliations for 1993," *Automotive Industries* 173, no. 2 (February 1993): 17; "VW to Increase Investment in Shanghai," *Agence France Presses* (21 October 1991); "Germany--VW to Expand Production," Xinhua news Agency, Peking *BBC Summary of World Broadcasts* (6 November 1991). S. Vines and J. R. Crate, "Car-Making Again on Track, But Experts Scoff at Goals," *AN* (4 March 1993): 3.

70. "Automakers Switch Focus to China"; S. Vines and J. R. Crate, "Car-Making Again on Track, But Experts Scoff at Goals," *AN* (4 March 1993): 3; "Hong Kong Company Sets up Office in Shanghai," *Xinhua General Overseas News Service* (3 July 199)1; "Suzuki to Enter China's Auto Market," *Japan*

Economic Newswire (5 November 1990); "Suzuki Pact to Make Small Cars in China," *Financial Times* (6 November 1990): 8; *CBR* 18, no. 2 (1991): 67.

71. *CBR* 13, no. 6 (1986): 61; *CTR* (September 1991): 11; *CBR* 18, no. 5 (1991): 55; R. Johnson, "Ford Calls China Report about Plant Premature," *AN* 3 May 1993, 22.

72. R. Johnson, "Ford Calls China Report about Plant Premature," *AN* 3 May 1993, 22.

73. *CBR* 13, no. 6 (1986): 61.

74. *CBR* 12, no. 3 (1985): 58; *CBR* 16, no. 1 (1989): 53.

75. "China's Largest Auto Meter Production Line Operational in Jilin," *Xinhua General Overseas News Service* (15 November 1990); "China to Build Largest Automobile Bearing Factory," *Xinhua General Overseas News Service* (17 September 1991); *CBR* 16, no. 3 (1989): 52.

76. M. Gurtov, "Swords into Market Shares: China's conversion of Military Industry to Civilian Production," *China Quarterly* (June 1993): 213-241.

77. Interviewed with Qiang Hua, Beijing, January 1992. Again, the name is fictitious to maintain the anonymity of the interviewee.

78. "No.1 Auto Plant Absorbs Three Qinghai Plants," *Xinhua General Overseas News Service* (13 March 1991); "No.1 Auto Plant Annex Mini-Vehicle Plant," *Xinhua General Overseas News Service* (28 June 1991).

79. Interviewed with Qiang Hua, Beijing, January 1992.

80. Interviewed with Hua Qi, Beijing, January 1992.

81. Interviewed with Qiang Hua, Beijing, January 1992.

82. L. Do Rasorio, "State Industrial Bosses Sign on for Profits," *FEER* (8 September 1988): 132-133; S. Vines, "Car Import Business Slips into Top Gear," *South China Morning Post* (28 March 1993): 3; "No Time to Waste on Theory," *Newsweek* (18 January 1993): 43; C. Raj, "China Companies Set for Listing on Singapore Exchange," *Business Times* (11 March 1993): 1.

83. These include the Three Bigs, in addition to the Three Smalls and probably Nanjing-Iveco and Changan-Suzuki. For the counts cited here, see S. Vines, "Industry Tastes Life in Fast Lane," *South China Morning Post* (28 March 1993): 3.

84. Interviewed with Hua Qi, Beijing, January 1992.

85. The State Planning Commission had reduced its control of the outputs of enterprises under the government's mandatory planning to ten to twenty percent of the total by the end of 1988. It had shifted control over the remaining 80-90 percent to the local authorities instead of enterprises. But the local governments turned out to be more rigid in administration. While they were now responsible for securing much of their inputs, comparable with their autonomy in production planning, marketing and so on, the enterprises found they had to listen to the local authorities. See Do Rasorio, "Too Many Cooks," *FEER* (8 September 1988): 128-130.

86. For consolidation, see J. Karp, "Back on the Road," *FEER* (26 March 1992): 49-50; Yuichi Takayama, "The Chinese Automobile Industry," *CN* 94 (September-October 1991): 16-21. To effectively support the localization programs of the joint venture assemblers, which China has already adopted 60 percent domestic content rule. That is, if the domestic content reaches A 60 percent then an assembler would be entitled to preferential tariff treatment

instead of having to pay 120 percent tariffs on the imported knockdown inputs. For 120 percent rate, see "No Time to Waste on Theory," *Newsweek* (18 January 1993): 43; Raj, "China Companies Set for Listing on Singapore Exchange," *Business Times* (11 March 1993): 1. For 60 percent domestic content rule, see "GATT Would Bring New challenge for China's auto Industry," *Xinhua General News Service* (22 November 1992).

87. China is certainly walking extra miles to ensure the success of the targeted joint ventures. At a conference on how China may work out the role of the state in managing the economy sponsored by the State Planning Commission in May 1993, China's President Jiang Zemin even consulted Carl Hahn, Chairman of Volkswagen, on the German view of China's reform. "China to Learn Foreign Experience in Market Economy: Jiang," *Xinhua General News Service* (12 May 1993).

88. L. Do Rasorio, "Driven away," *FEER*, (9 November 1989): 60; *Interviewed with Qiang Hua*, Beijing, January 1992.

89. The Chinese boast of having raised Cherokee's domestic content to 61 percent. See "Parts of Cherokee Jeep Made in China," *Xinhua General Overseas News Service* (20 February 1993).

90. *Interviewed with Hua Qi*, Beijing, January 1992.

91. "No.1 Auto Plant Absorbs Three Qinghai Plants," *Xinhua General Overseas News Service* (14 March 1991).

92. "Wuhan to Set up First Inland Bonded Warehouse," *Xinhua General Overseas News Service* (25 March 1993). Wuhan pioneered the trend of privatization in 1992 by allowing Hong Kong investors to buy up some of the local factories. The city then sent a delegation to Singapore, headed by officials of the local bureau of the Foreign Economic Relations and Trade Commission, to invite more capital to come in. Wuhan has targeted Singapore because its investors rank among the most aggressive in participating in China's privatization drive. One of them, Oei Hong Leong, reportedly took over 41 state enterprises in Fujian's Quanzhou and has formed a joint venture to buy 101 plants in Dalian in northeast China. In comparison, Wuhan had 11 deals with Singapore by early 1993. See Y. P. Ang, "Wuhan Woos Singapore Businessmen to Buy Its State Industries," *Business Times* (11 March 1993): 11; "Guangzhou Free Trade Zone to Focus on Re-Export Trade," *Xinhua General News Service* (17 April 1993).

93. China is attempting to narrow the gap between itself and world-class auto makers to ten years of difference when its total annual output hits three million at the turn of the century, with car production taking up two millions, or sixty-five percent (Table 4.1). See "China to Make Auto Industry Its Pillar," *Xinhua General News Service* (19 February 1993).

Chapter Five

The Evolving Automobile Industry in a Global Economy

In the post-Cold War world, conflicts and policy prescriptions for containing and resolving these conflicts are no longer as clear-cut as they used to be. Several reasons account for this change. In the first place, political conflicts are becoming harder and harder to resolve, because as long as they do not pose a direct threat, no nation wants to make the sacrifices and expend the financial resources to intervene or impose its own notion of the international rules. But more importantly, the world is now concentrating on the economic relations and management of the trade conflicts. It is in this area that nations are showing policy ambivalence.

On the one hand, they want to expand the global economy and tear down the economic boundaries by promoting free trade and reducing both tariff and non-tariff barriers. On the other hand, they want to protect either technological superiority or weak industries so as to safeguard national prosperity. Sometimes, this leads them to ambivalent and contradictory stands and policies. While they would like to expand trade and reduce or even eliminate economic nationalism, they are prepared to indulge in managed trade to resolve trade conflicts. Managed trade is generally used to protect economic boundaries and ensure national economic well-being as a high priority. The global economy, in comparison, tends to progress toward elimination of these boundaries. To some extent, it has succeeded in making them porous.

To be sure, there are always some conflicts between technonationalism and technoglobalism (Stevens 1990) in both purpose and policy. While the demands of the political economy and national security favor technonationalism, the need for corporate strategic alliances and economic competition will support technoglobalism. Further, there is some element of technoglobalism in every aspect of a modern industry. But some industries are more prone to depend on it than others. Automobile manufacturing is such an industry. Indeed, a major evolution in this industry has been that it is becoming more and more difficult to identify a purely national automotive product.

In the 1950s and 1960s, the extension of the value chain necessitated by fierce national competition made it necessary for the location of parts production to be based mostly on labor costs, labor peace, and other economic incentives. In the 1970s and 1980s, managed trade forced many automobile producers to further locate transplants in major consumer markets. Whether these transplants are established for market advantage and whether parts production is established for the extension of the value chain, neither involves simply an export of capital and technology. It is also an export of the corporate culture as well as organizational and management styles, which is ultimately more important than winning the competition in the domestic market of the other societies.

Economic strength, therefore, has in some cases become less important than organizational strength. The transplants have generally not only changed the interfirm relationship between assemblers and domestic parts suppliers, but also forced the domestic assemblers of the host countries to at least incorporate some of the interfirm linkages transferred by the transplants to compete successfully. It is, indeed, in diffusion of the management of interfirm structural relations more than elimination of the tariffs and non-tariff barriers that the globalization of the economy has led to the porousness of national economic boundaries.

As the world moves to the end of the twentieth century, the need for strategic alliances in the auto industry is becoming more and more critical, with computers, electronics, and other high-tech innovations being increasingly integrated into the auto manufacturing process. Three or four decades ago, such alliances were practically non-existent, because the world automobile industry was dominated by less than a dozen producers. These companies only assembled outside their national boundaries to enter foreign national markets. They limited their competition to third countries while retaining dominance in domestic markets. Strategic alliances have become possible only when both sides have something to contribute, especially in the area of technology. In pursuit of competitiveness in technology, innovative and strong auto companies increasingly turn to strategic alliances with their counterparts of equal capabilities.

This has led to technoglobalism, resulting in a difficulty in identifying a product in this industry as having 100 percent domestic content.   As brand names have evolved, they no longer coincide with national identity. On the other hand, technonationalism insists on promoting national competitiveness. It resents the growing separation of brand names from national identity. The pressure of the political economy to maintain national living standards as well as conserve and promote jobs is also forcing strong competitors to agree to managed trade, as in the case of voluntary export restraints against the Japanese.

Nowadays, managed trade is often practiced in the name of unfair competition and opening of closed markets. Top competitors like the Japanese companies are asked to import products from other societies while being forced to transplant their manufacturing operations into most societies in the world in order to meet the demands of national economic policies and politics. Yet measures like these that are designed to solve the problems of the political economy do not necessarily solve those concerning preservation of national boundaries--an original intent of managed trade. Indeed, national boundaries have become porous not only through transplants, which have affected interfirm relationships in both Europe and the United States, but also through policies like numerical quotas and pressure to improve imports of automotive parts, which have begun to influence the traditional culture of interfirm relations between parts suppliers and assemblers in Japan.

In international relations, there has always been a misunderstanding of international trade negotiations. Broadly speaking, most countries can be divided into two categories. On one side are countries like Japan which consider international trade as simply a matter of economic rationality. To them, the question is how to conduct a commercial relationship. On the other side, there are countries like the United States to whom economic relationships in the global economy involve more than trade or commerce. They are also for diplomacy and maintenance of a superpower aura. Therefore, negotiations on managed trade between these parties have become more and more difficult.

To the Chinese, and to most of Asian countries, the linking of the commercial relations to other goals such as human rights constitutes unwarranted interference in their domestic affairs. In contrast, the United States believes in linking these two objectives and in using trade to advance its diplomatic and national foreign policy objectives. The same holds true for numerical quotas and other similar demands. Yet diplomatic and ideological goals on the one hand and trade on the other have to be separated in a global economy. This is why corporate goals and actions often diverge from national policy objectives.

Corporations, left to themselves, would like to pursue economic rationality in the context of an increasingly global economy. They generally base their decisions to form strategic alliances and joint ventures on market considerations. In fact, corporations care more about freedom to invest and market their products than about the nature of the political system or the relationship of a particular government with its own citizens. The needs of the global economy, therefore, are always under some tension from the needs of national and foreign policy objectives. Certainly, this tension has been a major force in promoting ambivalence in national policy, as well as contradictory statements and results.

An example is the de-linking of the most-favored-nation status (MFN) from annual human rights certification. Such a de-linking can reduce ambivalence and contradictions as well as the need to retreat on stated national goals. Corporate interests demand such a de-linking and to some extent one can argue that globalization of the economy is slowly taking precedence over the promotion of national and ideological or policy goals. This is becoming evident in countries as far apart as China, India and the United States. If this trend continues, global linkages will increasingly dominate international relations, rendering national economic boundaries less and less relevant.

Until 1960, the automobile industry was predominately the preserve of the United States and a few western European countries. In organizational culture and interfirm relationships, most of them took their cue from either Ford or GM. Even communist countries like the Soviet Union and China mostly followed the two American auto builders in industrial organization. A sustainable auto industry remained the mark of an advanced industrial society. As such, it was difficult for other societies to compete through national auto industries.

Most of the non-European nations in the early postwar period either had colonial status or did not possess the capital and technology to develop an auto industry of their own. Multinationals in this industrial sector generally established assembly operations when national economic policies forced them to do so. A prime example was a country like Mexico. Even then, the bargaining power still rested with the multinationals rather than national economies of the lesser developed countries. The only non-Western country to enter this highly competitive arena was Japan. Most of the Japanese auto industry had not, however, evolved for the market or commercial sector. It had developed, instead, by supplying Japan's armed forces in the pre-WWII era and American forces in the Korean War period. The transition to passenger cars and commercial success in the postwar period needed, therefore, the combined effort of government policy makers and automobile companies.

The most successful company in the Japanese case turned out to be Toyota. Toyota had relied on its own capacity in product and process innovation, developed partly through forging a new paradigm in interfirm relationships. Through the process of associated learning and lean production method such as JIT, Toyota eventually became the quintessential Japanese auto company. Toyota not only became the most successful Japanese auto assembler, but also a formidable competitor to established auto companies in both the United States and Europe.

The transition which the Japanese auto companies made from producing military vehicles to civilian passenger cars was, of course, not an easy one. In some ways, it can be compared to the difficulties which most nations are facing in making successful transition from building military aircraft to building civilian airplanes. Decades later, the Japanese are using their capital and technology to help to proliferate auto production in several countries in the Pacific Rim. It has become increasingly easier for the lesser developed countries to have an auto industry with a relatively high level of domestic content. This proliferation in some cases, as in Malaysia, aims primarily to serve its regional market. In Korea, in comparison, it has developed to export in the lower end of the world market.

While the Japanese have changed the rules of interfirm relationships and, to a great extent, the nature of international competition in the automobile industry, many established multinationals in the western world are facing mounting difficulties. For example, the European car makers from Mercedes Benz to Saab and from Fiat to Renault and Volkswagen have had to seriously consider reorganization and protection mostly as a result of the Japanese competition. The British car industry has, on the other hand, become either foreign-owned or remains non-competitive. In the United States, a decade of heavy losses has also rendered extensive re-organization necessary. The U. S. automobile industry has had to abandon the egocentric and parochial thinking of GM as expressed by its Chairman in his famous 1952 statement "What's good for GM is good for the country." All of the U. S. automobile manufacturers have, in fact, had to establish joint ventures or adopt some form of interfirm relationship basically on the Toyota paradigm.

Recently, American auto makers are returning to profitability, but this has happened mostly to trucks and sports utility vehicles. They still have to struggle in the passenger car area. Evidence like this demonstrates that there are limits to the porousness of national boundaries. One can adopt, to some extent, the organizational framework and modes of lean production, but learning and reskilling have not been as easy and successful as generally assumed. This points to the necessity for more in-depth comparative study of the Japanese transplants and restructured American auto manufacturing plants.

While globalization has made national economic boundaries porous, the nature of interfirm relations has not become totally susceptible to external influences. Neither a universal nor global model has emerged nor have historically isolated national organizational relationships have endured. For a time, it may have appeared that the Japanese model would be utilized by everyone to some extent, as in the early period of the evolution of the automobile industry when the American model of mass production and interfirm relations were at least universally considered. What globalization has achieved, however, is to cause the impact of different national models on each other, loosening historical ties as well as national characteristics.

Thus, American corporations have had to look at semi-competitive long-term relationships with suppliers while moving towards some form of associated learning. By contrast, the Japanese are having a great deal of difficulty in keeping intact largely monopsonic relationships between assemblers and their suppliers. The suppliers can deal with other major customers now, including long-term national competitors, as in the case of Nippon Denso, which has finally received a green light to supply Nissan, Toyota's main rival. Nor can the Japanese maintain JIT in the national market as in the past, because of traffic jams and related difficulties in moving goods and services on demand. The ability of suppliers to expand their client base will therefore eventually affect the process of associated learning, the fundamental characteristic of historical relationship in the Japanese auto industry. Instead, neither the Japanese nor the Americans will be able to maintain the same interfirm relations, as global linkages continue to increase and the pressure of global competition, managed trade, and responsible economic behavior combine to force some form of accommodation on all societies.

Lastly, the Japanese automobile industry took shape in a developmental mode when Japan was trying to catch up with the other industrialized countries. In the developmental mode, there was considerable government-industry collaboration in the general economy and, to a great extent, government dictation and assignment of industrial functions and roles. This, however, is no longer possible, because Japan is no longer in the mode of catching up. A primary reason explaining Japan's continuing conflicts with a number of trading partners lies in the fact that what was acceptable from it in the developmental period is no longer acceptable after it has become a prime competitor.

In response, the Japanese auto industry has introduced significant change. First, more and more of its automobile production is located outside Japan now. This may result in a "hollowing out" of the Japanese industrial revolution. To compensate, the Japanese may have to move toward more advanced knowledge-based products. If they do so, then methods of production and relationships between management and labor, as well as between man and machine, will also significantly change. If Japanese industry hollows out, however, then Japan would find it difficult to continue to maintain nearly full lifetime employment as well as non-adversarial relationship between its management and labor.

Yet neither Japan nor the United States is really prepared at the moment for a society based on the knowledge revolution. By themselves, they are also unprepared to introduce very high-tech products in the auto industry. Both, therefore, need strategic alliances, because both will have difficulties in finding those workers who can produce such knowledge-intensive products. Indeed, the American auto companies are even having problems in finding an adequate number of engineers, because the American educational system is not producing enough technically skilled and advanced knowledge-intensive graduates. The Japanese system, in comparison, does not produce enough people who can analyze information and data to decide effectively on investment and aid projects. Finally, both societies are reaching a point where the growth of the domestic market will be limited. Neither will be able to sustain or increase its level of production for markets experiencing slow growth.

In the case of China, its reforms have neither eliminated the major aspects of the planned economy nor institutionalized their relationship between the center and periphery. Throughout the history of the People's Republic, it is the political center that has adjusted the relationship between the two levels of the decision-making units. Reforms have tried to give more freedom and flexibility to both the provinces and individual enterprises. But such freedom has at times led to somewhat runaway growth, inflation, and an uncoordinated national automobile industry. The central regulatory agencies have been unable to stop or control the provinces from developing their own auto industry. It seems that, in the 1980s, any growth was encouraged over systematic evaluation of the long-term aspects of chaotic growth.

It has been pointed out that the global auto assemblers have generally sought to forge investment partnerships with emerging and fast-developing economies by shifting production of standardized products to the domestic partners in these economies. This enables the global assemblers to stretch out the product life cycle by extending the life cycle of past innovations. For this reason, those countries which can help the global auto assemblers to recover past R&D costs are generally chosen as the recipients of technology transfer. China seems to fit the criteria for such transfer.

As they arrive with intra-industry investment and trade, the global linkages have not only affected Chinese assembly operations, but also their parts suppliers. Joint ventures in parts and components manufacturing that have mushroomed since the late 1980s have also led to accelerated localization and increased domestic content.

Thanks to globalization, structural relations between the auto makers and suppliers are changing not only in the United States and Japan, but also in the People's Republic of China.

In the past, China had very high barriers in the automotive supply chain. Unlike Japan, where the barriers resulted from a non-hierarchical method of managing contractual relations in the market, the barriers in China were erected by the government through regulation of relations between suppliers and auto assemblers. The indicator of any major structural change in China will, therefore, have to be whether auto manufacturers have the freedom and authority to purchase parts and supplies from the firms of their own choice instead of assigned enterprises.

It is fair to say that the structural relationship never significantly changed before the period of reforms in the 1980s, because the government always controlled the inputs or supplies. In periods of decentralization, the provincial and municipal governments took control of the industrial enterprises within their geographical administrative boundaries to promote import substitution production locally, including automotive parts makers. This explains why reforms in the past always gave rise to a "cellularized" pattern of trade between the auto makers and local parts and inputs suppliers without affecting the fixed nature of the matching relations in the national economy. The pattern received further reinforcement from the auto makers who sought integration in production in the periods of decentralization so as to reduce uncertainty of supplies and control the quality of the products.

In the first half of the 1980s, the Chinese auto makers did gain limited flexibility in procurement under such deals as compensation arrangements, but this involved only the above-plan portion of the production. As partnership with the global auto makers began to make inroads, the fixed relations between the Chinese auto assemblers and their suppliers were finally affected. The foreign partners demanded and secured control of the quality of inputs in exchange for providing capital and automobile technology. They would maintain knockdown assembly as long as the Chinese suppliers remain unable to meet the quality standards necessary for preserving the brandname image of the foreign auto producers. By the mid-1980s, the joint venture assemblers started to pursue a policy of nationwide bidding instead of sourcing with the regular matching suppliers of the Chinese partners. The local governments of those areas that were losing the matching deals were, of course, not happy with this situation, because they wanted to keep the parts supplies, jobs and tax revenues within their own geographical jurisdiction.

With rising global linkages, furthermore, the Chinese suppliers became exposed to the competitive pressure of the world market. This also highlighted the structural relations as well as domestic parts production as the key bottleneck in the expansion of auto assembly. The structural bottleneck has, indeed, hampered transfer of the mass production technology, and dampened international balance of payments. It has also made it necessary for China to switch to a national automobile industry strategy.

In the early 1990s, such a national automotive strategy began to emerge. The central government has begun to limit its role to supervising the consolidation of assembly operations and coordinating complementary development of the automobile and related industries. Within the auto industry itself, it has designated a few assemblers as candidates for establishing specialized production of such selected categories of motor vehicles as small cars, light trucks, and heavy-duty trucks. At the same time, it has left it largely to the joint venture assemblers to determine vendor selection criteria. The joint venture assemblers have thus gained some control of local procurement of parts and components. Increasingly, they are able to demand that supplier plants move towards standardization and specialization of production both to improve product quality and to achieve cost efficiency.

The entry of the joint venture assemblers has, therefore, had a great impact on Chinese automobile production. They have opened up equity investment in parts supply, thereby triggering competition among matching suppliers under the protection of local governments and forcing them to reorganize and change. The matching suppliers have to make the necessary changes to compete with joint venture suppliers as well as meet the demands of joint venture assemblers. Increasingly, the nature of the competition in the intermediate inputs market is also affecting both the administrative boundaries and interfirm relationships between auto assemblers and parts suppliers. To compete with limited funds in the quality and scale of parts and components production, local governments have had to select a few enterprises in which to concentrate their investment in support of modernization programs.

Global linkages have also compelled local governments to re-draw their geographical administrative boundaries to cooperate and regulate regional administrative markets. The joint venture assemblers are forcing them to lower territorial barriers and accept that parts supplies will cross the boundaries of the regional markets as well as erode the boundaries between defense and civilian industries.

In sum, global linkages are affecting all three economies of the United States, Japan, and China (Table 5.1). In the United States, individualistic competition in the intermediate market is increasingly being replaced by cooperation and associated learning, as between auto assemblers and suppliers. The Japanese auto assemblers, in comparison, have had to adjust the boundaries of the keiretsu system, which in turn is reducing the intensity of their relationships with the suppliers in the respective family groups while opening up the opportunity for alliances with world-class suppliers from other national economies. In China, partnership with global auto assemblers has helped Chinese manufacturers to break away from the control of the government and move towards procuring supplies from the enterprises of their own choice. The Chinese are also finally reducing the constraints of the local administrative barriers.

Table 5.1
Globalization and Change
in Manufacturer-Supplier Relations

	Historical Ideal Type	Under Globalization
U.S.:	individualistic market competition	collaborative competition and associated learning
Japan:	group-oriented collaborative competition and associated learning	reduction of keiretsu barriers in supplies
China:	fixed relationship under government assignment	reduction of government administrative barriers in supplies

For an emerging economy like China that wants to promote linkages with the global economy, an important question remains how much it is prepared to redraw interfirm relationships in order to achieve the objective of technology transfer. Although global linkages demand significant organizational change in all societies, emerging economies like China are at a much greater disadvantage, having less capacity to resist the demands for such change. Such societies do not possess the technological bargaining power to form a strategic alliance and run against the technonationalism of the advanced industrial societies.

Technonationalism tries to promote strategic trade theory, a theory which combines the principles of classical comparative advantage and industrial policy into an argument for promoting national competitiveness in technology. It believes that technology constitutes a critical factor endowment that determines the nations' positions in the global division of labor. From this perspective, countries like China are not graded very high in the hierarchy of the global division of labor. Moreover, these countries find it harder and harder to improve their relative position in the hierarchy of the global economy, because the physical inputs which in the past provided them with their comparative advantage are becoming less and less critical for national competitiveness.

Recently, there has been a growing attempt to argue that the lower level of costs in the emerging economies is achieved by suppressing labor's right to organize and violating fundamental human rights. Countries like China and other emerging economies look upon this argument as evidence of economic nationalism and protectionism promoted to deal a serious blow to the only comparative advantage they have. Though the use of technology as an instrument of diplomacy has considerably weakened in the post-Cold War era, it still poses an asymmetrical trading and investment paradigm disadvantageous to these emerging economies. To offset this disadvantage and increase their bargaining power to some extent, they try to take advantage of the competition between various multinational companies.

Many advanced economies are also using technonationalist policies to counteract negative employment effects from business restructuring. At times, they have promoted "buy national" movements as well as formation of regional free trade blocs. Yet the success of the technonationalist policies is by no means certain. This is because no government policy can substitute the domestic structural change necessary for realizing competitiveness in product and process innovation. If the comparative advantage is no longer in price competition with static product life cycles in relatively protected national markets and if corporations must, instead, depend on global linkages as the determinants of competitiveness, then they must aim for corporate comparative advantage rather than promoting national ideology.

For this reason, global corporations at times may find their policy position at odds with those of their headquarters' governments. They seek and select strategic alliances on the basis of their own interests instead of promoting certain foreign policy goals. Their interests dictate that they team up with those candidates who can pool internal know-how, human resources and capital needed for carrying on radical innovation. They also seek partners which can share market risks, provide market access, and allow them to recover R&D costs. In their selection criteria, therefore, national identity and past historical animosities do not have any place.

Technoglobalism promotes competition among global corporations through networks of alliances in every aspect of the global value chain. This includes R&D, intermediate parts and components sourcing, production and trade in technology, and the final products carried out across the national boundaries. The fundamental reason for the rise of technoglobalism remains, however, the radical nature of the technological competition, which progresses at an accelerating pace with escalating costs as well as consequent risks, rendering it impossible for any corporation to undertake on its own all the product and process innovations necessary. The competitive pressures of both market and technology, therefore, dictate that corporations turn to technoglobalism. But at the same time, they endorse technonationalist policies to a limited extent. Indeed, corporations want protectionist assistance from their respective national governments, as long as corporate competitiveness remains in question.

Thus, not only governments but also corporations show ambivalence and contradictions in the period of transforming from a purely national to a global economy. All nations try to promote such advanced factor endowments as human capital, high-tech infrastructure, and an innovative supply industry to maintain domestic prosperity and technonationalist superiority. On the other hand, global corporations would rather have the freedom to pursue a technoglobalist perspective to achieve their competitive advantage. They believe that the advanced resources necessary for their survival and success must be pooled from wherever they are located. Transborder alliances have thus become a critical factor in competitiveness. By pooling global resources, such corporations have the technology and capital to bargain successfully their terms of entry in the emerging economies when the latter greatly needs external investment and technology transfer to close the economic and technological gap both in their own domestic arena and with the advanced industrial nations. China is in such a position, with one of its bargaining points being its ability to let these corporations compete against themselves.

During the Cold War, economic conflicts were generally subordinated to ideological conflicts. It was for this reason that several Pacific Rim countries, including Japan, were given favorable access to the American market in return for diplomatic and foreign policy cooperation and coordination. But with the end of the Cold War, ideological conflicts have become less clear. Instead, trade and economic conflicts are now becoming more and more pronounced. In addition, there are arising what Professor Huntingon (1993) characterizes as "civilizational conflicts" which could see national and regional cultures predominate over globalization of the economy. Some have thus begun to argue that U. S. interests and economic cooperation should lie with Europe and not with Asia. This is another way of saying that, from the point of view of cultural values, societal organization and national interaction, the United States and Europe should become closer allies, which would find expression in their economic ties. The trade conflict between them should therefore be muted for the sake of larger civilizational interests.

Others argue, on the other hand, that the mature economies in Europe and the United States have reached their peak. While their growth prospects will remain modest, the fastest economic growth will occur in Asian societies. This is not only because most of the world's population resides there, but also because, in a period of rapid economic change, income distribution in these societies is fueling the growth of the affluent middle class. Indeed, the growth of such a middle class, with purchasing power rivaling that in the advanced economies in the west is becoming increasingly apparent in Southeast Asia and the Pacific Rim. But even poorer economies such as India, Indonesia and China now have a combined middle class greater than the entire population of the United States. If one looks at purchasing power instead of per capita income, then one will see, further, the emergence of a vast market. This is precisely why worldwide global investors are favoring these societies.

Ten or fifteen years ago, most of these societies had very little economic interaction among themselves. They were still an extension of the colonial period, trading bilaterally with the west. It was in that period when bilateral managed trade was the most effective. But intra-Asian investment and trade are rapidly increasing, as reflected in several Asian countries' decisions to take a more independent position versus the United States and its demands for managed trade. There is growing self-confidence among them as well as a continuous assertion that the civilizational differences between Asia and the rest of the world must be taken into account when the latter makes political and diplomatic demands or insists on any particular method of economic management.

Thus, China would not retreat on the stand that human rights is an internal matter. Similarly, Singapore would not retreat on the enforcement of its national laws. Most Asian countries would not support the idea of linking trade with human rights or political interference of any sort. In contrast, the United States has had to retreat on this issue by de-linking political goals and trade.

If the hypothesis of civilizational conflicts should gain widespread acceptance, it could result in regional trade blocs, with some degree of hostility expressed in civilizational terms towards other blocs. This could mean a widening of policy differences between corporations which want to build and maintain strategic alliances and governments which are moving towards civilizational solidarity. It would also mean a slowing down of the global linkages witnessed in the last decade or so.

But most analysts have missed a very important fact, namely, that Asian economies are again increasingly revolving around Japan. What the Japanese were not able to win with military force they have gained by divorcing politics and trade and continuously expanding their financial and industrial investment in other parts of Asia. In this exercise, the Japanese have refrained from practicing political interference. They make their investment decisions basically on purely economic grounds. Time-honored as it is, this Japanese policy is nonetheless encountering some difference this time: Japan has several Asian competitors for intra-Asian investment nowadays.

Since the future of globalization depends on how the contradictions between corporate and national policies will be resolved, the future of any industry for the next decade or so is hard to predict. If ideological conflicts are to be replaced by civilizational assertions leading to interference and, finally, to a new Cold War, then economic conflicts may result in further political tensions.

But the vast potential market continues to lure the European, American and Japanese auto companies increasingly to develop joint ventures or production facilities in various parts of Asia, including China. This would provide the major source of expansion in the world's automobile production in the long run. In the immediate future, these corporations will continue to use Asian locations for exporting either parts or assembled vehicles to take advantage of their comparative advantage in the costs of labor and raw materials. In the foreseeable future, however, it does not matter whether global linkages are forged or whether regional boundaries are established, because these corporations have already established their presence within various national and regional boundaries. This is where the maximum growth will lie between now and 2010.

Bibliography

Abernathy, W. J. *The Productivity Dilemma: Roadblock to Innovation in the Automobile Industry*. Baltimore: Johns Hopkins University Press. 1978.

Abernathy, W. J. A Dynamic Approach to the Problems of the Automobile Industry. Cambridge, Mass.: Center for Policy Alternatives. Mimeographed. 1981.

Abernathy, W. J. , K. B. Clark, and A. M. Kantrow. *Industrial Renaissance*. New York : Basic Books. 1983.

Adachi, F., K. Ono, and K. Odaka. Ancillary Firm Development in the Japanese Automobile Industry. In *The Motor Vehicle Industry in Asia: A Study of Ancillary Firm Development in Asia*, ed. E. Odaka, 325-396. Singapore: Singapore University Press. 1983.

Aguayo, R. *Dr. Deming*. New York: Simon & Schuster. 1990.

Allen, G. C. The Development of Industrial Combinations. In *The Industrialization of Japan and Manchukuo: 1930-1940*, ed. E. Schumpeter, 680-740. New York: Macmillan. 1940.

Anderson, J. C., and J. A. Narus. Partnership as a Focused Marketing Strategy. *California Management Reviews* (Spring): 95-113. 1991.

Andors, S. Factory Management and Political Ambiguity, 1961-63. *China Quarterly* 59: 435-476. 1974.

Andors, S. *China's Industrial Revolution: Politics, Planning, and Management, 1949 to the Present*. New York: Pantheon. 1977.

Andrea, D., M. Everett, and D. Luria. Automobile Company Parts Sourcing: Implications for Michigan Suppliers. *AIM Newsletter* 3, no. 2. 1988.

Aoki, M. ed. *The Economic Analysis of the Japanese Firm*. Amsterdam: North-Holland. 1984.

Aoki, M. Horizontal vs. Vertical Information Structure of the Firm. *American Economic Review* (December): 971-983. 1986.

Arnett, H., and D. Smith. *The Tool and Die Industry: Problems and Prospects*. Michigan Business Reports, New Series: 1. Ann Arbor: University of

Michigan. 1974.

Asanuma, B. Manufacturer-Supplier Relationships in Japan and the Concept of Relation-Specific Skills. *Journal of Japanese and International Economic Studies* 3: 1-30. 1989.

Ash, R. S. The Evolution of Agricultural Policy. *China Quarterly* 116: 525-555. 1988.

Baark, E. Commercialized Technology Transfer in China 1981-1986: The Impact of Science and Technology Policy Reforms. *China Quarterly* 111: 390-406. 1987.

Baranson, J. Transnational Strategic Alliances: Why, What, Where and How *Multinational Business* 2 (Summer): 54-61. 1990.

Barnet, R. J., and J. Cavanagh. *Imperial Corporations and the New World Order*. New York: Simon & Schuster. 1994.

Blechmer, M., and M. Meisner. Economic Growth and Equality in Rural China. *Comparative Political Studies* 13, no. 4: 505-527. 1981.

Bressand, A. Beyond Interdependence: 1992 as a Global Challenge. *International Affairs* 66, no.1: 47-65. 1990.

Broadbridge, S. *Industrial Dualism in Japan*. Chicago: Aldine Publishing Company. 1966.

Burt, D. N. Managing Product Quality through Strategic Purchasing. *Sloan Management Review* 30, no. 3 (Spring): 39-48. 1989.

Burt, D. N. , and W. R. Soukup. Purchasing's Role in New Product Development. *Harvard Business Review* (September-October): 90-97. 1985.

Byrd, W. A. Chinese Industrial Reform. In *Chinese Industrial Firms under Reform*, ed. W. A. Byrd, 1-32. Washington D. C.: Oxford University Press. 1992a.

Byrd, W. A. The Second Motor Vehicle Manufacturing Plant. In *Chinese Industrial Firms under Reform*, ed. W. A. Byrd, 371-426. Washington D. C.: Oxford University Press. 1992b.

Carlton, D. Vertical Integration in Competitive Markets under Uncertainty. *Journal of Industrial Economics* 27: 189-209. 1979.

Chamberlain, H. B. Party-Management Relations in Chinese Industries: Some Political Dimensions of Economic Reform. *China Quarterly* 112: 631-661. 1986.

Chandler, A. D., Jr. *Strategy and Structure: Chapters in the History of the Industrial Enterprise*. Cambridge, Mass.: MIT Press. 1962.

Chandler, A. D., Jr. *Giant Enterprise: Ford, General Motors, and the Automobile Industry: Sources and Reading*. New York: Harcourt Brace & World. 1964.

Chandler, A. D., Jr. *The Visible Hand : The Managerial Revolution in American Business*. Cambridge, Mass.: Belknap Press. 1977.

Chandler, A. D., Jr. with assistance of Takashi Hikino. *Scale and Scope: the Dynamics of Industrial Capitalism*. Cambridge, Mass.: Belknap Press of Harvard University. 1990.

Cheng, C. Y. Growth and Structural Changes in the Chinese Machine-Building Industry, 1952-1966. *China Quarterly* 41: 26-59. 1970a.

Cheng, C. Y. Dr. Chu-yuan Cheng Replies. *China Quarterly* 43: 132-133. 1970b.

Cheng, C. Y. Industrial Modernization in China. In *The Challenge of China and Japan: Politics and Development in East Asia*, ed. S. Shirk, 234-239. New York: Praeger. 1985.

Cheung, S. N. S. Privatization vs. Special Interests: The Experience of China's Economic Reforms. In *Economic Reform in China: Problems and Prospects*, eds. J. A. Dorn and X. Wang, 21-32.. Chicago: University of Chicago Press. 1990.

Clark, K. B. Competition, Technical Diversity and Radical Innovation in the U.S. Auto Industry. In *Research on Technological Innovation Management and Policy*, vol. 1, ed. R. S. Rosenbloom, 103-149. Greenwich, Conn.: JAI Press. 1983.

Clark, R. *The Japanese Company*. New Haven: Yale University Press. 1979.

Cohen, J. A. China Adopts Civil Law Principles. *China Business Review*, 13, no. 5: 48-50. 1986.

Cohen, J. A., and J. P. Horseley. The New Joint Venture Regulations. *China Business Review* 10, no. 6: 44-48. 1983.

Cusumano, M. A. *The Japanese Automobile Industry: Technology and Management at Nissan and Toyota*. Cambridge, Mass.: Harvard University Press. 1985.

Cusumano, M. A. and A. Takeishi. Supplier Relations and Management:: A Survey of Japanese, Japanese-Transplant, and U. S. Auto Plants. *Strategic Management Journal*. 12: 563-588. 1991.

Davis, D. Unequal Changes, Unequal Outcomes. *China Quarterly* 114: 223-242. 1988.

Deming, E. W. *Out of the Crisis*, 2nd ed. Cambridge, Mass.: MIT Press. 1986.

Dicks, A. The Chinese Legal System: Reforms in the Balance. *China Quarterly* 119: 540-576. 1989.

Ding, Z. H. A Year of Innovation and Development in China's Auto Industry. In *Zhongguo Jingji Nianjian, 1984 (Almanac of China's Economy, 1984)*, IV56-IV57. Beijing: Jingji Guanli Chubanshe. 1984.

Dittmer, L. "Line Struggle" in Theory and Practice. *China Quarterly* 72: 675-712. 1977.

Dittmer, L. The 12th Congress of the Communist Party of China. *China Quarterly* 93: 108-124. 1983.

Donnithorne, A. China's Economic Planning and Industry. *China Quarterly* 17: 111-124. 1964.

Donnithorne, A. *China's Economic System*. New York: Praeger. 1967.

Donnithorne, A. China's Cellular Economy: Some Economic Trends Since the Cultural Revolution. *China Quarterly* 52: 605-619. 1972.

Donnithorne, A. Centralization and Decentralization in China's Fiscal Management. *China Quarterly* 77: 328-340. 1976.

Doolin, D. The Revival of the "Hundred Flowers" Campaign: 1961. *China Quarterly* 8: 34-41. 1961.

Drucker, P. F. *Concept of the Corporation*. New York: The John Day Company. 1946.

Drucker, P. F. *The Effective Executive*. New York: Harper & Row. 1967.

Drucker, P. F. *Post-Capitalist Society*. New York: Harper Business. 1993.

Eckstein, A. *China's Economic Development: The Interplay of Scarcity and Ideology*. Ann Arbor: University of Michigan Press. 1975.

Eckstein, A. *China's Economic Revolution*. Cambridge: Cambridge University Press. 1977.

Eisenstadt, S. N. Tradition, Change, and Modernity. In *China's Heritage and the Communist Political System*, vol. 1, book 2, eds. P. T. Ho and T. Tsou. Chicago: University of Chicago Press. 1968.

Ericson, S. J. Private Railways in the Meiji Era: Forerunners of Modern Japanese Management? In *Japanese Management in Historical Perspective*, ed. T. Yui and K. Nakagawa. Tokyo: University of Tokyo Press. 1988.

Field, R. M. Changes in Chinese Industry since 1978. *China Quarterly* 100: 742-761. 1984.

Fischer, W. A. Update on Enterprise Reforms. *China Business Review* 13, no. 5: 42-45. 1986.

Fraser, A. Hachisuka Mochiaki (1846-1918): From Feudal Lord to Modern Businessman. In *Japanese Management in Historical Perspective*, ed. T. Yui and K. Nakagawa, 209-248. Tokyo: University of Tokyo Press. 1988.

Friedman, E. The Politics of Local Models, Social Transformation and State Power Struggles in the People's Republic of China. *China Quarterly* 76: 873-890. 1978.

Friedman, M. Using the Market for Socialist Development. In *Economic Reform in China: Problems and Prospects*, ed. J. A. Dorn and X. Wang, 5-11. Chicago: University of Chicago Press. 1990.

Fujimoto, A. The Economic Responsibility System in China's Industrial Sector. *China Newsletter* 41: 2-8. 1981.

Fujimoto, A. Progress in China's Enterprise Reform. *China Newsletter* 68: 2-6. 1987.

Fujimoto, A. Market Disorder and Reforms in the Distribution System. *China Newsletter* 86: 7-11. 1990.

Gaenslen, F. Culture and Decision-Making in China, Japan, Russia and the United States. *World Politics*. 39, no. 1: 78-103. 1986.

Galbraith, J. K. *American Capitalism: The Concept of Countervailing Power*, 4th Ed. New York: M. E.. Sharpe. 1980.

Garvin, D. What Does "Product Quality" Really Mean? *Sloan Management Review* 25 (Fall 1984).

Garvin, D. *Managing Quality: The Strategic and Competitive Edge.*. New York: The Free Press. 1988.

Gerschenkron, A. *Economic Backwardness in Historical Perspective*. Cambridge, Mass.: Belknap Press. 1962.

Gilpin T. *The Political Economy of International Relations*. Princeton, N.J.: Princeton University Press. 1987.

Gold, T. B. The Business Climate in the PRC. In *Two Societies in Opposition: The Republic of China and the People's Republic of China After Forty Years*, ed. D. H. Meyers, 159-173. Palo Alto: Hoover Institute Press. 1991.

Goodman, D. S. G. The Second Plenary Session of the 12th CCP Central Committee. *China Quarterly* 97: 84-90. 1984.

Goodman, D. S. G. *Groups and Politics in the People's Republic of China*. Armonk, N.Y.: M. E.. Sharpe. 1985.

Goodman, D. S. G. The National CCP Conference of September 1985 and China's Leadership Changes. *China Quarterly* 105: 123-130. 1986.

Goodman, D. S. G. ed. *China's Regional Development*. New York: Routledge. 1989.

Griffin, K. Income Differentials in Rural China. *China Quarterly* 92: 706-711. 1982.

Gross, I. G. Partnering: Games Businesses Play. *Marketplace: The ISBM Review* (Spring 1989): 1-4.

Grossman, S. and O. Hart. The Costs and Benefits of Ownership. Cambridge, Mass.: MIT. Mimeographed. 1985.

Grow, R. F. How Factories Choose Technology. *China Business Review* 14, no. 3: 35-39. 1987.

Gugler, P. Building Transnational Alliances to Create Competitive Advantage. *Long Range Planning* 25, no. 1: 90-99. 1992.

Hanami, T. Conflict and Its Resolution in Industrial Relations and Labor Law. In *Conflict in Japan*, ed. E. S. Krauss, T. P. Rohlem, and P. G. Steinhoff. 107-135. Honolulu: University of Hawaii Press. 1984.

Harding, H. *Organizing China: The Problem of Bureaucracy, 1949-1976*. Palo Alto: Stanford University Press. 1981.

Harding, H. From China, with Disdain: New Trends in the Study of China. *Asian Survey* 22: 934-958. 1982.

Harding, H. The Study of Chinese Politics: Toward a Third Generation of Scholarship. *World Politics* 36, no. 2: 284-307. 1984.

Hare, P. What Can China Learn from the Hungarian Economic Reforms? In *Transforming China's Economy in the Eighties: Vol. 2*, eds. S. Feuchtwang, A. Hussain and T. Pairault, 51-66. Boulder, Colo.: Westview Press. 1988.

Hayes, R. H., and W. J. Abernathy. Managing Our Way to Economic Decline. *Harvard Business Review* (July-August). 1980.

Hayes, R. H., and S. G. Wheelwright. Link Manufacturing Process and Product Life Cycles. Harvard *Business Review* (January-February): 133-140. 1979a.

Hayes, R. H., and S. G. Wheelwright. The Dynamics of Process-Product Life Cycles *Harvard Business Review* (March-April): 127-136. 1979b.

Helper, S. Comparative Supplier Relations in the U.S. and Japanese Auto Industries. *Business and Economic History*, second series 19: 153-163. 1990.

Helper, S. How Much Has Really Changed between U. S. Auto Makers and their Suppliers. *Sloan Management Review* 32, no. 4 (Summer): 15-28. 1991.

Helper, S. Strategy and Irreversibility in Supplier Relations. *Business History Review*. 1992.

Helper, S. and D. I. Levine. Supplier Participation and Worker Participation. Paper presented at International Motor Vehicle Program Researchers' Meeting, December, at Cambridge, Mass. Photocopy. 1993.

Helper, S. and M. Sako. *Supplier Relations in the Auto Industry: A Limited Japanese-US Convergence*. Paper Presented at International Motor Vehicle

Program Researchers' Meeting, January, at Cambridge, Mass. Photocopy. 1994.

Hervey, R. P. *Preliminary Observations on Manufacturer/Supplier Relations in the Japanese Automotive Industry*, Working Paper series 5. Ann Arbor: U. S.-Japan Automotive Study. 1982.

Hill, R. C. Flat Rock, Home of Mazda: The Social Impact of a Japanese on an American Community. In *The Auto Industry Ahead: Who's Driving*, ed. Arnesen, Ann Arbor: Center for Japanese Studies. 1989.

Hirschmeier, J. Shibusawa Eiichi: Industrial Pioneer. In *The State and Economic Enterprise in Japan*, W. W. Lockwood, ed., 209-248. Princeton, N. J.: Princeton University Press. 1965.

Hoffman. C. Work Incentive Policy in Communist China. *China Quarterly* 17: 92-110. 1964.

Horie, Y. Modern Entrepreneurship in Meiji Japan. In *The State and Economic Enterprise in Japan* W. W. Lockwood, ed., 183-208. Princeton, N.J.: Princeton University Press. 1965.

Howe, C., and K. R. Walker. Introduction: The Readjustment in the Chinese Economy. *China Quarterly* 100: ii-v. 1984.

Hsiao, K. H. Y. H. Money and Banking in the People's Republic of China: Recent Developments. *China Quarterly* 91: 462-277. 1982.

Hu, T. W., M. Li, and S. S. Shi, Analysis of Wages and Bonus Payments among Tianjin Urban Workers. *China Quarterly* 113: 77-93. 1988.

Huntington, S. The Clash of Civilization? *Foreign Affairs* 72, no. 3: 22-50 (Summer 1993).

Ikeda, M. An International Comparison of Subcontracting Systems in the Automotive Component Manufacturing Industry. Unpublished Manuscript. International Motor Vehicle Program. Cambridge, Mass.: Photocopy. 1987.

Ishida, T. Conflict and Its Accommodation: Omote-Ura and Uchi-Soto Relations. In *Conflict in Japan*, eds. E. S. Krauss, T. P. Rohlem, and P. G. Steinhoff, 16-38. Honolulu: University of Hawaii Press. 1984.

Iwagaki, M. The State of China's Automobile Industry. *China Newsletter* 63: 9-12, 16. 1986.

Jackson, B. B. *Winning and Keeping Industrial Customers*. Lexington, Mass.: Lexington Books. 1985.

Jackson, S. Reform of State Enterprise Management in China. *China Quarterly* 107: 405-432. 1986.

Johnson, C. Political Science and East Asian Area Studies. *World Politics*, 26, no. 4: 560-575. 1974.

Johnson, C. What's Wrong with Chinese Political Studies. *Asian Survey* 22: 919-933. 1982.

Jorde, T. M., and D. J. Teece. Competition and Cooperation: Striking the Right Balance. *California Management Review* (Spring): 25-37. 1989.

Kagawa, S. China's Enterprise Management and Japan-China Technological Cooperation. *China Newsletter* 44: 13-18. 1983.

Kallgren, J. The Concept of Decentralization in Document No. 1, 1984.

China Quarterly, 101: 104-142. 1985.

Kambara, T. China's Energy Development During the Readjustment and Prospects for the Future. *China Quarterly* 100: 762-782. 1984.

Kamien, M. I., and N. L. Schwartz, *Market Structure and Innovation*. Cambridge: Cambridge University Press. 1982.

Kiichi, K. Plant Exports and Technology Transfer to China. *China Newsletter* 55: 17-28. 1985.

Kindleberger, C. The Monopolistic Theory of Direct Foreign Investment. In *Transnational Corporations and World Order*, ed. G. Modelski, 91-107. San Francisco: W. H. Freeman & Co. 1977.

Koerner, E. Technology and Planning at General Motors. *Long Range Planning* 32, no. 2. 1989.

Kojima, R. Agricultural Organization: New Forms, New Contradictions. *China Quarterly*. 116: 706-735. 1988.

Korzec, M., and M. K. Whyte. Reading Notes: The Chinese Wage System. *China Quarterly* 86: 248-273. 1981.

Kotabe, M., and J. Y. Murray. Linking Product and Process Innovations and Modes of International Sourcing in Global Competition. *Journal of International Business Studies* (Third Quarter): 383-408. 1990.

Koziara, E. C., and C. S. Yan. The Distribution System for Producers' Goods in China. *China Quarterly* 96: 689-702. 1983.

Krafcik, J. Learning from NUMMI.. Working Paper. International Motor Vehicle Program. Cambridge, Mass. Photocopy. 1986.

Krafjic, P. Purchasing Must Become Supply Management. *Harvard Business Review* (September-October): 109-117. 1983.

Kueh, Y. Y. Economic Reform in China at the Xian Level. *China Quarterly* 86: 665-688. 1983.

Kueh, Y. Y. The Maoist Legacy and China's New Industrializing Strategy. *China Quarterly* 119: 420-447. 1989.

Kumpe, T., and P. T. Bolwijin. Manufacturing: The New Case for Vertical Integration. *Harvard Business Review* (March-April): 75-81. 1988.

Laaksonen, O. *Management in China*. New York: Walter de Gruyter. 1988.

Lamming, R. *The International Automotive Components Industry: The Next "Best Practice" for Suppliers*. Paper Presented at International Policy Forum, International Motor Vehicle Program, June, at Cambridge, Mass. Photocopy. 1989.

Lardy, N. R. Centralization and Decentralization in China's Fiscal Managment. *China Quarterly*. 61: 25-60. 1975.

Lardy, N. R. Nicholas R. Lardy Replies. *China Quarterly* 66: 340-354. 1976.

Lardy, N. R. Consumption and Living Standards in China, 1978-83. *China Quarterly* 100: 849-865. 1984.

Lardy, N. R. Economic Developments in the PRC. In *Two Societies in Opposition*. ed. R. H. Meyers, 180-190. Palo Alto: Hoover Institute Press. 1991.

Lee, P. N. S. Enterprise Autonomy Policy in Post-Mao China: A Case Study of Policy-Making, 1978-83. *China Quarterly* 105: 45-71. 1986.

Leedner, M. R., and D. L. Blenkhorn. *Reverse Marketing: The New Buyer-*

Supplier Relationship. New York: The Free Press. 1988.

Lei, D. Strategies for Global Competition. *Long Range Planning*. 22, no. 1: 102-109. 1989.

Leonard, H. J. *Pollution and the Struggle for the World Product*. Cambridge: Cambridge University Press. 1988.

Lieberthal, K. and M. Oksenberg. *Policy Making in China*. Princeton, N.J.: Princeton University Press. 1988.

Little, D. Rational-Choice Models and Asian Studies. *Journal of Asian Studies* 50, no. 1: 35-52. 1991.

Lustgarten, S. The Impact of Buyer Concentration in Manufacturing Industries. *Review of Economics and Statistics* 57: 125-132. 1975.

Lynch, R. P. Building Alliances to Penetrate European Markets. *Journal of Business Strategy* (March-April): 4-8. 1990.

Manion, M. The Cadre Management System, Post-Mao: The Appointment, Promotion, Transfer and Removal of Party and State Leaders. *China Quarterly* 102: 203-233. 1985.

Manion, M. Policy Implementation in the People's Republic of China: Authoritative Decision versus Individual Interests. *Journal of Asian Studies* 50, no. 2: 253-279. 1991.

Mann, J. *Beijing Jeep*. New York: Simon & Schuster. 1989.

March, R. M. *The Japanese Negotiutor*. New York: Kodansha International. 1988.

Marler, D. L. The Post Japanese Model of Automotive Component Supply: Selected North American Case Studies. Paper Presented at International Policy Forum, International Motor Vehicle Program, June, at Cambridge, Mass. Photocopy. 1989.

Maruyama, N. China's System of Economic Management and Its Impact on Joint Ventures, *China Newsletter* no. 26: 3-16. (June 1980).

Mateyka, J. A. et al. *Profiles of Major Suppliers to the Automotive Industry*, vol. 1. Washington, D. C.: National Highway Traffic Safety Administration. 1982.

Marshall, B. K. *Capitalism and Nationalism in Prewar Japan: The Ideology of the Business Elite, 1868-1941*. Palo Alto, Calif.: Stanford University Press. 1967.

McMillan, J. Managing Suppliers: Incentive Systems in Japanese and US Industry. *California Management Review* 32, no. 4: 38-55 (Summer 1990).

Michalet, C. A. Strategic Partnerships and the Changing Internationalization Process. In *Strategic Partnership* ed. L. K. Mytelka, 35-50. Rutherford, N.J.: Fairleigh Dickinson University Press. 1991.

Monteverde, K., and D. J. Teece. Supplier Switching Costs and Vertical Integration in the Automobile Industry. *Bell Journal of Economics* 13 : 206-213 (Spring 1982).

More, R. A. Developer/Adopter Relationships in New Industrial Product Situations. *Journal of Business Research* 14, no. 6 (December 1986): 501-518.

Nathan, A. J. Policy Oscillations in the People's Republic of China: A Critique. *China Quarterly* 68: 720-733. 1976.

Naughton, B. The Profit System. *China Business Review* 10, no. 6: 14-18. 1983.

Nee, V., and D. Stark, eds. *Remaking the Economic Institutions of Socialism*. Palo

Alto, Calif.: Stanford University Press. 1989.

Newman, R. G. Single Source Qualification. *Journal of Purchasing and Materials Management* (Summer 1988): 10-17.

Nishiguchi, T. Competing Systems of Automotive Components Supply: An Examination of the Japanese "Clustered Control" Model and the "Alps" Structure. Unpublished Manuscript. International Motor Vehicle Program. Cambridge, Mass. Photocopy. 1987.

Nishiguchi, T. Good Management is Good Management: The Japanization of the U.S. Auto Industry. *The JAMA Forum* 7, no. 4. 1989a.

Nishiguchi, T. Japanese Subcontracting: A "Post-Commodity" Contracting Model. Unpublished Manuscript. International Motor Vehicle Program. Cambridge, Mass. Photocopy. 1989b.

Nishiguchi, T. Governing Competitive Supplier Relations: New Auto-Industry Evidence. Paper Presented at International Motor Vehicle Program Annual Sponsors' Brief Meeting, January, at Cape Cod, Mass. Photocopy. 1993.

Nobeoka, K. Strategy of Japanese Automobile Manufacturers: A Comparison between Honda Motor Co. Ltd., and Mazda Motor Corporation. M. A. Thesis, Sloan School of Management, Massachusetts Institute of Technology. 1988.

Nobuto, O. Mazda in America. In *The Auto Industry Ahead: Who's Driving*, Arnesen, ed. 11-18. 1989.

Nonaka, I. The Knowledge-Creating Company. *Harvard Business Review* (November-December): 96-104. 1991.

Nueno, P., and J. Oosterveld. Managing Technology Alliances. *Long Range Planning* 21, no. 3: 11-17. 1988.

Ohmae, K. *Triad Power: The Coming Shape of Global Competition*. New York: The Free Press. 1985.

Oi, J. C. Peasant Grain Marketing and State Procurement: China's Grain Contracting System. *China Quarterly* 106: 270-290. 1986.

Oksenberg, M. China's Developmental Experience. *Proceedings of the Academy of Political Science* 31, no. 1: New York: Columbia University. 1973.

Ono, T. *Toyota Production System: Beyond Large-Scale Production*. Cambridge, Mass.: Productivity Press. 1988.

Oshima, T. Technology Transfer of Japanese Automakers in the United States: Mazda Motor Corporation Case Study. Paper Presented at International Policy Forum, International Motor Vehicle Program, June, at Cambridge, Mass. Photocopy. 1989.

Perkins, D. *Market Control and Planning in Communist China*. Cambridge, Mass.: Harvard University Press. 1966.

Perkins, D. Ed. *China's Modern Economy in Historical Perspective*. Palto Alto, Calif.: Stanford University Press. 1975.

Perry, M. Vertical Integration: The Monopsony Case. *American Economic Review* 68: 561-570. 1978.

Perry, E. J. State and Society in Contemporary China. *World Politics*, 41, no. 4: 59-91. 1989.

Petrick, R. L. Policy Cycles and Policy Learning in the People's Republic of

China. *Comparative Political Studies* 14, no. 1: 101-122. 1981.

Pfeffer, R. M. The Institution of Contracts in the Chinese People's Republic (Part I). *China Quarterly* 14: 153-177. 1963.

Pfeffer, R. M. The Institution of Contracts in the Chinese People's Republic (Part II). *China Quarterly* 15: 115-139. 1963.

Pfeffer, R. M. Contracts in China Revisited, with a Focus on Agriculture, 1949-1963. *China Quarterly* 28: 106-129. 1966.

Porter, M. *Competition in Global Industries*. Cambridge, Mass.: Harvard Business School Press. 1986.

Porter, M. E. *The Competitive Advantage of Nations*. New York: The Free Press. 1990.

Porter, M. E. How Competitive Forces Shape Strategy. In M. E. Porter, and C. A. Montgomery, eds. *Strategy: Seeking and Securing Competitive Advantage*. Cambridge, Mass.: Harvard Business School Press. 1991.

Prybyla, J. S., ed. *Comparative Economic Systems*. New York: Appleton-Century-Crofts. 1969.

Prybyla, J. S. *The Chinese Economy: Problems and Policies*. Columbia, S.C.: University of South Carolina Press. 1978.

Pu, S. Planning and the Market. In *Economic Reform in China: Problems and Prospects*. eds. J. A. Dorn and X. Wang, 17-20. Chicago: University of Chicago Press. 1990.

Pye, L. W. Forward. In *China: Management of a Revolutionary Society*. Ed. Lindbeck, J. M. H. Seattle, Washington: University of Washington Press. 1971.

Reynolds, B. L. Two Models of Agricultural Development: A Context for Current Chinese Policy. *China Quarterly* 76: 842-872. 1978.

Richman, B. *Industrial Soceity in Communist China*. New York: Random House. 1969.

Roberts, J. G. *Mitsui: Three Centuries of Japanese Business*. New York: Weatherhill. 1973.

Ross, L. Market Reform and Collective Action in China. *Comparative Political Studies* 19, no. 2: 217-232. 1986.

Roth, G. Private Provision of Government Services. In *Economic Reform in China: Problems and Prospects*. eds. J. A. Dorn and X. Wang, 193-219. Chicago: University of Chicago Press. 1990.

Rubenstein, A. H., and J. E. Ettlie. *Analysis of Federal Stimuli to Development of New Technology Suppliers to Automobile Manufacturers: An Exploratory Study of Barriers and Facilitators*. Washington, D.C.: U.S. Dept. of Transportation. 1978.

Sabel, C. F., H. Kern and G. Herrigel. Collaborative Manufacturing: New Supplier Relations in the Automobile Industry and the Redefinition of the Industrial Corporation. Paper Presented at International Policy Forum, International Motor Vehicle Program, June, at Cambridge, Mass. Photocopy. 1989.

Sakiya, T. *Honda Motor: The Men, the Management, the Machines*. Tokyo: Kodansha International. 1982.

Sandholtz, W. ESPRIT and the Politics of International Collective Action.
    Journal of Common Market Studies, vol. 30, no. 1: 1-21 (March 1992).

Sakurai, M. Investment-Related Laws and Regulations. *China Newsletter*
    48: 2-9, 24. 1984.

Sawai, M. The Development of Machine Industries and the Evolution of
    Production and Labor Management. In *Japanese Management in Historical
    Perspective*, eds. T. Yui and K. Nakagawa. Tokyo: University of Tokyo
    Press. 1988.

Schonberger, R. J., and J. P. Gilbert. Just-in-Time Purchasing. *California
    Management Review* 26, no. 1: 54-68. 1983.

Schram, S. R. China after the 13th Congress. *China Quarterly* 114: 177-197. 1988.

Schurmann, H. F. Organizational Principles of the Chinese Communists, I.
    China Quarterly 2: 47-58. 1960.

Schurmann, H. F. Organizational Principles of the Chinese Communists, II.
    China Quarterly 17: 65-91. 1964.

Schurmann, H. F. *Ideology and Organization in Communist China*. Berkeley:
    University of California Press. 1968a.

Schurmann, H. F. The Attack of the Cultural Revolution on Ideology and
    Organization. In *China in Crisis, vol. 1 Book II*. P. T. Ho and T. Tsou,
    eds. Chicago: University of Chicago Press. 1968b.

Shambaugh, D. L. The Fourth and Fifty Plenary Sessions of the 13th CCP
    Central Committee. *China Quarterly*. 120: 852-862. 1989.

Sharp, M. The Single Market and European Technology Policies. In
    Technology and the Future of Europe. Freeman, C. M. Sharp and W. Walker,
    eds., 59-78. New York: Pinter Publishers. 1991.

Shapiro, R. C. Toward Effective Supplier Management: International
    Comparisons. Working Paper 9-785-062, Harvard Business School,
    Cambridge, Mass. 1985.

Shimokawa, K. Honda's Entry in the Worldwide Automobile Industry.
    In *Government, Technology, and the Future of the Automobile*, eds. D. H.
    Ginsburg and W. J. Abernathy, 305-313. New York: McGraw-Hill. 1978.

Shirk, S. L. Recent Chinese Labor Policies and the Transformation of
    Industrial Organization in China. *China Quarterly* 88: 575-593. 1981.

Shirk, S. L. ed. *The Challenge of China and Japan: Politics and Development in
    East Asia*. New York: Praeger. 1985.

Shirk, S. L., and J. B. Stepanek. The Problem of Partial Reform In *The Challenge
    of China and Japan*, ed. S. L. Shirk, 240-243. New York: Praeger. 1985.

Shook, R. L. *Honda: An American Success Story*. New York: Prentice-Hall. 1988.

Sicular, T. Agricultural Planning and Pricing in the Post-Mao Period.
    China Quarterly 116: 671-705. 1988.

Simon, D. F. China's Drive to Close the Technological Gap. *China Quarterly*
    119: 597-630. 1989.

Smith, D. N. Challenges to Michigan's Automotive Stamping Industry. *AIM
    Newsletter* 1, no. 3. 1986.

Smitka, M. J. The Invisible Handshake: The Development of the Japanese
    Automotive Parts Industry. *Business and Economic History*, second series,

19: 163-171. 1990.

Smitka, M. J. *Competitive Ties: Subcontracting in the Japanese Automotive Industry*. New York: Columbia University Press. 1991.

Snead, W. G. Self-Reliance, Internal Trade and China's Economic Structure. *China Quarterly* 62: 302-308. 1975.

Solomon, R. *Mao's Revolution and the Chinese Political Culture*. Berkeley: University of California Press. 1971.

Stevens, C. Technologlobalism vs. Technonationalism: The Corporate Dilemma. *Columbia Journal of World Business* (Fall 1990): 42-49.

Stigler, G. J. The Division of Labor is Limited by the Extent of the Market. *Journal of Political Economy* 59: 185-193. 1951.

Stone, B. The Basis for Chinese Agricultural Growth in the 1980s and 1990s: A Comment on Document No. 1, 1984. *China Quarterly* 101: 114-121. 1985.

Stopford, J., and S. Strange. *Rival States, Rival Firms: Competition for World Market Shares*. Cambridge: Cambridge University Press. 1991.

Strange, S. Reconsiderations: The Name of the Game. In *Sea-Changes*. N. X. Rizopoulos, eds. 238-273. New York: Council on Foreign Relations Press. 1989.

Strange, S. States, Firms and Diplomacy. *International Affairs* 68, no. 1: 1-15. 1992.

Sullivan, L. R. Assault on the Reforms. *China Quarterly* 114: 198-222. 1988.

Takahashi, K. *The Rise and Development of Japan's Modern Economy*. J. Lynch., Trans. Tokyo: The Jiji Press. 1969.

Takai, K. Current Reforms in China and the Outlook for the Future. *China Newsletter* 87: 17-22. 1990.

Tam, O. K. Rural Finance in China. *China Quarterly* 113: 60-76. 1988.

Tang, J. Z., and L. J. C. Ma. Evolution of Urban Collective Enterprises in China. *China Quarterly* 104: 630-632. 1985.

Teece, D. J. Profiting from Technological Innovation: Implications for Integration, Collaboration, Licensing and Public Policy. *Research Policy* 15, no. 6. 1986.

Teece, D. J. Reconceptualizing the Corporation and Competition. In *European Economic Integration*. G. R. Faulhaber, and G. Tamburini, eds. Boston: Kluwer Academic Publishers. 1991.

Thomson, G. Inter company Technical Standardization in the Early American Automotive Industry. *Journal of Economic History* 14 : 1-20. (Winter 1954).

Thurow, L. C. Who Owns the Twenty-First Century? *Sloan Management Review* (Spring 1992): 5-17.

Townsend, J. R. Democratic Management in the Rural Communes. *China Quarterly* 16: 137-150. 1963.

Townsend, J. R. *Politics in China*. Boston: Little, Brown and Company. 1974.

Toyota Jidosha Kabushiki Kaisha. *Toyota: A History of the First 50 Years*. Toyota City, Japan: Toyota Motor Corp. 1988.

Tsou, T. *China's Heritage and the Communist Political System*, vol. 1. Book 2. Chicago: University of Chicago Press. 1968.

Tsou, T. Western Concepts and China's Historical Experience. *World Politics*,

21, no. 4: 655-691. 1969.

University of Michigan. *U.S.-China Automotive Industry Cooperation Project: Final Report*, vol. 1 Task 1.2. 1989.

Vanderwerf, P. A. Product Tying and Innovation in U.S. Wire Preparation Equipment. *Research Policy* 19. 1990.

Vermeer, E. B. Income Differentials in Rural China. *China Quarterly* 89: 1-33. 1982.

Vernon, R. International Investment and International Trade in the Product Cycle. *Quarterly Journal of Economics* 80, no. 2: 190-207. 1966.

Vernon, R. The Product Cycle Model. In *Transnational Corporations and World Order*, ed. G. Modelski, 108-117. San Francisco: W. H. Freeman & Co. 1977.

Wada, J. A Case History of Guidance and Upgrading of Subcontracting Firm. In *Intra-National Transfer of Technology*. Tokyo: Asian Productivity Organization. 1976.

Walder, A. Wage Reform and the Web of Factory Interests. *China Quarterly* 109: 22-42. 1987.

Walder, A. Factory and Manager in an Era of Reform. *China Quarterly* 118: 242-264. 1989.

Wallace, W. The Chinese Machine-Building Industry. *China Quarterly* 43: 130-132. 1970.

Walter, C. E. Chinese Agriculture during the Period of Readjustment. *China Quarterly* 100: 783-812. 1984.

Walter, C. E. Dual Leadership and the 1956 Credit Reforms of the People's Bank of China. *China Quarterly* 102: 277-290. 1985.

Wang, C. C. Some Notes on Tax Reform in China. *China Quarterly* 97: 53--67. 1984.

Watson, A. The Reform of Agricultural Marketing in China since 1978. *China Quarterly* 113: 1-28. 1988.

Whalley, J. CUSTA and NAFTA. *Journal of Common Market Studies* 30, no. 2: 125-141 (June 1992).

White, G. The Politics of Economic Reform in Chinese Industry: the Introduction of the Labor Contract System. *China Quarterly* 111: 365-389. 1987.

Williamson, O. *Corporate Control and Business Behavior*. Englewood Cliffs, N.J.: Prentice-Hall Inc. 1970.

Williamson, O. *Markets and Hierarchies*. New York: The Free Press. 1975.

Williamson, O. *Economic Organization: Firms, Market and Policy Control*. New York: New York University Press. 1986.

Wilson, R.W. Chinese Studies in Crisis. *World Politics* 23, no. 2: 295-317. 1971.

Wilson, R. W. Reconciling Universalism and Relativism in Political Culture: A View Based on Economic and Psychological Perspectives. *Journal of Asian Studies* 50, no. 1: 53-66. 1991.

Winckler. E. A. Political Management of the Development Process: Assessing the Chinese Development Experience. *China Quarterly* 55: 560-566. 1973.

Winckler. E. A. Policy Oscillations in the People's Republic of China: A Reply. *China Quarterly* 68: 734-750. 1976.

Womack, J. P. The Decline of the American Auto Industry and the Search for Industrial Policy. Working Paper. Cambridge, Mass.: Massachusetts Institute of Technology. 1980.

Womack, J. P., and D. T. Jones. From Lean Production to the Lean Enterprise. *Harvard Business Review* (March-April): 93-103. 1994.

Womack, J. P., D. T. Jones, and D. Roos. *The Machine that Changed the World*. New York: Harper Perennial. 1992.

Wong, T. T. The Salary Structure, Allowances and Benefits of a Shanghai Electronics Factory. *China Quarterly* 117: 135-144. 1989.

Wray, W. D. Kagami Kenkichi and the N.Y.K., 1929-1935. In *Managing Industrial Enterprise: Cases from Japan's Prewar Experience*. Ed. W. D. Wray, 183-228. Cambridge, Mass.: Harvard University Press. 1989a.

Wray, W. D. Afterward. In *Managing Industrial Enterprise: Cases from Japan's Prewar Experience*. W. D. Wray, ed. , 317-374. Cambridge, Mass.: Harvard University Press. 1989b.

Xu, P. F. Comment: Establishing a New Order of the Socialist Commodity Economy. In *Economic Reform in China: Problems and Prospects*, eds. J. A. Dorn and X. Wang, 33-38. Chicago: University of Chicago Press. 1990.

Xue, Q. Chinese Motor Vehicle Industry: Technology, Strategy for the Future. M. A. Thesis, Sloan School of Management, Massachusetts Institute of Technology. 1988.

Yabuchi, M. Technology Transfer and Technological Reform of Existing Enterprises in China. *China Newsletter* 64: 7-10. 1986.

Yakushiji, T. Dynamics of policy Interventions: The Case of the Government and Automobile Industry in Japan: c. 1900-c.1960. Ph. D. disc. Massachusetts Institute of Technology. 1977.

Yakushiji, T. The Government in a Spiral Dilemma: Dynamic Policy Interventions vis-a-vis Auto Firms: C. 1900-1960. In *The Economic Analysis of the Japanese Firm*, ed. M. Aoki, 266-310. Amsterdam: North-Holland. 1984.

Yuann, J. K. Negotiating a Technology License. *China Business Review* 14, no. 3: 50-53. 1987.

Yue, K. C. Macroeconomic Changes in the Chinese Economy during the Readjustment. *China Quarterly* 100: 691-716. 1984.

Zhai, L. Y. Current Situation and Problems of China's State Enterprises. *China Newsletter* 98: 8-12. 1992.

Zhou, M. W. Comment: The "Socialization" of Public Services. In *Economic Reform in China: Problems and Prospects*, eds. J. A. Dorn and X. Wang, 219-222. Chicago: University of Chicago Press. 1990.

Zipkin, P. H. Does Manufacturing Need a JIT Revolution? *Harvard Business Review* (January-February 1991): 40-51.

Index

About the Author

XIAOHUA YANG is an independent consultant and a participant in the International Motor Vehicle Program at MIT. She is the contributor of a recent IMVP report, "China in the Globalizing Automobile Industry." As an extension of her interests in the political economy of globalization, she is investigating the intra-Asian capital flow in the Asian Pacific region.

ISBN 0-275-94837-4

EAN

9 780275 948375

HARDCOVER BAR CODE

UNIVERSITY OF MAINE AT AUGUSTA

3 2304 00060125 0

APR. O 1 1996